Alexander McKee was selling aviation articles to flying magazines by the age of eighteen. During the Second World War he wrote for a succession of army newspapers and later became a writer/producer for the British Forces Network.

Since 1956 he has been researching and writing books on all branches of naval, military and aviation history. He instigated the excavation of the Tudor ship *Mary Rose* in the seabed off Portsmouth, which he describes in *King Henry VIII's Mary Rose*. In all he has written over twenty books. .

ALEXANDER McKEE

Strike from the Sky

The Story of the Battle of Britain

GRAFTON BOOKS

A Division of the Collins Publishing Group

LONDON GLASGOW
TORONTO SYDNEY AUCKLAND

Grafton Books
A Division of the Collins Publishing Group
8 Grafton Street, London W1X 3LA

Published by Grafton Books 1990

This revised edition first published in Great Britain by
Souvenir Press Ltd 1989

A CIP catalogue record for this book
is available from the British Library

ISBN 0-586-21022-9

Printed and bound in Great Britain by
Collins, Glasgow

Set in Times

Contents

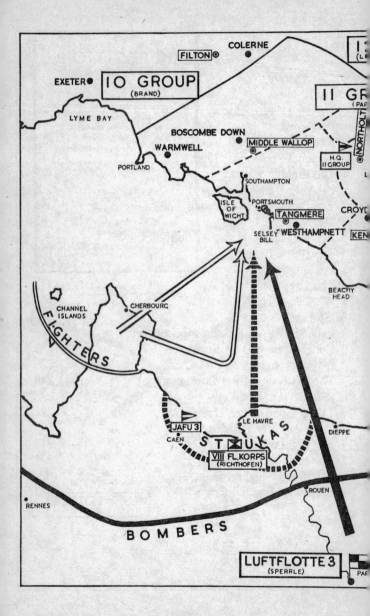

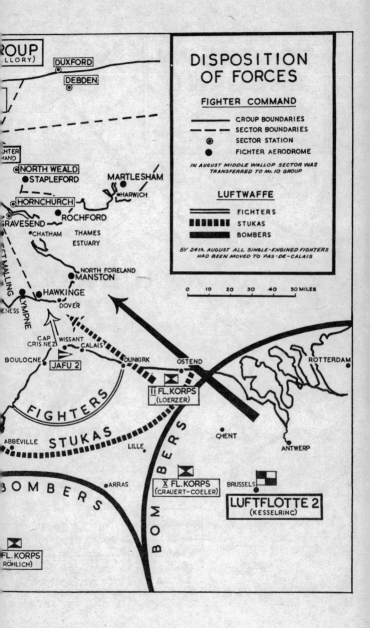

SOUTHERN ENGLAND
THE MAIN TARGETS

0   10   20   30   40 MILES

12

10 GROUP

11 GROUP

CARDIFF

BRISTOL CHANNEL

FILTON
BRISTOL

OXFORD

READING

ANDOVER

ODIHAM

MIDDLE WALLOP

WORTHY DOWN

SALISBURY

WINCHESTER

SHAFTESBURY

EASTLEIGH

SOUTHAMPTON

WOOLSTON

LEE-ON-SOL

YEOVIL

GOSPORT
PORTSMO

WARMWELL

POOLE

BOURNEMOUTH

ISLE OF WIGHT

THORN
ISLAN

LYME BAY

WEYMOUTH

PORTLAND BILL

VENTNOR

GROUP BOUNDARY

SECTOR BOUNDARY

MANSTON AERODROME

DEBDEN SECTOR STATION

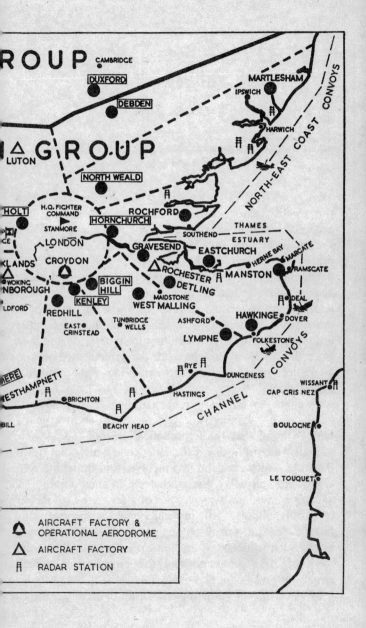

ROUP

CAMBRIDGE

DUXFORD

DEBDEN

MARTLESHAM

IPSWICH

HARWICH

NORTH-EAST COAST CONVOYS

GROUP

LUTON

NORTH WEALD

HOLT

H.Q. FIGHTER COMMAND

STANMORE

ROCHFORD

LONDON

HORNCHURCH

CROYDON

GRAVESEND

SOUTHEND

THAMES

ESTUARY

EASTCHURCH

HERNE BAY

MARGATE

ROCHESTER

MANSTON

RAMSGATE

WOKING

NBOROUGH

DETLING

DEAL

KENLEY

BIGGIN HILL

MAIDSTONE

DOVER

LDFORD

REDHILL

WEST MALLING

HAWKINGE

EAST CRINSTEAD

TUNBRIDGE WELLS

ASHFORD

FOLKESTONE

LYMPNE

CONVOYS

MERE

WESTHAMPNETT

RYE

DUNCENESS

WISSANT

CAP CRIS NEZ

BRIGHTON

HASTINGS

CHANNEL

BILL

BEACHY HEAD

BOULOCNE

LE TOUQUET

Symbol	Legend
⬡	AIRCRAFT FACTORY & OPERATIONAL AERODROME
△	AIRCRAFT FACTORY
⊞	RADAR STATION

Foreword

'God of battles, was ever a battle like this in
the world before.'

Tennyson's line evokes precisely the epic quality which
the English associate with the Battle of Britain: the
emotional impact of war on a country which had not
known a foreign invader for 800 years, the lack of
precedent involved in the spectacle of the first air campaign in history, the feeling that England stood alone
against fearful odds. In thus writing on a subject about
which many others have much of value to say, I must
make clear my intention, which was to show the battle
unfolding blow by blow, seen first from one side and then
from the other, as well as from the ground, not only as
a matter of machines and methods but individual
experiences.

I sought to obtain a representative cross-section of
fighter pilots, varying widely in their skill and fortune; I
bore in mind that the hypothetical case of the Messerschmitt which shot down the Hurricane which shot down
the stuka which sank the ship involves four quite different
viewpoints, all valid, the truth lying in their totality. A
narrative based on the successes of a few 'aces' of one air
force only, although true in detail, would be demonstrably
false in general. On the other hand, I have passed over
briefly such subjects as 'Sealion', the London 'Blitz', the
work of AA Command and the Fire Service, which
already are well enough known.

Most clashes of opinion were within the rival air forces

and not between them; where witnesses on opposing sides met each other in combat their accounts are substantially the same. The fighting men showed no tendency to minimize defeats. The planners, however, tended to differ because the information available to them was not always identical; in particular they knew their own strengths and weaknesses better than the enemy could ever hope to do. Which is only to say that history written from one side alone is not history at all.

Inevitably, some cherished illusions are thereby lost or modified, mostly those which were not contemporary, but grew up afterwards. The affair was no less an epic for that – a great adventure for all those who fought in, or were witnesses of, one of the decisive battles of the world.

ALEXANDER MCKEE
Rowlands Castle, May 1960

Acknowledgements

I have first to acknowledge the very kind co-operation of both the British and German Air Ministries and their respective Historical Departments; a number of people went to a great deal of trouble in helping me to contact witnesses and in answering queries where these arose. Indeed the facilities offered not infrequently exceeded my capacity to take advantage of them as, by choice, I preferred to talk to witnesses rather than to study records. What documentation there is was largely supplied by the witnesses themselves, in the form of logbooks, victory report sheets, private or official studies, diaries and unpublished MSS. These were intelligible in terms of the general battle largely because the framework had already been established by Mr Basil Collier in the official *The Defence of the United Kingdom*. Among the documents particular mention must be made of a detailed postwar study by Generalleutnant Galland, a staff study made during the war by Major Bechtle, a detailed day-to-day diary kept by Wing Commander Constable Maxwell, an unpublished squadron history by Group Captain Satchell, a number of MSS by Squadron Leader Clarke, the complete records of 303 (Polish) Squadron kindly made available by the squadron historian, Major Bienkowski, the unpublished official history of the Bristol company, the published histories of Shorts, Supermarine and Vickers-Armstrong, and a number of German papers concerning the radar and radio interception stations set up in Pas de Calais. I also consulted Barry Sutton's *The Way of a Pilot* (Macmillan, 1942).

I am exceedingly grateful to Air Chief Marshal Sir Keith Park, formerly Air Officer Commanding 11 Group, and to Generalfeldmarschall Albert Kesselring, formerly commander of *Luftflotte* 2, for so readily clarifying and resolving a number of apparent disagreements which had arisen by the time the British and German viewpoints had been closely compared.

The bulk of the narrative is based, not on documents, but on the recollections of the following witnesses, to whom I am deeply grateful for their interest and the invaluable help they afforded me:

Fighter Command

Air Vice-Marshal J. Worrall, DFC, OC 32 Squadron.
Air Commodore F. E. Rosier, OBE, DSO, OC 229 Squadron.
Air Commodore J. M. Thompson, OBE, DSO, DFC, AFC, OC 111 Squadron.
Group Captain J. B. Coward, AFC, 19 Squadron.
Group Captain A. C. Deere, DSO, OBE, DFC, 54 Squadron.
Group Captain R. Dutton, DSO, DFC, 145 Squadron.
Group Captain C. F. Gray, DSO, DFC, 54 Squadron.
Group Captain C. B. F. Kingcome, DSO, DFC, 92 Squadron.
Group Captain E. J. Morris, CBE, DSO, DFC, 79 Squadron.
Group Captain W. A. J. Satchell, DSO, OC 302 Squadron.
Group Captain F. B. Sutton, DFC, 56 Squadron.
Group Captain J. W. White, MBE, Fighter Interception Unit.

Wing Commander M. V. Blake, DSO, DFC, MSc, OC 238 Squadron.

Wing Commander R. Frankland, Controller, Biggin Hill.

Wing Commander R. J. B. Jackson, OBE, Eng Offr, Biggin Hill.

Wing Commander M. C. Maxwell, DSO, DFC, MA, 56 Squadron.

Wing Commander R. M. Milne, 151 Squadron.

Wing Commander R. W. Oxspring, DFC, 66 Squadron.

Wing Commander A. G. Page, DSO, DFC, 56 Squadron.

Wing Commander D. F. B. Sheen, DFC, 72 Squadron.

Wing Commander A. R. Wright, DFC, AFC, 92 Squadron.

Squadron Leader E. D. Glaser, DFC, 65 Squadron.

Squadron Leader W. A. K. Igoe, Controller, Biggin Hill.

Major Z. Bienkowski, 303 Squadron.

Flight Lieutenant B. Malinowski, DFC, VM, CV, CG, 501 Squadron.

Flight Lieutenant J. K. Quill, OBE, AFC, 65 Squadron.

Mrs Pamela Grice, Cypher Offr, Biggin Hill.

Mr H. Noaks, 600 Squadron.

Mr Trevor Tarr, 600 Squadron.

Bomber Command

Group Captain R. J. Oxley, DSO, OBE, DFC, 50 Squadron.

Wing Commander W. G. Gardiner, DFC, AFC, 50 Squadron.

Coastal Command

Squadron Leader D. H. Clarke, DFC, AFC, 2 AA Co-operation Unit.

Acknowledgements 15

Luftflotte 2

General der Flieger P. Deichmann, EKI, EKII, RK, Chief of Staff, II Flieger Korps.

General der Flieger J. Fink, EKI, EKII, RK, DK (Gold), Kommodore, KG 2 and Kanalkampfführer.

Generalleutnant K. B. von Döring, EKI, EKII, DK (Gold), JAFU 2.

Generalleutnant A. Galland, SK (Gold), RK (ESB), OC III Gruppe/JG 26.

Generalmajor P. Weitkus, OC II Gruppe/KG 2.

Brigade-General J. Steinof, JG 52.

Oberst C. Viek, Chief of Staff, JAFU 2.

Major O. W. Bechtle, EKI, III Gruppe/KG 2.

Hauptmann R. Lamberty, EKI, EKII, I Gruppe/KG 76.

Herr W. Klein, EKI, EKII, KG 26.

Dr W. Schaufuss, KG 27.

Luftflotte 3

Oberst W. Andres, JG 27.

Oberstleutnant W. Berlin, KG 55.

Oberstleutnant B. Dilley, EKI, EKII, DK (Gold), RK (E), Immelmann St G.

Major H. M. Wronsky, EKI, EKII, III Gruppe/KG 55.

Hauptmann E. Bodendiek, EKI, EKII, JG 27.

IX Flieger Korps (Maritime Warfare)

Generalleutnant (Seeflieger) E. A. Roth, Kommodore, KG 126.

[Decorations given only where known: EK – Iron Cross, DK – German Cross, SK – Spanish Cross, RK – Knight's Cross, in four grades.]

Aircraft Factories

Shorts, Rochester
Mr H. G. Bramwells, Mr W. Capps, Mr R. T. Fryer, Mr D. Robins.

Croydon Airport
Mr H. C. Robinson, Mrs Norah Robinson.

Vickers-Armstrong, Brooklands
Mr C. F. Andrews, Mr S. Brierly, Mr A. G. Budgen, Mr F. W. Hackney, Mr J. Hilyard, Mr C. Pipe, Mr F. Stevens.

Supermarine, Southampton
Mr E. L. Cooper, Mr L. Gooch, Mr N. Jackson, Mr D. Webb.

Bristols, Filton
Mr W. Avery, Mr G. E. Catley, Mr F. Hackwell, Mr N. Harris, Mr E. W. King, Mr H. W. Pitt, Mr W. Seal.

Miscellaneous

Commander F. C. Broderick RN (HMS *Brilliant*), Mr A. Duke (HMS *Wilna*), Captain D. Connacher (*Henry Moon*, *Fulham V*, *Charles Parsons*), Captain J. H. Potts, MBE (*Betswood*), J. R. Gallagher, BEM (*Tanworth*), Mrs E. C. Hollands, Mr M. K. Tither, Mr E. H. Shaw, Mr G. W. Ross, Mr R. E. Vince, and several dozen witnesses whose accounts were noted down at the time in a 1940 diary.

Personal Preface for 1990

I have kept detailed diaries only three times in my life: during the Battle of Britain and the 'Blitz', plus the first waves of V1 attacks; during the Normandy campaign of 1944–5 and the first year of the military occupation of Germany; and from the time I first started to explore the underwater scene off Portsmouth in 1958.

In all three cases I believed I was witnessing something unusual and important, which I felt most people would not bother to record.

I made it a principle to note down everything, particularly the trivia; for while great events are remembered, the little things which anchor them to everyday life tend to be forgotten.

I wrote for no one but myself, but this did not mean I was preoccupied with self, for I made a point of obtaining other people's impressions, too. Nor did I fall into the opposite trap of forgetting self, for war takes place on two levels – the external events, and the internal, psychological reactions which, to me, were the really interesting aspect.

Keeping a diary does not always guarantee accuracy. Sometimes the witness needs technical knowledge. In the case of the Battle of Britain I did have some qualifications: I had studied the aerial warfare of the Great War of 1914–18; I had started learning to fly in 1933, at the age of 15; I was adequate at aircraft recognition; and above all I had a collection of books published in the 1920s and 1930s, professing to predict the shape of the 'next war'. It would be interesting to find out which of them was right.

However, as I was soon to learn, while it is possible to observe and accurately remember a simple, single combat – one fighter against one bomber, for instance – to observe a whole skyful of whirling, diving, climbing aeroplanes, manoeuvring under stress at very high speeds, is impossible. There is no question of fallible memory – the human eye and brain simply cannot take it all in. Either you get a vague idea of the general pattern or you decide to follow closely one section of the combat and understand that.

Rereading a diary many years afterwards, and comparing it with memory, you find that time has acted to sieve out the facts or scenes you personally felt unimportant. The big events are never forgotten, although after twenty years or so there may be some confusion in remembering the precise order of a series of very similar actions occurring at about the same time. When you open an old diary, much of it reads like new – because the detail has gone from your recollections.

My own diary opens on 25 May, 1940, with Holland and Belgium in German hands and the Battle of France half lost. Poland, Norway and Denmark had already gone.

I was worried at this time about my friends in the BEF (British Expeditionary Force), who were retreating upon Dunkirk, but it was actually the Luftwaffe who prompted me to start recording my impressions. One of their minelaying aircraft either blew up over the Solent, off Portsmouth, or one of its parachute mines exploded prematurely. As I was writing for my eyes only, I had no hesitation in noting that the explosion shook my parents' house in Southsea and 'gave me the hell of a scare!'.

But a few nights later, when a similar aircraft flew down Southsea front, with red, yellow and green tracer going up at him, and so low that I managed to take a photograph (forbidden) of the converging searchlight beams which were holding him, I suffered only from excitement, not fright. And on the third occasion – although this time the sirens sounded – I did not even bother to get out of bed.

The diary establishes quite convincingly that, although the Belgian Army had just surrendered, everything was normal in Southsea – except for Dutch Navy uniforms and the blackout. The pubs were full, there was no rationing and everyone was enjoying themselves. But on 1 June I suffered my first war wound. When helping to escort some women from the bar of the Queen's Hotel to the Cut Loaf restaurant, I quite failed to see the bumper of a blacked-out car and tripped over it, gashing one leg severely.

There were a lot of 'armchair strategists' about and, inevitably, I was one of them. On 28 May, for my eyes alone, I wrote: 'We are well able to fight on alone, even if the French suffer total defeat and thus get no terms at all, and France is completely occupied by the enemy. After all, Napoleon had a better view of England for a much longer time – and the Grand Army was backed by a large navy.' As it turned out, my youthful assessment proved to be right.

The French did collapse three weeks later. But it was just as well that I had confined my doubts about the battle to my diary only, because – strange as it may seem now – to have said this publicly would have been regarded officially as 'spreading alarm and despondency'. This says much about the nervousness and incompetence of the men at the top, which, fortunately, the mass of the people did not share.

Now, one can almost sympathize with the leaders in London. They had worked out their solemn, strategic plans to protect Poland from Nazi aggression, and had seen their grand designs erased from the board by a common corporal's command. Naturally, they felt their authority threatened by doubt.

By the end of June, there was an atmosphere of tremendous events impending. I noted that it was rather like watching some enormous stage for the beginning of the first act, as the curtain went up. The appropriate scenery was being hurriedly rushed into position. Pill-boxes were appearing by main roads and in towns (poorly sited, I now realize), there were guards on railway tunnels, trench lines were being dug far inland from Portsmouth.

A French battleship and a flotilla of French destroyers lay at Spithead – and then vanished, taken over by the Royal Navy (not without resistance, it was said) and moved to the back of Portsmouth Harbour to prevent their escape. And my brother could produce an actual German tracer bullet which he had recovered from our grandmother's front garden, near the cesspit. (He assumed the Germans had been firing at balloons, not Granny or her cesspit.)

The orchestra was warming up in the pit, too. For this was the first war to be fought *on* the air as well as *in* it. And the media were heavily engaged, at it hammer and tongs every night. They took themselves, and each other, very seriously. But I, according to my diary, apparently thought neither of them was really earning their money, and devoted a page to a crude parody of, respectively, Lord Haw-Haw and the BBC.

And so it began. After nine months of 'Phoney War', the reality had arrived on our doorstep – in my case quite literally, for my parents' house was only a few hundred yards from the sea, and that sea was soon to be No-Man's-Land.

In September 1939 few people had welcomed the war – not in Britain, not in France, not even in Germany (despite Hitler's propaganda). The shadow of the Great War, of the trench lines which had swallowed so many millions only twenty years before, lay upon all of us. We had expected a senseless mass slaughter, settling little; in my own family, eleven close relatives had been killed during 1914–18. We had not suffered afterwards, except from the gaps, but millions as a reward for their suffering had been thrown on the scrapheap as useless hands, once victory had been won, by 'the hard-faced men who had done well out of the war'.

Now all that was forced into the background. For the British, not years of mud and carnage on foreign soil, but a direct and deadly threat, from apparently invincible forces, poised only just over the water for the first all-powerful invasion of England for a thousand years. For the Germans, the euphoria of swift and continual victory with small loss, and the end of the war already in sight – just over the water.

At some time during the war I decided to write a book about the raids and people's reactions; on leave from an infantry battalion (having failed aircrew medical), I typed out my hand-written notes and painted watercolours from rough sketches made at the time. In late 1943 and early 1944, when I was in London, I began to keep a detailed diary again, reporting the night raids and then the arrival of the first V1s. And very shortly after that, I experienced something which in 1940 I had never expected: I was in a landing craft approaching a beach in Normandy with the continuous drumfire of the guns in a half-circle ahead, from horizon to horizon. They had never come to us, but now we had gone to them.

Less than a year after that and we were in Germany, where there was a Home Guard (the *Volksturm*) and antiquated, improvised defences quite unlike the neat, perfectly concealed positions of the regular *Wehrmacht*. Both these experiences, naturally, gave an added perspective to any book about the Battle of Britain.

The major change, however, arose from my four-year stint with the British Forces Network in Hamburg, as a writer-producer of 'feature' programmes. A new type of documentary was being introduced from the BBC – for instance, the Battle of Midway done by quoting from the orders and reports of the American and Japanese commanders, instead of employing the tired BBC seagull and loud splashes and fake dialogue. I was enormously impressed.

When I came to write books instead of radio features, I planned to use the same method, but immensely expanded to obtain not only the commanders' points of view, but those of many humbler but necessary people. I reckoned that about a hundred should do (before it became unwieldy and bitty), and that the concentration should be on a smaller number, whom we would follow throughout the battle, for as long as they lasted (for, unlike TV or film, in war the hero may well fall in the first act). This book, when it first appeared in 1960, was, I believe, the first to employ this method to show the action taking place on both sides. Up to that time, either we had government-sponsored lies or the ghost-written autobiographies of various 'aces', which were necessarily untypical. But I did not intend to restrict the narratives to those of aircrew only – far from it. The people of Britain were part of the battle as well.

The time was right. After approximately twenty years there were few forbidden secrets and people could talk freely. Normally, even if one wanted to tell the whole truth, sixty per cent might be helpful to the enemy and therefore could not be mentioned. Consequently, newspaper readers and radio listeners in wartime received a partial and distorted view of the situation. I well remember one of the British fighter pilots I was interviewing telling me at once that he hoped I agreed that it was high time to tell the truth, even if it was more ragged and less flattering than the tidy tales most people had come to accept.

The time was also right in another sense. Another British fighter pilot made the point that after twenty years most people had put the war behind them and had determined to make new careers. Had I, too, done this? I agreed I had. When I interviewed General Galland, he sighed politely and said that he had thought he had said his last word on the war, but nevertheless refreshed his memory from his logbooks. He, clearly, had already made the break with the past.

To leave it fifty years would have been decidedly too long. Many of the potential witnesses, particularly the commanders, would no longer be available for interview or correspondence, being dead. The living might long since have put the war behind them, and their recollections would lack immediacy. I felt it was almost a positive duty to obtain the recollections and answers to questions, before too much time passed.

Accordingly, this is in essence the same book as first published in 1960, bar a few minor corrections and this preface written for a new audience, many of whom might not have been born when we were 20. For this reason, the ranks or the jobs held by the witnesses are those of 1960, twenty years after the battle was fought.

ALEXANDER MCKEE
Hayling Island, 1988

1

The Prelude

September, 1939–June, 1940

'What General Weygand called the Battle of France is over. I expect that the Battle of Britain is about to begin . . . The whole fury and might of the enemy must very soon be turned on us. Hitler knows that he will have to break us in this island or lose the war . . . Let us therefore brace ourselves to our duties, and so bear ourselves that, if the British Empire and its Commonwealth last for a thousand years, men will still say, "This was their finest hour."'

A few hours after Mr Churchill had spoken, as darkness fell on 18 June, 1940, German bombers began to come in towards London from the direction of the Thames Estuary. It was not an attack; it was a navigational exercise, carried out to train the new crews of the *Löwengeschwader – Kampfgeschwader* 26 – in the operational use of scientific methods of target finding by night. A staffel of Heinkel 111s took part; one came back. The rear-gunner of that machine was Willibald Klein. For him it was his 110th operation; he had flown most of them over the British Isles during the first nine months of the war. It was also his last, as he was immediately afterwards posted to Linz as an instructor. In the briefing room, earlier in the day, he and the flight mechanic of the aircraft had been virtually the only experienced airmen present; when the newly appointed staffel kapitan had introduced himself and stated that he was going to lead them all to London at 4,500 feet, the flight mechanic had glanced at Klein and significantly tapped his head. But both were NCOs and no protest was possible, and indeed the

purpose of the exercise most probably could not have
been carried out at a high altitude.

'However,' said Klein, 'we crewed ourselves quietly up
to 20,000 feet.' They could not see much of London
because it was a dark night and the searchlights cast a
blinding glare up at them, but there was a dim shimmer
from the Thames which reflected the storm of flak bursting around their companions lower down. It was impossible to identify a target so, like most British night bombers
at that time, they released their bombs at random and
turned for home. 'On that night,' said Klein, 'the whole
of our staffel was killed over there. They either flew
straight into the barrage or were shot down by the light
flak. Our plane was the only one to come home; then,
we could safely say that the operating height had been
too low.'

But the radio beam method of target finding, with
which they had been experimenting almost from the start
of the war, was potentially very efficient and a great
advance on the equipment of their opponents. RAF
Bomber Command had then no specific aids and bombed
by the primitive methods of the first world war. This raid
convinced the British that the Germans had some means
of blind bombing based on the radio beam and they at
once began counter-measures; at the same time, the heavy
losses of the Germans resulted in an over-optimistic
estimate of the capabilities of the night defences. It was
not realized that, if all the bombers had flown as high as
Klein's aircraft, all would have got home. There was, as
yet, no scientific defence against the night bomber. On
the other hand, the defences against the day bomber,
based on long-range radar warning and clear-speech radio
communication with the fighters while they were in the
air, was extremely effective. Quite early on Klein had had
unmistakable evidence of that; it had resulted in an air

fight in which he had caused RAF Fighter Command's first casualty of the war.

Willibald Klein, then an Oberfeldwebel, was an East Prussian who had joined the police force in 1931 and had subsequently been transferred to the Luftwaffe 'by order of the Führer' when, in 1935, Göring was rapidly creating, virtually from nothing, an air force which was soon to dominate Europe. He quickly mastered his new trade of Radio Operator/Air Gunner and was subsequently employed on a number of secret missions for Hitler; he had no pilot's licence, but the crews trained each other, and he could in an emergency fly the aircraft. Klein has now returned to his old job and is a Polizeiobermeister in Duisburg.

When war broke out, neither side was yet prepared to initiate a bombing campaign against cities, thus flatly contradicting every word which had been written, spoken or filmed in prophecy of the 'next war'. Apart from co-operation with the ground forces in Poland, the Luftwaffe was restricted to shipping targets; similar restrictions were placed on Bomber Command. In spite of the frenzied predictions, neither side was actually strong enough in the air to make the effort worthwhile. The German force devoted to shipping strikes was commanded by General Hans Ferdinand Geisler and consisted of *Kampfgeschwader* 26, equipped with the Heinkel 111, and *Kampfgeschwader* 30, equipped with the first of the fast, modern Junkers 88s, which had dive-bombing capabilities.[1] These, together with some Heinkel 115 seaplanes, carried out the early attacks around the British Isles.

[1] A *Kampfgeschwader*, or bomber unit, was organized in multiples of three: Kette – 3, Staffel – 9, Gruppe – 27, Geschwader – 74 (i.e. three Gruppen plus HQ Flight), plus a reconnaissance staffel of 9 aircraft and three reserves to each staffel – 27 reserve aircraft in all. A *Jagdgeschwader*, or fighter unit, was organized in multiples of two: Rotte – 2, Schwarm – 4, Staffel – 12, Gruppe – 40, Geschwader – 120.

While Poland was being over-run, KG 26 was at Lubeck. 'The old fanatics of the Party wanted war,' recalled Klein, 'but we didn't have any with us. We weren't even the type of soldier who fought in order to be shot dead, hoping that posterity would erect a beautiful monument to him. Those who believed in having a lot of blood flowing usually preferred the blood to belong to someone else. Nevertheless, when the real shooting started, we would not be prepared to sit and look on.' On 27 September his staffel took off on its first operation, against a British taskforce escorting home a damaged submarine. Klein was in the leading aircraft. As they broke cloud cover in a dive, glowing fire-balls came up at them from *Nelson*, *Rodney* and *Ark Royal*, and Klein thought blankly, 'What's that?' They climbed back into the clouds after bombing, and Klein radioed to base: 'All aircraft to this position.' In reply, a single bomber from KG 30 was sent. Its pilot, Adolf Francke, overnight became famous as the first man to claim to have sunk the *Ark Royal*, which he had near-missed. Klein heard him, on his return, saying that he was almost certain she must have been sunk.

During October KG 26, now based on Sylt, began night experiments with the beam by flying to Scapa Flow in the Orkneys; the main difficulty was that the earth curved one way and the beam curved the other, so that as they flew out along the beam – which was simply one continuous note in the earphones, with dots on one side and dashes the other – they began to lose it; it was necessary to climb in order to continue to receive the signal. Some British experts considered that long-distance navigation by such methods was impossible, and therefore discounted it. KG 26 also flew daylight missions, known as 'armed reconnaissance', over Scotland, Orkney and Shetland; there were virtually no British defences in these areas, and when they flew over Lerwick in staffel strength, the sole opponent which rose to meet the nine bombers was an old flying boat. There was a very brief air battle, in which Klein used his camera and not his gun, and then all that was left of their gallant opponent was a funeral pyre rising from the still waters of the harbour.

Their interest in Scotland had not gone unnoticed on the British side and the Spitfires of 72 Squadron were shortly afterwards moved to Drem, in Scotland, to deal with them.[2] Two members of the squadron, Desmond Sheen and Jimmy Elsdon, had already been in action from their previous base at Leconfield against Heinkel 115 seaplanes attacking a convoy off the Humber. Sheen, now a Wing Commander and still serving in the RAF, had attacked one and killed the rear gunner. He was at Drem when the squadron were scrambled to meet a German raid on 7 December.

That day Klein's staffel had flown across the North Sea to Scotland and turned south for the Firth of Forth, searching for warships; with the over-confidence of inexperience, they were at only 1,500 feet. Over Scotland it was as quiet as ever, but as they came down from the north past Aberdeen, Klein took in a code message from base, 'You have been detected by the defence.' The Germans had of course been picked up by the British radar and almost certainly the RAF controller's instructions to the fighters were being monitored in North Germany. Klein knew nothing of any of this, and simply passed the message to his staffel kapitan, who replied,

---

[2] An RAF fighter squadron consisted of 12 aircraft, organized in Sections of three, two Sections making a Flight. Theoretically, an equal number of aircraft and pilots was held in reserve, but the total was usually between 14 and 18. A Wing could be any number – it might be two squadrons, it could be seven. After the Battle of Britain, the German system was adopted.

'Oh, rubbish, the English defences are no good.' But he took them up to 3,500 feet, adding, 'We won't go back, we haven't fulfilled our mission – we will go on to the Firth of Forth.'

Radar gave the British an enormous advantage; there was no need to keep aircraft on endless patrols on the off chance that something might happen; they were scrambled only for a definite threat and then, while in the air, directed on to the bombers by the ground controller on the basis of radar reports depicted in front of him on a plotting table. There was a slight time-lag involved, and the numbers and height of the enemy were not always correctly reported, but it was an enormous improvement on the system of short-range sound locators which had been used until quite recently. The Germans were working on a similar system, but were a little behind technically; neither side knew that the other had discovered it, and no one else in the world had. Over the Firth of Forth, the interception was achieved, and Sheen found himself looking down on Klein's staffel. 'These aircraft were obviously flown by picked and experienced crews,' he said. 'They flew in two very tight vics at low level.'

At the same time, Klein saw the Spitfires high above him and gave a sighting report: 'Behind us – fighters.' The staffel kapitan's answer was laconic. 'All right, we'll turn away to the North Sea; we can fly for a long time, they can't – we'll shake them off.' The Heinkels turned out to sea, the wing machines of each kette closing in tightly; they were called the kettenhunde, or 'chained dogs', because they had to conform to the movements of their leader. Klein folded his hands for a short, sharp prayer. Nobody noticed it. He was sure that some of them would not survive the action but that he would. 'Get hold of the machine-gun calmly,' he told himself. 'Load, release safety catch – just as you've been taught so often.' His position faced to the rear, where the cockpit was open; he had a single machine-gun only against the eight-gun batteries of the British fighters. 'Afraid I was not, I've always been an excellent shot,' he recalled. 'I was nervous only the first time, when we attacked the ships.'

Sheen led his section down on the bombers, aiming at the Heinkel flying close alongside Klein and on his right, fired at very close range, and broke away. The bombers went down to sea-level with the Spitfires streaming after them, putting in attack after attack. Sheen remembered the pursuit passing the Bell Rock lighthouse; to the best of his belief it was above them when they went past it. Then he came down again on the bomber flying to the right of Klein. 'The Spitfires let fly with what they'd got, and it was a hell of a lot,' said Klein, wryly, 'and I let fly with what I'd got.' As Sheen came in for his final attack, he flew into a cross-fire from the starboard kettenhund and from Klein in the staffel kapitan's aircraft. As the Spitfire flew right across his sights, Klein fired. 'I really let him have it. Smoke came out of him, he went down and made for the coast.'

'My aircraft took a pasting and I was wounded in the leg and ear,' said Sheen. 'I was lucky enough to make landfall near Leuchars, where I landed. I believe I had the doubtful distinction of being Fighter Command's first casualty of the war.'

The remaining Spitfires pressed the attack. 'I couldn't pay much attention to the other He. 111s,' said Klein. 'Spitfires came from above and rear – fired – dived past – climbed up – and attacked again. For a fraction of a second I looked at the two kettenhunde, left and right, and noticed that in the rear cockpit of the one on the right the machine-gun was just wobbling up and down, giving no return fire; I assumed the gunner was wounded or dead. A few seconds later the aircraft turned away, diving

slowly and then with increasing steepness, until it went
into the sea.

'In the other aircraft, on our left, the rear-gunner was a
very young man, very inexperienced, slack and slow; he
hardly shot at all, so of course the Spitfires had great fun
with him; they came so close that they literally hung on to
his tail, riddling him, before they turned away – and only
then would he shoot. This machine was going slowly,
because of the hits, and as the battle progressed it was
gradually pushed closer and closer to the sea until it was
almost touching the waves. We stayed with it and when it
finally ditched we were so low that the splash touched us.
The crew got out, but they had no dinghy, only Mae
Wests, and the last I saw of them was their heads bobbing
in the water.'

Because he was firing so energetically Klein was soon
out of ammunition, so he shouted forward to the staffel
kapitan, 'All the ammo you have – back to me at once!'
He waited impatiently for the officer to crawl back
between the bomb racks. 'You've no idea!' he recalled.
'The tension, it was nerve-racking, we were all jumping
with excitement.' He snatched a drum, whipped it on the
gun, yelling, 'More – quickly. Quickly!' For some minutes
Klein carried on firing while the staffel kapitan crawled
along the catwalk, burdened with ammunition, until
eventually the Spitfires turned away for home.

The Germans relaxed, wiping sweat from their brows.
The staffel kapitan's uniform was worn through at the
knees from crawling and the inside of the bomber resembled a 'Robbers' Cave'; empty drums and cartridge cases
littered the floor or rattled about in the 'Tub' – the lower
gun position; the metal skin of the fuselage was ripped
and torn by bullets. One of Klein's wide floppy boots felt
uncomfortable. When he took it off and tipped it upside
down an odd assortment of enemy bullets and his own

cartridge cases fell out; none of the ricochets had touched him, so he put it on again. None of the Germans was wearing a parachute. 'We used them only as cushions,' explained Klein. 'We felt we would rather fall into the sea than into the hands of the English. Partly that was because of the propaganda stories, but also it was because when you are a POW, you are out of it all, you can't fly again; I'd rather be drowned.'

The battered bomber banked slowly and headed back to where the last Heinkel had ditched; the men were still there, still swimming, with their heads bobbing up and down in the waves, but their aircraft had sunk. Klein stood at the lower hatch and opened it, to throw out a dinghy and survival equipment, but what poured out first was a cascade of empty drums and cartridge cases. They circled once, waved to the men below in the icy sea, and turned for home, their own aircraft labouring heavily despite the jettisoning of the bomb load. The radio had been shot up, so they could neither report what had happened nor ask for their own position. The direction-finding apparatus was their only hope of getting home – if the engines would last that long. One stopped after a while, and with hundreds of miles still to go the bomber dragged along only a hundred feet above the waves.

The Heinkel eventually reached Sylt and made a belly landing on Westerland airfield. They got out and counted the bullet holes – 350. The men left swimming in the North Sea were never found although a search was made.

This action, and a few similar occurrences which took place about the same time, made it clear that the whole theory on which the German bomber force was based was twelve months out of date. A year previously, there would have been no radar chain to detect the bombers and no Spitfires to attack them. Apart from a few Hurricanes, the British fighter force had consisted only of old biplanes,

armed with four guns, which were too slow to overtake
the fast German bombers. The latter had been designed
to out-run the fighters, range, bomb-load, and armament
being sacrificed to speed; they were 'evader' bombers,
unstoppable by any air defence at the time they came into
service, but exceedingly vulnerable now. Mr Baldwin's
dictum, that 'the bomber will always get through', which
he had made public in 1932, might now well be amended
to read: 'Without fighter escort, a depressingly high
proportion of the bombers will never get back.'

This, it was now realized, also applied to the British
bombers which, in general, sacrificed a certain amount of
speed for a heavier armament; for in a number of daylight
penetrations into Heligoland Bight in search of warships,
which RAF Wellingtons made in the second half of
December, the losses were prohibitive. The German
fighter pilots paid tribute to the cold-blooded courage and
doggedness of the crews, but to them shooting Wellingtons was not war but sport. Both sides had learned by the
end of the year that, against modern fighter opposition,
directed by radar, the unescorted bomber was not the
shining sword of the air power theorists, nor the terror
weapon of the peace propagandists, but a tin dagger.
Before the bomber could operate freely in daylight there
would have to be a battle after all, the enemy fighters
would have to be beaten down and what was to be called
'air superiority' established; it was this concept which was
to be the dominating factor in that series of operations
known as the Battle of Britain. The battle must precede
the bombardment and therefore the fighter arm was
initially far more important than the bomber force. This
came as something of a shock to both sides, because the
theories of an Italian thinker, General Douhet, had much
influenced policy. Briefly, Douhet, basing his theories on
the experience of the first world war, held that the bomber

would indeed 'always get through', and that fighters could therefore be dispensed with and everything concentrated on the bomber force. Both the British and the Germans, although not accepting his proposition in its entirety, had believed in it sufficiently to build only one fighter to every two bombers; and this was to be a root cause of German failure in the Battle of Britain.

The British and German bomber forces had however been built up on two totally different conceptions. Basically, the British accepted Douhet's proposition that in land warfare defence had overcome offence, that the trench deadlock of the Western Front was unlikely to be broken in a future war, and that the solution was to pass a large force of bombers over the ground defences and destroy the enemy nation's war potential at source; in short, to lay his industrial centres in ruins. Taken to extremes, this meant that air power would play the major rôle, armies and navies being reduced to the status of holding forces; air power would win the war outright. The killing of civilians was accepted, because it could not possibly be as ultimately damaging as the slaying of the pick of a nation's manpower in the slaughterhouse of the trenches; and anyway, except in England, civilians always did get killed in wars. The weapon needed to accomplish so mighty a task could not possibly be a short-range bomber carrying a small load, such as the Germans had; a long-range, four-engined heavy bomber, operating probably by night, was the obvious vehicle, and the first of these, the Short Stirling, was due to go into production at Rochester, in Kent, in the summer of 1940. The Americans had somewhat similar ideas, except that they insisted on day bombing, because of the vastly increased accuracy, and were prepared to sacrifice bomb load for an exceedingly heavy armament – the four-engined Flying Fortress was literally to fight its way through without fighter escort, whose short range would anyway limit the extent of the penetration. Some Germans also thought along these lines, but they made no headway.

The proposed German solution to the problem of trench deadlock was not to go over, employing heavy bombers, but to go through, using tanks in mass, immediately preceded by pin-point dive-bomber attacks and with fast short-range bombers attacking targets farther away to disorganize the enemy rear. Basically, it was a much less ambitious concept of the use of air power than the rather grandiose schemes of the British and the Americans, and more in keeping with the needs of a great land power. Air power was simply to be one essential component of the Blitzkrieg, the lightning war; into the disorganization created by the bombing the fast-moving armoured spearheads would erupt, increasing that disorganization; if a sufficiently fast tempo could be achieved, the enemy's organization would collapse, he could be not so much hammered to death as hamstrung and made helpless. The Germans had just demonstrated this theory in Poland, where it had worked perfectly, aided by the fact that the Poles lacked both a radar warning system and a force of modern fighters.

The storm burst without warning on 1 September, 1939. Bruno Malinowski, flying a P. 11 fighter, took off from his base near Warsaw in a cloud of dust raised by German bombs and found that the Dorniers were so fast that he could not keep up with them, let alone overtake. He never saw his base again, but landed at one of the emergency airfields – they were literally fields – which the Poles had already prepared against this contingency. What shocked the Poles, said Major Bienkowski, another Polish pilot who later joined the RAF, was not the size of the Luftwaffe, which had been expected, but its sheer technical superiority over the Polish air force. They had known that their enemy possessed some excellent aircraft; they had not anticipated that virtually the whole Luftwaffe would be equipped with them. The Polish air force finally collapsed from the disorganizing element of the Blitzkrieg and the bombing of aircraft factories; aircraft were not replaced, petrol became short, and so on. They were not destroyed on the ground.

In fact, it was to prove very difficult, if not impossible, to destroy a fighter force by attacking its bases. Other targets also proved unexpectedly hard to knock out. Another airman who took off at first light on 1 September was Hauptmann Bruno Dilley of the *Stukageschwader Immelmann*; with two other pilots, he managed in the morning to keep Polish engineers away from the Bridge of Dirschau, a crossing point which the Germans wanted, but when an armoured train arrived to make it secure, Polish guns put it out of action and the Poles blew the bridge. In the afternoon he flew with a gruppe-strength raid on the transmitters of Warsaw radio station, but although he saw the masts rock from the blast, Warsaw continued to broadcast. With the bombs then available targets of this sort, which included the stations of the British radar chain, were obviously unprofitable.

The Luftwaffe finished the Polish campaign in a blaze of glory which concealed the fact that a number of units had not completed their training and that virtually everything had been 'in the shop window'. Its rate of expansion had been astonishing. The first fighter gruppe formed at Döberitz in 1935 had by 1939 fathered thirty similar fighter units, ten two-seater fighter units, and nine stuka units. The bomber force had been expanded at a similar rate, by the relentless driving tempo of the Nazi régime. The Germans, however, had the advantage of recent operational experience in Spain where a loose fighter formation had been evolved which was in marked contrast to the tight vics of three flown by the RAF squadrons. The new idea was for the entire formation to consist basically of pairs – number one watched the sky ahead for the enemy and concentrated on killing him, number two kept his tail clear by watching the sky to the rear; and they flew wide apart so as to cover a greater area of sky and avoid the distraction of strict formation keeping. The method has stood the test of time and is still in use.

Not only did the British fly in a rigid drill formation but they also intended to attack in the same parade ground way, although many of the pilots themselves felt that it was nonsense. RAF Fighter Command was also deficient in bad weather flying experience, but here the Germans obliged by sending Klein and others throughout the winter to attack convoys off the east coast, and because the bombers had been shown to be vulnerable they now operated mainly when cloud cover was available. The result was that Fighter Command was forced to fly convoy patrols in bad weather and therefore gradually became used to it, where a sudden change from peace conditions would have led to a high accident rate, as it subsequently did with the Americans. The nine months of the 'phoney war' also enabled a number of minor operating 'bugs' to be ironed out. Flight Lieutenant M. V. Blake, a New Zealander, was one of those who discovered quite early the unexpected difficulties which the blackout now imposed on night flying. On his first practice night flight from Croydon, four Hurricanes failed to get off the ground at all – two taxied into each other, one taxied into a searchlight, and the fourth had engine failure; Blake got airborne but found that accurate navigation was impossible, because a high wind was blowing, and finally that the approach and landing procedure was ill-adapted to the new conditions. After his third attempt he had engine failure and went into Purley Hospital at about 100 mph.

The Hurricane lost a wing, turned over, and finished up with the cockpit over a deep ditch, thus saving Blake's life. Now a retired Wing Commander and a successful business executive, he summed up the training position as: 'In 1938 we were hopeless, in 1939 better, in 1940 we had nearly caught up.'

The radar and control system similarly needed 'working up', and this was demonstrated within minutes of Mr Chamberlain's declaration of war on 3 September. A technical fault caused the radar plot to be read the wrong way round and for an hour the RAF intercepted itself and the Chatham guns fired at the defending fighters in what became known as the Battle of Barking Creek. For 'Tommy' Rose of 56 Squadron it was a morning of embarrassment for he was shot down by a Spitfire while wearing only pyjamas and had to hitch-hike back in that condition; another Hurricane pilot who had been flying with him was not only shot down but killed.

On 9 April, 1940, the Germans invaded Denmark and Norway, which were beyond the range of all except carrier-based fighters; both Dilley and Klein took part in attacks on major units of the Royal Navy, but the results were not nearly so great as had been hoped, although they forced the British Admiralty and War Office to realize that such operations required an air 'umbrella'.

On 10 May the long-delayed German offensive broke in the west; close-phasing, the inter-action of dive-bombing and bombing with the headlong rush of armour, tore the front apart and shivered the organization behind it into ineffective splinters. This was how the Luftwaffe was designed to work. The German fighters and flak shot the Allied fighters and bombers out of the air and the German bombers attacked them on the ground, shortly before the tanks over-ran their airfields. The French had no scientific system of air defence. Many of the fighters were scattered in flights of three to five on local defence, and the warning to take off was often the civilian air raid siren operated from the roof of the local Fire Station. Bienkowski and Malinowski, who had both escaped from Poland and were now flying fighters in France, found themselves operating under these primitive conditions. The Hurricane squadrons based in France had mobile radar stations to aid them but they were nevertheless consumed at an alarming rate.

Air Marshal Sir Hugh Dowding, head of Fighter Command, saw the danger of his force being poured into France and prematurely crippled and on 15 May secured the vital agreement from the War Cabinet that no further fighter squadrons should be sent out of the country. But French pressure was insistent and next day additional reinforcements were sent; they included a flight from 56 Squadron, led by Ian Soden, and a flight from 229 Squadron, led by F. E. Rosier. They arrived in France on the evening of 16 May and by the afternoon of the 18th had been destroyed.

'Tommy' Rose was with 56 Squadron; he was killed, and so was Soden. Barry Sutton, now a Group Captain and still serving, was wounded, and Michael Constable Maxwell, now a Wing Commander, and also still in the RAF, was twice shot down. Rosier, now an Air Commodore, led the last sortie by 229 Squadron; they had now been reduced to three aircraft. As they took off on an escort mission they were attacked by Messerschmitt 109s, but Rosier managed to climb up several thousand feet and attack in turn a 109. Almost immediately another 109 came at him from behind. The Hurricane caught fire, the hood jammed, and then the aircraft must have exploded, for Rosier's next recollection was of falling. He pulled the ripcord, drifted slowly down, and has a dazed memory of waking up on the ground and of being taken to hospital on a motor bike.

But no sooner had Dowding at last obtained a firm agreement that no more of his force should be dissipated in this fashion than he was almost at once compelled to expend not only Hurricanes but Spitfires in an attempt to put an air 'umbrella' over the evacuation of Dunkirk from 25 May to 4 June. They would be operating beyond the range of radar, at near the limit of their fuel, and frequently over enemy-held territory; they would have to fly standing patrols instead of directed interceptions. Consequently, a rain of bombs poured through the gaps in the air 'umbrella'; the Germans were more hampered by the cloudy weather and the smoke from the burning oil tanks than they were by the RAF. When the British fighters did engage, they were highly effective, however, as the Germans admitted. 'The RAF were first rate,' said Generalmajor Paul Weitkus, now retired, who led the Dorniers of II *Gruppe* of *Kampfgeschwader* 2 over the beaches. 'But Dunkirk was a stroke of luck for you. We saw you getting the troops away in rowing boats, yachts, rubber boats, everything – but the ocean was quiet and our airfields were covered in fog much of the time. It was so bad that even the artillery, which had been brought forward, couldn't see the target.'

Bomber Command was also operating over the Dunkirk area. On 29 May they provided Generalleutnant Adolf Galland, then a Hauptmann, with two victories in six minutes, both being Blenheims. 'Quite easy, no escort, and the bomber not armoured,' was his comment. This was paralleled exactly by Brian Kingcome's summary from the British side. Kingcome, now a director of a television film company, was then flying daily over Dunkirk with 92 Squadron. 'The bombers were easy meat; a short burst from behind – the rear gun would tilt up, meaning the gunner was dead; then the rest were dead. Later, when they were armoured, it took too long, long enough for their fighters to come down.' By night also, Bomber Command had been operating over the battle-field; almost from the start, W. G. Gardiner, now a Wing Commander and then flying a Hampden of 50 Squadron, had carried out night interdiction above the German breakthrough at Sedan. But neither the fighters, the day bombers nor the night bombers were in sufficient force to have notable effect; and most of the troops waiting patiently on the beaches for embarkation, watching the German bombers and occasionally relieving their anger by firing rifles at them, seeing the rescue ships sunk and the oil-blackened corpses drifting in with the tide to ground in the shallows, were not even aware that the RAF were anywhere in the sky. The Navy, despite the Luftwaffe, was doing its job magnificently, but it seemed that they had been abandoned by the RAF. The bitterness created in both services reached such a pitch that Churchill was forced to claim that Fighter Command had achieved at Dunkirk 'a victory within a deliverance', which was of course a gross exaggeration. The customer, as ever, was right. Fighter Command was by no means fully committed, because Dowding wanted to build up his force for the impending decisive battle over England; even if it had been, it could not conceivably have obtained the sort of air superiority with which it was later to guard the Normandy beaches.

The real victory of Dunkirk was won by the Navy, but desperate efforts were made both by the RAF and the Fleet Air Arm, with totally unsuitable – and therefore expendable – aircraft, to aid the evacuation. At Detling an amazing collection of long-forgotten machines was assembled. Pilot Officer D. H. Clarke reported there for duty on 31 May, flying a target-towing Skua of No. 2

Anti-Aircraft Co-operation Unit, Gosport. He was told that he was to patrol each night west of Dunkirk, towing powerful flares to light up any attempt by the German Navy to interfere with the evacuation; he had precisely two hours' night-flying experience. During the morning of 1 June, as his operation was not timed until after nightfall, he assisted the ground crews who were working on about fifty Fleet Air Arm Swordfish, which were shortly due to take off on a fighter patrol over Dunkirk. The Swordfish was an obsolete biplane torpedo-bomber and it was hoped that the German bombers would mistake them for equally obsolete Gladiator biplane fighters, and be frightened off. They had already done one such patrol without being attacked, but the Germans were not fooled a second time.

Clarke noticed some Blenheim IVs which never left the ground, asked why, and was told: 'Gas! We're fitted with tanks for spraying gas, just in case the Jerries start using it.' There was also an Anson with what appeared to be an enormous rod sticking out of its nose. 'What on earth have you got there?' he enquired of the pilot.

'Cannon, old boy – like it?' He almost purred. 'Got a 110 and a 109 on the last trip, plus a 109 damaged.'

'But where did you nick it from?' asked Clarke, whose own aircraft was unarmed.

'Ah, now there's a thing . . . plenty of guns if you know where to go to, old boy.' The pilot was evasive. 'Got some Vickers gas-operated, too – look.' He pointed to the bullet-splashed side of the Anson, where a twin-barrel was poking out of a side window.

'Another one on the starboard side, a Lewis in the turret – and we cut a hole in the floor to fire at the silly clots who try to sneak in underneath. No mounting, we just hold a Vickers, and spray – works like a charm!'

The second 'fighter patrol' of the morning was flown by Fleet Air Arm dive-bombers and two-seater fighters. 'The thirty-seven Skuas and Rocs were a splendid sight as they took off in mass formation,' recalled Clarke. 'They looked a bit more operational than some of the others, even if their maximum speed was only 225 mph. They came back just before lunchtime, so I stayed to watch them land. There were not many – I counted six; where were the others? One belly-flopped and I went across to see what had happened, the blood-wagon passing me on the way. That aircraft was a complete write-off. Bullets and cannon shells had ripped the fuselage from end to end – the after cockpit was sprayed liberally with blood, the inside of the glasshouse reddened throughout by the forward draught. The front cockpit, if anything, was worse. Two bullet holes through the back of the pilot's seat showed where he had been hit, and his parachute, still in position, was saturated with blood. The instrument panel was shattered wreckage, and on the floor was a boot – and the remains of a foot.

'I was nearly sick with the horror of it. How that pilot flew home will never be known, for I found out that he was dead when they dragged him out. Of those thirty-seven Skuas and Rocs, nine came back; of the nine, only four were serviceable.'

The morning was not quite over yet. A shot-up fighter-Blenheim came in and landed; the pilot, Reg Peacock, was a friend of Clarke's. His lean face was grimy and sweat-stained, his black hair plastered down from the pressure of his helmet. 'I think I'm the last of the squadron, Nobby,' he said. 'We were attacking a crowd of Dorniers when a whole swarm of 109s jumped us . . .'

'He went along to the Mess with his crew for a beer,' recalled Clarke. 'An hour and a half later they were airborne once more. The starboard wheel was not fully retracted and they disappeared at low level with a decided list to port – too much rudder bias countering the drag of the wheel, I thought. They looked very pathetic limping back to Dunkirk all alone . . .'

The British Army had now, in effect, been disarmed; all that remained was a Navy weakened by the loss of many destroyers and an air force weakened both by the Battle of France and the fighting over Dunkirk. As improvised defences began to appear along the south coast, there was a sense of enormous events impending, of a stage set for the enactment of a stupendous drama. But the Germans had made no preparation for an invasion and there was a breathless lull, during which Fighter Command prepared for the decisive battle which must result from the totally unexpected appearance of an enemy air force actually on the Channel coast instead of hundreds of miles away beyond the Rhine.

The first line of defence would be the Spitfires and Hurricanes. In the first month of the war the factories had produced only 93 single-engined fighters, but by May, 1940, the monthly total was 325. This was the result of the planned expansion directed by Air Marshal Sir Wilfrid Freeman. Lord Beaverbrook became Minister of Aircraft Production halfway through that month, gathered around him a brilliant team which included Sir Charles Craven of Vickers, Trevor Westbrook, Frank Spriggs of Hawkers, Lord Austin, and Sir William Rootes, and gave the production of single-engined fighters over-riding priority. In June 440 were produced, in July 490 – British production caught up with German production and then surpassed it, while the battle was actually being fought. Dowding's caution, in not allowing his force to be prematurely weakened, and Beaverbrook's dynamic personality at MAP, combined to produce a situation in which the British were never at any time short of fighter aircraft but only of the pilots to fly them; and the country owes an immeasurable debt to these two men.

It was not a matter of production only but also of quick-change technical improvements to keep up with the Germans – the fitting of armour, of self-sealing petrol tanks, of constant-speed propellers, and a device to prevent the engines faltering when negative 'g' was applied. Both Spitfires and Hurricanes had now been matched against the Messerschmitt 109. The latter had one marked advantage over both the British fighters, because its direct-injection engine enabled it to nose over into a dive and simply drop away from them; neither Spitfire nor Hurricane could follow until their float-type carburettors had been modified. The 109 had a higher ceiling than the Spitfire I but the Spitfire II, equipped with the Rotol constant-speed propeller, had a markedly improved rate of climb, ceiling and manoeuvrability at height.

Johannes Steinhof, a leading German fighter pilot now a Brigade-General in the new Luftwaffe, made this comparison: 'At the start the 109 had a certain advantage, except for its turning radius, but the later Spitfire had a higher ceiling and better climb.'

Adolf Galland summed up: 'The Spitfire was dangerous, on account of its armament, climb, manoeuvrability, and the courage of its pilots.'

Jeffrey Quill, Spitfire test-pilot who fought in the Battle of Britain, said: 'It was certainly necessary to pull out all the stops in order to fight the 109, but at altitude we had the edge on them and they treated the Spitfire with respect.' Both Germans smiled when the Hurricane was mentioned. 'The Hurricane was a big disadvantage to you, the rate of roll being bad – we were lucky to meet Hurricanes,' commented Steinhof. 'The Hurricane was hopeless – a nice aeroplane to shoot down,' said Galland.

M. V. Blake, who flew both types, said: 'The Spit was an infinitely superior aircraft, although I loved the Hurricane. The Spit was like a fine blade cutting through the air – a precision instrument; it and the 109 were so close that the chap who had the height advantage would be the victor.'

Al Deere, who flew Spitfire IIs with 54 Squadron, said: 'The Hurricane and the Spitfire were complementary. The Hurricane was the better gun platform and therefore more effective against bombers, but it could not have lived without Spitfires to take on the 109s, whereas the Spitfires could have lived without the Hurricanes.'

Two-thirds of Dowding's fighters were Hurricanes and at the time of Dunkirk most of the Spitfires were of the early type; he was not therefore anxious to engage in an all-out fighter battle except in the most favourable circumstances – that is, over England, not over France or the Channel, and even then, only when a bomber threat to an important target made it imperative.

The British were in no doubt as to what Hitler would do now – he would attack them as soon as possible. In this they were quite wrong. The crucial point, they thought, would be the capacity of the aircraft industry to replace battle losses; aircraft and aero-engine factories were the vital targets – if they were destroyed, Fighter Command by battle wastage would be beaten down. And if the German bombers could roam as they pleased, relatively untroubled by fighters or decimated by losses, they could clear the way for invasion. Whether or not this would be practical depended in large measure on the ability of the Luftwaffe to hit such small fast targets as destroyers and so prevent the Royal Navy from intervening. That was still a matter of opinion. The Air Ministry was not prepared to defend these destroyers at the cost of uncovering its aircraft factories and believed that it did not have enough fighters to protect both targets. In point of fact, it had insufficient fighters to protect either the one or the other. However, as long as Fighter Command remained in being it could certainly restrict attacks to southern targets only – those which were within range of the Messerschmitt 109; but if it were to be crippled, then unescorted bombers could come north to attack the main centres of the armament industry. Production was concentrated in only a few centres – there was virtually no dispersal and they were exceedingly vulnerable. As far as the land battle was concerned, there was no divergence of opinion whatever – if the Germans could land and maintain in England a small number of armoured divisions, the largely immobile and unarmed British forces could not drive them out.

The aircraft factories would be the crux of the air battle and the panzer divisions the crux of the land battle; what was still uncertain was the ability of the German bombers, once air superiority had been gained, to drive the Royal Navy out of the Channel. If that could be done, then invasion stood a chance of success; but it would have to be done by the Luftwaffe, for the German Navy was impotent in the face of the vastly superior Royal Navy. The matter was never put to the final test of invasion, but it was certainly put to a test – and the destroyers fared badly.

Hitler was not in fact thinking of an immediate attack on the British Isles – he was hoping to avoid it; in any case, it would take many weeks to move the entire Luftwaffe forward from its German bases to the Channel, and many months before even a makeshift invasion could be prepared. In the meantime, while the German leaders were considering what to do next, Johannes Fink, the Kommodore of *Kampfgeschwader* 2, was given the

additional command of some stuka units and two Jagdgeschwader under Theo Osterkamp, the resounding title
of *Kanalkampfführer*, or Channel Battle Leader, and told
– to secure air superiority over the English Channel in the
area of the Straits of Dover and to use it, when won, to
see that nothing moved on the waters there. Fink retired
as a General of the Air Force, his last command being
Luftflotte 1 in Courland at the end of the war. Further
down Channel, between Dieppe and Cherbourg, Richthofen's Stuka Corps, supported by its own fighters, would
achieve air superiority and close the Channel to English
shipping in the area between Portsmouth and Portland.
Dover was the right flank and Portsmouth the left flank
of the invasion plan in its original form, so that this move,
if successful, would facilitate matters; at the same time,
as it had not yet been decided whether or not there was
in fact to be a Battle of Britain at all, both Fink and
Richthofen were rigidly restricted to shipping targets.
England was not to be attacked, and therefore this first
phase is more accurately described as the Battle of the
Channel, but because Fighter Command was very soon
heavily engaged, the RAF date the Battle of Britain as
beginning on 10 July. More precisely, the German operations order was dated 2 July, and the attacks began on
the following day.

PHASE I:
Shipping

2

The Battle of the Channel

July

The Luftwaffe operations order of 2 July specified two objectives, necessarily inter-related, which may be summarized as:

(a) Sweep the Channel of British shipping.

(b) Sweep the air of British fighters.

The combats were waged with limited forces – limited on the German side, because the bases of their main force were not yet ready, limited on the British side from choice. Dowding considered that this phase of the battle could not be decisive and that his forces would be relatively at a disadvantage; he chose therefore to commit no more than token numbers and meanwhile to build up the strength of his command in readiness for the decisive battle which must take place later when the Germans came inland and the relative advantage would lie with the British. His position was much the same as that of Jellicoe at Jutland, able to lose the war, if not in an afternoon, then at least within a short time, and unlike Jellicoe he had no superiority of force with which to cushion any reverse.

When the order to close the Straits of Dover was received by Loerzer's II *Flieger Korps* it was not thought necessary to commit the whole of this force, a small battle group should be quite sufficient. The command of it was given to Johannes Fink, whose *Kampfgeschwader* 2 in the campaign just concluded had achieved the best results of any geschwader combined with the least losses. Fink was now 45; he had been an infantry officer in the first world war and had learned to fly at the age of 32 as one of the five pilots allowed under the Versailles Treaty to be trained in any one year. He had spent some time at the Engineering Academy, where a fellow student, Walter Dornberger, was just beginning to experiment with the rockets which were to lead to the V2. Two years before the war, Fink had done a course in accident prevention, to the results of which he ascribed the low losses suffered in action by his geschwader. During the forced growth of the Luftwaffe the accident rate was high, twenty-eight pilots being killed in one year in Fink's own unit. Fink cut this sharply by finding the basic causes, the most important of which were bad flying training, the tendency of pilots to drink too much when the weather was too bad for flying, and – the girl friend. The latter probably accounted for more fatal accidents than all the other reasons put together, and not in the German Air Force only; Fink forbade pilots to deviate from the courses laid down, so that they could not stunt over their friends' houses, and the accident rate fell at once. Theo Osterkamp gently deprecated this, saying that one should not take all the romance out of flying. Osterkamp was now to command the fighter component of Fink's battle group; this consisted of the *Schlageter Jagdgeschwader* 26 in which Adolf Galland led a gruppe, and *Jagdgeschwader* 53 in which Werner Mölders was the brightest star. Mölders, who had fought with distinction in Spain, had developed many of the new fighter tactics used by the Luftwaffe and was also well-known as a fanatical anti-Nazi. The striking force consisted of the Dornier 17s of *Kampfgeschwader* 2, now based at Arras, some distance from the coast, and two or three stuka gruppen from Loerzer's Corps, based on Pas de Calais, which could be in action within a short time of any warning of approaching convoys. The operational force amounted to about seventy-five bombers, sixty or more stukas and about 200 fighters.

Down Channel to the west Richthofen's Corps could supply a roughly equal force, but without the twin-engined bombers; they had long distances to fly over the sea and only single-engined machines with which to do it. The British fighter defence, concentrated in Air Vice-Marshal Keith Park's 11 Group, was so based that it was able to concentrate much more rapidly over Kent than over Hampshire and Dorset, owing to the pre-war orientation.

When it first went into action, however, Fink's system was only a week or so old and improvisation was the keynote. He set up his command post in an old omnibus on the cliffs at Cap Blanc Nez near Wissant; directly behind it was the Blériot statue commemorating the first cross-Channel flight ever made, an ironical reminder of the change brought about by air power. Inside the omnibus were four telephones and when an action was in progress and all were simultaneously in use for giving orders or taking down messages, concentration was difficult. Underground quarters were being dug in the chalk but these were not ready when Kesselring, commanding *Luftflotte* 2, came round on his first inspection; he looked shocked, and muttered, 'This is impossible!' The position did, however, give a direct view over the Straits of Dover, so that Fink could watch the battle with his own eyes. Attached to his staff was a naval officer, with whom Fink sat down to work out how to catch the convoys in spite of the delay caused by his bombers being back at Arras; what at first seemed complicated soon proved quite simple – the ships sailed in accordance with the tide mechanism and it became possible to anticipate sailings and send over a reconnaissance aircraft at the right time. Nevertheless, this was a primitive method and during July the system was improved.

One of the first officers to arrive in Pas de Calais was Generalmajor Kurt Bertram von Döring, the JAFU 2 (*Jagdfliegerführer*, or fighter commander, of *Luftflotte* 2); sometime in June he set up his headquarters at Wissant and could see the white cliffs of England from his window. Von Döring, who retired as a Generalleutnant and is now in business, was a former pilot of the Richthofen Circus in the days when it flew the Albatros, the Pfalz and the Fokker D. VII; afterwards, he had gone into business in South America and had only come back to rejoin the air force when war seemed likely. His first task after the French campaign had been to reconnoitre the airfields in Pas de Calais and decide what measures would be necessary to turn them into operational bases for the fighters of the Luftwaffe. His second task was to set up at Wissant a W/T Interception Station to monitor the control system of Fighter Command; on 7 July an *H-Sonderformation* provided by III/*Ln Rgt* 2, under the direction of General Wolfgang Martini, the radio and radar specialist, was operating, and henceforward the orders given by the RAF Sector Controllers to the fighters and the conversations of the pilots were known to the Germans. The information gained was varied; later it included the fact that British pilots were becoming exhausted through having to make so many sorties per day, and sometimes it gave the Germans a good laugh, as for instance when von Döring heard some British pilot yell, 'Fighter-bombers dropping eggs!' His third task was to see to the installation of a system of radar watch and towards the end of July a *Freya Gerät* had been brought from Dieppe, where *Luftflotte* 3 had been using it, and set up on the cliffs at Wissant. This enabled the Germans to watch all convoy movements in all weathers, and at all times; it showed also the movements of aircraft, although it was more primitive in this respect than the British radar. It was not, however, linked to any complicated system of control, necessarily impossible to set up in the time available, which would have enabled the Germans to conduct air operations by radar; additionally, although the German fighter and bomber formations could talk among themselves, they could not talk to each other and often enough could not talk to base while in the air. The fully developed British system, primitive and short-ranged as it was, gave the RAF a great advantage, although this was not so apparent over the Straits, where the warning time was short, as it was to be later on.

When Fink, as *Kanalkampfführer*, began operations on 3 July, these arrangements were still being made, so that matters worked up gradually to a climax on 25 July, after which date his task had been achieved. '*Kanal*' has two meanings in German, one being that strip of water separating England from France, the other being a drain or sewer. Hence, among his intimates, Fink was immediately dubbed the *Kanalarbeiter*, or Sewage Worker. It was in this light-hearted mood that the Germans took over on the Channel coast. They had just won a stunning series of victories – and deserved to win them; as a result, they thought the war was over. Clearly, the position of England was hopeless – driven out of the Continent, her allies poleaxed, she stood no chance ever of gaining a decision over Germany, and must surely come to terms. Hitler was in fact waiting for the British Government to open peace negotiations and when none was made, endeavoured to initiate them, without the least success. Meanwhile, his advisers were divided in their opinion as to what to do if the British proved obstinate: to attempt an invasion for which no preparations had been made, or to strike at the British Empire in the Mediterranean – thereby choosing the enemy's weakest point instead of his strongest for the attack and at the same time leaving the British, unbraced by the threat of personal peril and national crisis, to consider the pass to which their leaders had brought them. In these circumstances, Fink and Richthofen were forbidden to attack England; their targets must consist exclusively of ships, at sea or in harbour. There must be no unwarranted provocation to imperil the peace negotiations, but rather a sharp reminder to the British Government of what Hitler could do if he chose.

From 3 July on, RAF pilots operating over the Straits found increasing activity by small groups of bombers hunting for ships, the German fighters flying offensive rover patrols, or 'free-hunts', over the area at the same time, in order to catch the British fighters by surprise while they were so engaged. On 4 July Colin Gray, a New Zealander of 54 Squadron, flew no fewer than five patrols, mainly against bombers dodging in and out of the clouds, the weather in the Straits being bad during this first week. Two of the British fighters were surprised, and destroyed. Down Channel that day the weather was better and this enabled Richthofen's Stuka Corps to strike a decisive blow within forty-eight hours of the opening of the Channel Battle.

Convoy OA 178, which was an Atlantic convoy consisting of large merchant ships, had come through the Straits on the 3rd and was off Portland on the 4th, when it came under attack by two stuka gruppen, losing four ships sunk and nine fired or damaged. A third gruppe attacked Portland, damaging two ships, and during the night E-boats sank one ship and damaged two more out of the convoy. The cost to VIII *Flieger Korps* was one aircraft – shot down by the AA guns of the convoy. An entire stukageschwader, approximately ninety bombers, had been employed, but this first major blow is not counted by RAF historians as being part of the Battle of Britain, because the Royal Air Force was not present at the action. Its results were considerable for the sea war – the Channel was closed to all ocean-going ships using the Port of London, and these had to be diverted either to west coast ports or sent 'north about' round Scotland instead. Henceforward the only convoys to use the Channel were made up of small coasters, mainly colliers.[1]

On 7 July a small force of stukas from Richthofen's Corps visited Portsmouth, 'trailing their coats' over the city and Spithead before putting in a perfunctory attack on a coastal battery in the Isle of Wight; the object throughout this phase was to draw Fighter Command on to the bombers while the 109s, waiting high above in the sun, chose their moment to attack. It was by this means that the Germans hoped to gain their second objective – air superiority. The pilots of the Messerschmitts, looking down, could fairly easily see the British fighters, climbing laboriously, whereas the British pilots found the 109s hard to see against the glare of the sky and impossible to see if they were in the sun.

The Germans were now flying a regular Channel reconnaissance at least twice a day when the weather permitted. On this day the morning reconnaissance was flown by one of Fink's pilots, Leutnant Otto Wolfgang Bechtle, in a Dornier, with an escort of two 109s. Bechtle, who retired as a Major, is now a publisher. His task that morning was to note position and course of any convoys and to count the ships in the harbours between Dover and Plymouth; he remembered it particularly well because the weather was glorious and as he flew down between France and England he could see inland as far as London.

---

[1] Their story is described in detail in *The Coal-Scuttle Brigade*, by Alexander McKee (Souvenir Press, 1957).

On 10 July good weather and a convoy in the Straits coincided; the bombing which resulted earned Bechtle a bottle of champagne and the consequent air fighting was on a sufficient scale for the RAF to make it their official opening date for the Battle of Britain. On 3 July a Fighter Command representative had informed a conference at the Admiralty that their rôle was the defence of Britain and not the defence of shipping; but the events of 4 July had caused Mr Churchill to pen one of his celebrated 'action this day' memos, which forced Dowding to compromise to the extent of giving token air protection to convoys. Sometimes squadrons were used, but often merely flights or even sections, whereas the 'free-hunting' German fighters were operating in large formations of two or three dozen machines. Galland, who day after day led such a formation over the Straits, commented on this first phase of the Battle: 'The English got their fighters up as soon as we started, but they were in little groups, and they had heavy losses.' The losses were not quite so great as he believed, because of the tendency to over-estimate the numbers of the enemy who are shot down, but the massed German formations were a daunting sight to the handful of British pilots, usually in inferior machines, climbing to the attack.

The procedure now adopted was for one flight of a squadron to be employed daily on convoy protection; in the morning, they flew down to a forward aerodrome near the coast, where the accommodation usually consisted of bell tents, and waited at 'readiness' beside their machines; in the evening, having done their 'stint' in the front line, they flew back to base, and next day the other flight would be on duty. On this day, 'A' Flight of 56 Squadron, based on North Weald, had flown to Manston, near Ramsgate, and were at readiness. One of the six pilots was Pilot Officer A. G. Page, now a retired Wing Commander and Assistant Sales Manager of Vickers-Armstrong at Weybridge. 'Page is the keenest member of the squadron,' wrote Constable Maxwell in the diary he was keeping then. 'He hates going on leave and can only think of fighting.' Unlike Maxwell, who had gone to France and been twice shot down without getting anything himself, Page had never been in action at all, the nearest to it being when he had dived after a Ju. 87 over St Valéry and lost it in the haze. Page himself described his attitude as being that of most of them – 'A careless optimism, you were enjoying yourself, because you were young and didn't think about what might happen – until something hit you.' As they were climbing the voice of the controller unemotionally reported, 'Large formation of bandits bombing the convoy and another large formation higher up.' Then they saw them – about twenty bombers, thirty 110s, and twenty 109s. Against six Hurricanes. Page's mounting excitement was instantly lost in the necessary cockpit drill – engine to full power, set guns to 'fire', set camera gun, adjust sights for the wingspan of the target – no time at all to feel or to think.

The 110s, instead of attacking, went at once into a defensive circle, flying in a ring, so that the guns of each machine covered the tail of the machine in front. Page remembered almost closing his eyes – that was the sensation – and diving right through that circle of thirty twin-motor fighters. Then the 109s, flying 2,000 feet above the two-seaters, came down on the three Hurricanes which had attacked the 110s – the other section had gone after the bombers. A 109 came curving straight down on Page – along the leading edges of its wings was a sight which fascinated him, the apparent rippling of electric light bulbs which were the flashes of its guns firing at him. Page was determined not to give way, and the two fighters missed each other by a matter of feet. The German's tracer had gone below him, but Page had the impression his tracer had connected; then the 109 had rocketed past below, and there was a 110, going down vertically with flames coming out of the port engine and the crew baling out.

Five of the Hurricanes landed intact at Manston, the sixth, flown by the Flight Commander, crash-landed on the airfield, but he was safe. They were all utterly surprised that it had been possible at all to attack so many and still get away with it, apart from the fact that they calculated that they had shot down five of the enemy; they felt considerably better after that. 'I think their vast numbers confused them,' said Page. 'They got in each other's way and couldn't tell who was who.'

As Bechtle came in to bomb with 9 *Staffel* of KG 2, he saw this combat in progress – 'The fighters were in a proper dogfight to the west, as thick as grapes.' At the head of the convoy was a warship of some kind, Bechtle thought possibly an AA cruiser, but more probably a destroyer, and this he hit. As the Dorniers turned away in a wide sweep to the west and headed back for France, the Hurricanes of 111 Squadron arrived, tried to put in a head-on attack and, closing speed being so high, found themselves slightly out of position. As they turned to correct the angle, the Dorniers appeared to skid sideways through the air at them. Then they were blazing through the formation and the severed wing of a Hurricane was seen fluttering down 6,000 feet towards the sea – one of the pilots had misjudged by a fraction the closing angle and at a combined speed of 500 mph had momentarily touched wings with a bomber. Squadron Leader J. M. Thompson then re-formed his squadron and led them in a stern chase of the Dorniers which, with empty bomb racks, made surprisingly good speed; at the French coast he broke off the pursuit. Squadron Leader Thompson, who is now an Air Commodore, was then based at Croydon in the Kenley Sector; his squadron usually operated from Hawkinge.

The most significant event of the day was probably the way in which the Messerschmitt 110s had promptly gone into a defensive circle when attacked by three Hurricanes and had had to be rescued by the 109s. This was early tacit acceptance of the fact that the Luftwaffe's long-range fighter, flown by the pick of the fighter arm, was as defenceless as a bomber and equally in need of fighter protection. It meant that penetration by escorted bombers would be limited to the 105 minutes' flying time of the single-engined Messerschmitt – that is, to just beyond London, and no further. This was the first weakness of the Luftwaffe to be revealed – although the Germans realized it some time before the British did, naturally enough.

The following day, 11 July, it was the turn of *Luftflotte* 3, which was now able to spare small numbers of twin-engined bombers as well as stukas; they attacked warships at Portsmouth and Portland and a convoy off Portland, sinking the 530-ton *Warrior*, a vessel of the Inner Patrol against invasion, which the Germans estimated at 2,500 tons. At 6 o'clock in the evening, about a dozen Heinkel 111s carried out the Portsmouth attack, streaking in over the Isle of Wight with the wind behind them and a lone fighter, ignoring the AA fire, hanging on to the formation and firing at close range. The bombs fell on and around the naval dockyard, the explosions shaking the windows of the forts on Portsdown Hill, to the north of the city, and causing a great pall of smoke to hang over the houses. Some witnesses saw a Heinkel fall away towards Selsea, with men baling out; 601 Squadron had in fact attacked, but too late to interfere with the bombing. The pattern had 'boxed' a battleship in drydock, without damaging her, and the 'overs' had fallen several thousand yards beyond, killing about twenty people. The public reaction was quite different to the predicted one: it was composed of excitement and pride, excitement because the city was now in the front line, pride at having been singled out by the Germans as important enough to attack.

The damage also contradicted the 'known facts', supported by photographs, which had come out of Spain, though at first sight it looked much worse than it was. Each bomb had blown out hundreds of windows and stripped slates off the roofs, so that the superficial aspect of the buildings and of the small rubble in the streets gave the impression of a savage wound. Barricades prevented sightseers going near unsafe buildings, but the roads were not blocked by the predicted impassable piles of rubble and traffic flowed past normally; possibly the fact that English houses are only two or three storeys high helped to account for this, possibly also the Spanish photographs had been distorted by clever selection of viewpoint. The damage was not at all impressive. A three-storey public house had taken a 550-lb bomb in its front wall; the result was to leave the ground floor intact, the rear wall and sides intact, and the roof, somewhat battered, still in place over the gap where the explosion had taken place. Part of an upper floor had not fallen away completely and a corner of a room, stripped to the public gaze, showed the unfamiliar picture of blast – furniture and pictures quite intact and undisturbed. This much, from the Spanish reports, was correct – first came the blast wave, spreading outwards, then the suction wave, collapsing inwards. The reality had a reassuring quality because the effects of bombing, instead of being a matter of imagination, could now be measured precisely; not only could lessons of personal survival be drawn but it could be seen what sort of force would be needed to do really significant damage.

Although the small striking forces on the Channel coast concentrated on shipping targets, there was throughout this phase a form of 'armed reconnaissance' inland; single bombers, flying by night or using cloud cover by day, tested the British defences, then virtually an unknown quantity to the Germans, and tried to attack aerodromes, dockyards and armament factories in the south and in the Midlands. On 12 July one of these aircraft, a Heinkel 111 from III *Gruppe* of *Kampfgeschwader* 55 at Villacoublay, near Paris, had flown straight into a radar-assisted reception; as he ducked down out of the clouds above the boom defences at Spithead, off Portsmouth, he was intercepted by seven Spitfires which put in a succession of beam attacks. The bomber jettisoned its load in the sea and the battle moved north across the housetops; after a few miles, as the Heinkel dived out of cloud with three Spitfires hanging grimly on to it and four more coming up, its port engine stopped and it was seen to disappear, losing height, over Portsdown Hill.

With one engine spluttering and banging it came in towards a field near the village of Southwick; wheels up, it passed over a hedge, and went skidding and bumping wildly across a ploughed field, coming to a stop fifty yards from a public house. Both engines and propellers were riddled, also the starboard petrol tank, there were large rents in the starboard wing where bullets had struck at a flat angle, and the observer, shot through the head, lay dead across the bomb-sights. A subaltern from one of the forts on Portsdown Hill took the surrender of the crew, about an hour after they had come down – owing to the winding country lanes it took some time to find the crash. The crew, aged about eighteen to twenty, were just getting out; the pilot staggered as far as the gate leading to the main road, gave the Nazi salute, said 'Heil Hitler', and practically collapsed, while the others supported each other across the field. It must have been a shattering experience to be on the receiving end of so many eight-gun batteries, although an attempt had been made to improve the fire power of the bomber by fitting two extra machine-guns in the rear compartment, aft of the bomb bay, as some sort of protection against beam attacks.

The wreck was a local attraction for some days after-wards, although not many people were actually allowed to go over it; luckily, I was one of them, as I had begun to keep a detailed diary of these events. The Heinkel was painted grey and green on top, light greenish-blue below; the geschwader crest was a red griffon with blue wings, on a shield. It had been hit by several hundred bullets, three of which had struck the cockpit. 'I crawled in through a small hatch on the port side and walked up to the nose; a sweet, sickly smell pervaded it. I settled down in the pilot's seat, tried out the controls, and then had a look at the instrument panel; a gyro, larger than ours, artificial horizon, Lorenz indicator, for blind flying, with kicker and one neon light only, and most interesting of all, a vertical compass with no grid wires or north-seeking needle, instead a miniature aeroplane pointing to the bearing. A well-equipped panel, in some respects better than ours, in others perhaps not so good; interesting, because stories were being passed round that, so poverty-stricken were the Germans, that only one aircraft in a formation had instruments . . .

'I got into the front gunner's position – the nose was entirely perspex, now rather blood-spattered; there was a trapdoor in the floor on which he lay when firing the gun. I slid back the trapdoor, revealing a blood-drenched bomb-sight and compass – the blood must have pumped out, every cranny was thickly saturated with it. I think he must have been shot through the head when actually gazing down through the bomb-sight. Strangely, I felt no emotion whatever, only curiosity. The man had died an honourable death, in battle, and I felt that that was perfectly in order. Yet I won't look at a street accident, so raw and pointless and perhaps the people still kicking . . .'

It was forty years before I learned his name – Oberleutnant Walter Kleinhaus of Stab/KG 55.

Meanwhile, Fink's bombers were demonstrating that the merchant ship, as opposed to the heavily armoured larger warship, was a vulnerable target. On 13 July two convoys were attacked off Harwich, and on the 14th a convoy off Dover. On the 15th Constable Maxwell was patrolling a convoy with 'Jumbo' Gracie and Sergeant Higginson, with cloud ceiling at 2,000 feet, when the bombers dived out of it, there was a shout of 'There they are!' and the three Hurricanes were after them flat out. 'It is the most sickening and awful sight seeing these angels of death diving upon the ships,' wrote Maxwell that evening. 'There is a huge blast of flame from the biggest ship and a smaller blast from another.' There was a confused dog-fight in the clouds, Gracie and Higginson both claiming a bomber. On 18 July there was an attack on ships between Ramsgate and Deal, and on the 19th against a convoy off Dover, now beginning to earn its nickname of 'Hellfire Corner'. 141 Squadron, equipped with the two-seater Defiants, had just been brought south into the battle area and their patrol on this morning was their first action and their last. Nine Defiants took off from Hawkinge, three returned. Most crashed in the Channel but one, burning furiously, came whining down over Dover and blew up in a gout of flame and smoke. In its last seconds, it had been followed by a newsreel camera and the sequence was widely shown, with a commentator screaming out, 'There goes another Messerschmitt!'

Among those who saw this newsreel were some of the surviving members of the squadron.

The Germans, incidentally, claimed twelve Defiants shot down – three more than the total force present. The Defiant had in fact shot its bolt over Dunkirk with one successful action in which the Germans had pounced gleefully from behind on what they thought were unsuspecting Hurricanes and had found themselves looking down forty-eight machine-gun barrels. However, the answer was only too obvious – to attack from below in the blind spot; as a result, the Germans fancied that the Defiant would soon be transferred to night fighting. It was not, because the British were almost as stubborn as the Germans in refusing to recognize the uselessness of their two-seater fighters.

In the afternoon of 20 July another convoy reached the Straits, escorted by the destroyer *Brazen* and the Hurricanes of 32 Squadron from Biggin Hill. They were operating from their forward aerodrome at Hawkinge and kept a close escort of three machines over the convoy the whole afternoon, one section being replaced by another as it came to the end of its flying time. At 5.40 P.M. Green Section, led by the squadron commander, 'Baron' Worrall, had reached the tail of the convoy. Worrall, who is now an Air Vice-Marshal and still serving, continues to retain his nickname; until May, he had been Senior Controller at Biggin Hill but had then gone back to flying. Over the Straits, the warning time being so short and the radar unable to tell the difference between a bomber and a fighter, surprise was always likely, and it was achieved on this occasion. The controller announced that a raid was on its way and that Blue Section was coming out to reinforce, and at that moment Worrall, astern of the ships, saw the bombers approaching the head of the convoy.

Worrall ordered his section into line astern and reached the first Ju. 87 as it was actually starting to dive. He throttled right back, fired a two-second burst, and went headlong towards the ships. The 109s and 110s came down at once, and in between dodging them and getting in damaging bursts at several stukas, he saw the escorting destroyer under dive-bombing attack; then a 109 hit his engine and gravity tank, and glycol streamed back over the windscreen, blinding him. Glycol was a coolant fluid held in a small tank in the nose; if this was holed, the aircraft was liable to catch fire within a few minutes. Worrall tried to get into the very crowded circuit at Hawkinge, but his engine seized up and he had to put down in a field with wheels retracted, the Hurricane skating over the rough surface with such violence that Worrall's straps broke and he was thrown forward, having his head cut open. Then the engine caught fire and he got out very quickly indeed.

His squadron lost two pilots and three aircraft, plus two aircraft damaged. The Germans claimed to have got two hits on the destroyer; they reported it as last seen on fire and out of control. In fact, she sank in tow next day. They did not claim to have done more than damage some of the merchant ships, but the 960-ton collier *Pulborough I* sank off Dover. They had themselves lost nine aircraft this day in operations all round the British Isles, a Ju. 88 (shot down by Page), a Dornier 17, an Fw. 200 four-motor aircraft and six 109s; they thought the RAF had lost more than twice that number, half of which were British bombers attacking Germany and Occupied Europe.

On 21 July Richthofen's Corps attacked a convoy off Bournemouth, and by 24 July Fink's efforts were rising to a climax. At dawn a Channel convoy was spotted off Hastings and subjected to waves of attack as it entered and passed through the Straits; at the same time, an East

Coast convoy was attacked in the Thames Estuary. Two escorted raids put in simultaneously against shipping targets widely separated split 54 Squadron, which was one of those sent up, and they were heavily outnumbered. Colin Gray got involved over the Estuary, thought he had probably got a 109 and, having ammunition left, remained behind. Hearing another pilot calling for help, he climbed up through the clouds and found directly in front of him a 109, turning gently. Over-anxious not to miss, he pressed the firing button inadvertently – and down went the 109, the pilot baling out. He had not sufficiently allowed for deflection and if he had fired when he intended to, the bullets would have passed behind the Messerschmitt.

Gray followed the German down until he hit the sea, saw that he had a dinghy, then flew to the North Foreland to see if he could attract rescuers. Later in the day he was in action over Deal against Dorniers, still bombing the unfortunate convoy. Galland was also in action over the convoy, escorting the Ju. 87s; he got a Spitfire over Margate – the pilot baled out but his parachute did not open.

By 25 July Fink's radar had been installed. He could now watch the convoys assembling off Southend Pier; a glance at a Tide Table would tell him in advance when to expect them in the Straits. The Wireless Interception Station was now of practical value; its reports were passed at once by radio to the fighter airfields, and from there to the German fighters in the air. It was neither so quick nor so accurate as radar, but was useful in that it told the Germans when the British fighters had taken off and allowed deductions about their movements to be made.

The convoy which sailed from Southend on the morning of 25 July was steaming into fame in the annals of the coastal trade – it is not often that a convoy suffers a fifty per cent loss in a matter of hours and in full view of tens of thousands of people. Its designation was CW8 and it consisted of twenty-one merchant ships escorted by two armed trawlers. The passage of the Estuary was made under close escort by six Hurricanes, with a German reconnaissance aircraft circling in the distance – the 'snooper', the seamen called him. By mid-afternoon they had turned to starboard round the North Foreland, through the swept channel in the minefields, and had begun to approach the Straits; they now came under direct observation from Fink's command post in the crowded omnibus on Cap Blanc Nez. He planned to attack as the convoy passed between the Goodwins and the shore, with three waves of stukas escorted by the 109s of *Jagdgeschwader* 26; the Dorniers of KG 2 would be in reserve.

When the first wave came in, the collier *Henry Moon*, at the rear of the convoy, was in the Downs off Deal. Her second mate was Donald Connacher, a North Shields man now master of the modern collier *Pompey Light*; he was below at the time, being served with afternoon tea, when the banging of gunfire brought him up on deck. The collier's 12-pounder was in action, manned by the crew under command of a naval gunner, and the officer on watch had already gone up to 'Monkey Island', the open bridge above the wheelhouse, and got in behind the old Lewis machine-gun mounted there inside a concrete emplacement. The steward, Tommy Dawes, was running up and down the ladder, bringing him fresh drums of ammunition, so Connacher took over the third job, which was to stay under cover in the wheelhouse and reload the empty drums; he saw very little of this wave of attack, merely a general 'state of chaos'. The attack had developed, as it usually did, at the head of the convoy. Vast columns of water, tinged with smoke, rose to six and seven times the height of the mastheads, as the stukas peeled off like divers from a board and came hurtling down.

Witnesses in the collier *Tamworth*, near the head of the line, registered a series of impressions which they could remember in no coherent order: the ship astern of them, the *Leo* of Hull, one moment steaming steadily ahead, the next moment her bottom plates showing and the figures of two men standing on the upturned hull; a Dutch 'schoot' ahead of them one moment, gone the next, with a rowing boat coming out of the smoke; then the *Tamworth* herself rising bodily out of the water from bombs dropping alongside and exploding below her, falling back, listing, engines stopped, wreathed in steam – and another Ju. 87 diving, the gunner on the 12-pounder getting a direct hit on it, and the stuka vanishing in an instant, leaving only a drifting cloud of smoke; and more stukas, bombs gone, sweeping over them at sea-level, machine-guns going; then the collier wallowing out of control while an escort vessel made smoke and a tug came out from Dover.

As the second wave of attack developed, Connacher's ship, still plugging ahead, passed the Dutch 'schoot', falling back through the convoy, bottom up; nearby, the cement carrier *Summity*, hit, sinking, plastered to her truck with cement from a bomb which had exploded in her cargo, was going hell-bent for the shore to beach herself, and did so. Up above was a vicious snarling dog-fight punctuated by the whine of diving fighters, the drum-roll of the British eight-gun batteries and the slower pop-pop-pop of the German cannon; Colin Gray was there, attacking with the Spitfires of 54 Squadron, and so was Galland with his 109s, protecting a stuka gruppe. Connacher, now on watch, was walking up and down the wing of the bridge and as he turned to face France, he caught sight of the next wave of stukas coming towards him. He rang the alarm klaxon and ran up the ladder to the Lewis gun; Tommy Dawes, who had been walking along the deck with cups of tea for the Master and Mate, put them down, followed him up the ladder, then lay down on his stomach ready to take fresh ammunition pans from the Mate, who was in the wheelhouse.

As Connacher peered up along the barrel of the Lewis, the stukas coming up from astern seemed to be splitting into flights of four or five, each flight picking a particular ship for its target; as the convoy had now lost all semblance of formation, it was hard to tell who the planes were after – to Connacher they looked just like a flock of rooks with black, crooked wings. Above him, a flight of five suddenly heaved into disturbed movement, rolling over on to their backs and then pouring down one after the other in a steady stream, directly for the *Henry Moon*, their silhouettes vaguely like birds of prey, growing larger in the sights, and the big bomb slung under the fuselage suddenly falling away and coming at him. There was too much vibration from the bombs exploding around them, of bombs exploding around other ships, and of the gunfire that replied, for Connacher to be able to distinguish the howl of the dive-bombers, or to be intimidated by it if he had. There were British planes up there and they were diving, there was the whistling, whining scream of thrown bombs, somewhere he thought also the sound of machine-gun fire, possibly from the Ju. 87s, and above all his ears were ringing with the clatter of his own Lewis, replying, the cartridges exploding a few inches from his ears. A burst of twenty at the first stuka, a burst of twenty at the second, and the gun stopped.

As he changed drums and cocked the gun, the fourth stuka, possibly the fifth, came falling like a plummet down the sights – its engine cowling steadily expanding in size and directly aligned in the cross-ring, not moving across the sights in any way. This one was going to score a hit. He saw the bomb leave. 'Christ!' he thought. Then he was struck a stunning blow on the mouth by the butt of the Lewis, the ship shuddered violently, enough to throw every man to the deck, vibrating for many seconds after the explosion.

Connacher staggered to his feet, his lip split open. He was now right aft by the funnel instead of on top of the wheelhouse forward, with no recollection of how he had covered both the distance and the drop. He found himself shouting for men to get into a boat which was being lowered, empty, from the davits; no one took any notice, probably because his damaged mouth made him incoherent. As the boat came level with the bulwarks he scrambled in, followed by the Bo'sun, an Able Seaman and a Fireman. The boat touched the water and began to list at once, part of the bottom having been blown out, and it began to sheer out from the ship's side, for the *Henry Moon* was still under way, her engines going ahead. The boat filled, capsized, and threw them into the water, but they clambered back on to the half-submerged keel and watched their ship steam away from them; there was no smoke from her hull, no sign of fire, the *Henry Moon* just steamed slowly ahead, turned quietly over, and then sank. They were left behind, four men on a broken boat waiting for rescue, with an air battle raging overhead as the third wave of stukas came out to strike at the convoy.

The radar had picked up the stukas early and one flight of 54 Squadron was already patrolling Dover when the first wave, escorted by Galland's 109s, approached. Colin Gray, flying one of the five Spitfires of this flight, heard the controller report bandits coming in from Cap Gris Nez, and then saw them – a stuka gruppe of about thirty Ju. 87s, with the three-dozen 109s of III *Gruppe* of JG 26, led by Galland, flying 3,500 feet above them. They looked enormously impressive and the Spitfire leader reported them as 120-plus. For five Spitfires effectively to interfere was impossible; nevertheless, said Gray, 'We were ordered to attack this armada – but in fact it was a hell of a job just to avoid getting shot down.' Gray's section was led by 'Wonky' Way, a gallant, ex-Cranwell type, who took the Spitfires straight at the bombers and was himself immediately 'bounced' by 109s. Gray called out to him, 'Break, break!' and then was forced to dodge. Galland recalled that the Spitfires got to the bombers just before they began to peel off, that he took his gruppe down on them, and that he selected one Spitfire for himself; the pilot did not get out and the burning aircraft struck the sea near the harbour mole at Dover.

'This was not a particularly successful time for the 109,' said Galland. 'We were too fast to escort stukas and they had a bad time, so we were not satisfied with our own performance. But in this combat we had clear superiority, the English aircraft fighting almost without exception singly.' 'Two out of our five were shot down,' said Gray, 'and I spent the next twenty minutes trying to avoid being shot down, in fact I was able only to fire at one of them. They kept telling us help was coming, and a Hurricane squadron arrived as the scrap was ending – they came sniffing round me, to make sure I wasn't a 109.' 'All this fighting was between the convoy and Dover,' said Galland, 'new English fighters coming from the land to join battle. I next attacked a Hurricane, but he escaped by half-rolling away. In a space of about fifteen minutes I saw four fighters hit the sea and one parachute.'

Galland's gruppe had the difficult job of direct escort, while other 109s provided the high cover for the operation; their task was easier. The Hurricanes of 111 Squadron, which were based forward at Hawkinge that day, had to climb up underneath the waiting German fighters; they were attacked when they had reached 18,000 feet and although they claimed a 109, were unable to get near the bombers. The Air Staff were pressing Dowding to make still more use of these forward aerodromes, not realizing that, as Squadron Leader Thompson said, 'You never had time to get height before you were attacked.'

The convoy was now scattered and Fink could see E-boats emerging from Calais to complete the destruction which his bombers had wrought – then two destroyers were coming boldly out of Dover, heading for the French coast at thirty-five knots; 'two little boats', Fink called them. In a little while, they were within gun range, the E-boats making smoke and turning away, their attack broken up in a storm of gunfire before it had hardly begun, and the destroyers' shells were slamming into the cliffs around Fink's command post. 'Cheek,' Fink called it, 'the limit of cheek! We felt strong and secure then; after all, we'd just won two wars. I'd been watching the battle on the radar, and now I sent out stukas against them – they disappeared quickly!'

'The E-boats put up such a smoke screen that it was difficult to see what was happening,' said Lieutenant-Commander F. C. Broderick, senior captain of the two destroyers *Brilliant* and *Boreas*. 'I think three or four were damaged – at any rate, the E-boats never appeared again. Then we were fired on by shore batteries from Gris Nez – quite small stuff and no damage done – and were ordered to return to Dover; while returning, we were attacked by twenty-four stukas, lots of near misses and *Boreas*'s steering gear out of action for five minutes.'

Looking down on the scene from high above the Straits were Geoffrey Page and Barry Sutton, patrolling with 56 Squadron; the CO's voice began to crackle in the R/T. 'Flashes from the guns of a couple of destroyers out in the Channel had held our attention for some minutes,' recalled Sutton, 'but what the target was had not been apparent. Now, swarming above the ships and about 12,000 feet below us, were aircraft in two layers. Three Hurricanes on my right heeled over until I could see the light blue of their bellies before they plunged down into the attack – they were "A" Flight machines, carrying out the CO's orders to attack that upper layer, which must be fighters. A second later, Gracie, Page and myself followed, diving almost vertically towards the destroyers, which had now ceased fire. That lower layer, which as we thought, consisted of Junkers 87s, had already begun to disperse. Two Ju. 87s in front of me turned steeply and headed for home. Their fighter escort was no use to them now.'

'We had been drenched on the bridge by near misses,' said Broderick, 'then we had a signal that fighter cover was over us now – which it wasn't, as the fighters flew right over to France.' 'It was musical comedy procedure,' recalled Page. 'It was like flicking a pack of cards: a Ju. 87, a Hurricane behind, followed by another Ju. 87, followed by another Hurricane, the two formations interlocking.' The whole pack tore for the French coast, leaving the destroyers behind and unprotected, the pilot of the Ju. 87 in front of Page kicking right and left rudder alternately to get the big fin out of the way and let his gunner have a chance.

The pilot of the Ju. 87 Sutton was following was doing the same, then he steep-turned to starboard and flew right across his sights. 'The worst shot in the world couldn't have missed,' said Sutton. 'In less than a second it was all over. It plunged in like a stone and made little splash. Something wound up in my stomach. It was my first Hun but there was no feeling of elation; I was conscious of a sickly, nauseating wave of sympathy for the wretched men I had sent to their doom. Then a second Ju. 87 flashed over my head, but he was already being dealt with by another Hurricane, snapping at his heels like an angry terrier. The evening sun picked out the cliffs east of Calais ahead of us, so that they shone gold above the cobalt water of the Channel. Against this background the end of the fugitive, which came a moment later, presented its brief, fantastic scene.'

The rear-gunner fired a last burst at Page, who was pursuing the stuka, then it caught fire, the flames lengthening in the slipstream to a huge, red banner, tinged with smoke. Page pulled out to one side and watched: it seemed to fly for a long time before it went in, possibly the crew were already dead; all that came up was one tyre and some burning oil.

The Channel was dotted with the funeral pyres of Ju. 87s, but the survivors were bombed up and immediately sent out again; about two-dozen of them caught *Brilliant* and *Boreas* three miles from Dover, the destroyers leaving huge, zig-zag wakes as they altered course to avoid the bombs. In the *Brilliant* the main AA armament consisted of one single-barrel pom-pom which in cold weather had to be heated by an electric kettle and in action had continually to be struck with a mallet, as this cleared the jam which occurred at every fifth round; and there were no fighters now to interfere with the bombing. Two bombs struck the quarter-deck of the *Brilliant*, missing the propeller shaft by about a foot and failing to explode; two bombs hit *Boreas* on the bridge, exploding below in the galley flat, killing or wounding fifty men. The convoy was still being bombed, but the last gruppe of Dorniers to set out turned back while over the Channel, as no fighter escort had arrived; Otto Bechtle, who was flying one of them, saw the scattered ships on the waters and the other Dorniers returning empty, before his formation abandoned the attack. Fink had no intention of throwing away the lives of his crews on a gamble; he had certainly won air superiority over the Straits this day, but not air supremacy.

That night, Donald Connacher was in a Dover hospital which was completely swamped by wounded merchant seamen and naval men from the *Boreas*. He and the three others had been rescued from the upturned lifeboat by a motor launch manned by Norwegians wearing German-type helmets; the sight of these, and the sound of the foreign language, had convinced them for a moment that they were all booked for a prison camp.

Of the twenty-one merchant ships which had sailed from Southend that morning, five were on the bottom of the Straits and six were left crippled on the waters, by the time the sun went down; both the destroyers were damaged, and one would be out of action for some time. During the night the E-boats ventured out again and under cover of the darkness successfully attacked the surviving ships, sinking three. 'Suicide lads' was the half-joking description the survivors of CW8 gave to themselves. Since 10 July the Channel convoys had lost 24,000 tons sunk by air attack alone; in all, one ship in every three which sailed became a casualty. The Admiralty cancelled all sailings of merchant ships through the Channel, and the convoys stopped; only destroyers and mine-sweepers moved in what was now no longer a highway but, in truth, the front line.

This position lasted for four days more. On 27 July, in the space of two hours, two destroyers were sunk and one damaged. One sinking, that of the *Wren*, was off Lowestoft on the east coast; the other two were Dover destroyers. The flotilla leader *Codrington* was first damaged and then put down, the Germans calculated, in thirty-five seconds; she was in the Channel off Dover. Inside the harbour, the *Walpole* was damaged – she was

towed to Chatham next day, 'B' flight of 56 Squadron
escorting her from the North Foreland on. On 29 July the
Delight, which the Germans mistook for a cruiser, was
reported to them by one of their E-boats to have sunk off
Portland some hours after an attack by Richthofen's
Corps; they were right – she had. After that, the Channel
was empty except for minesweepers and the small vessels
of the Inner Patrol, which had also suffered during this
period. Dover was abandoned as a base for destroyers
and when destroyers moved out of Portsmouth they did
so by night. By day, the Channel was German.

Fink and Richthofen had carried out the directive of
2 July. After 4 July, all big-ship convoys on world routes
in and out of the port of London had been driven out of
the Channel; after 25 July, all coastal convoys had been
stopped; on 28 July, the withdrawal of the Dover destroyers had been forced; after 29 July, the use of destroyers
in the Channel by day had been prohibited.

The victory was tactical, not strategic, because Britain's
seaborne communications with the world were uninterrupted, the ships being loaded and discharged at ports
inaccessible to the Luftwaffe in daylight. Even as a tactical
victory it was incomplete, because the British destroyers
prowled night after night off the Channel ports, hopeful
of catching an invasion fleet as it set out. The Luftwaffe
could do nothing about that, nor could the German Navy,
fatally weakened by its losses in the Norwegian campaign.
Also, the German Channel victory was in part an illusion
– the Luftwaffe had met only a fraction of Fighter
Command, whereas invasion would bring in the whole of
it. If the victory was to be exploited for invasion purposes,
then it would have to be extended; the destroyers would
have to be driven, not merely from Dover, but out of
every naval port in the south-east in order that they could
no longer intervene by night. As long as the British

retained some three dozen of them within striking distance of the Channel ports, any German invasion attempt must sail to disaster.

In Fink's view, 'My force could have dominated the Straits by day, granted that we had air superiority; but in no circumstances by night. My force alone could not have dominated a wider area than this. But if the RAF had been beaten, we certainly could have kept British warships out of the invasion area during daylight and kept our army supplied.'

Because the forces used in the Channel Battle were limited on both sides, and not merely on one side, the verdict applied to a full-scale clash: first the British fighters must be destroyed, then the British Navy – and then invasion was possible. Anything else was wishful thinking.

3

The Silent Sea

1–11 August

During July, parallel with the Channel Battle, while anti-invasion measures were pushed forward on the British side with a sense of desperate urgency, Hitler was metaphorically scratching his head. On 2 July, the day on which orders were given for the Channel Battle to begin, another order asked for information to be collected regarding a possible invasion of the island; on 11 July, by the time the Channel Battle was in full swing, Hitler agreed with Admiral Raeder that without air supremacy, nothing could be risked; on 6 July, Hitler issued his Operational Directive No. 16, which began, unenthusiastically, 'As England, in spite of the hopelessness of her military position, has so far shown herself unwilling to come to any compromise, I have decided to begin to prepare for, and if necessary to carry out, an invasion of England . . . and, if necessary, the island will be occupied . . .'; on 19 July, Hitler appealed to the British Government for a negotiated peace; at the end of July the German Naval Staff, who had been studying the crux of the matter, the seaborne preparations, recommended that invasion be postponed until next spring; and on 1 August the Luftwaffe was ordered to beat down the RAF, destroy its bases, and attack harbours – except those on the south coast which would be needed by the invading troops. There is plenty of evidence of vacillation on the German side, as of men confronted with a chasm which must be jumped but appears to be a fraction too wide. Above all, it was the leader who hesitated.

Generalfeldmarschall Albert Kesselring, now living in

retirement in South Germany, who then commanded *Luftflotte* 2 and would have had the most important part of all the air commanders in the invasion, was convinced that success was a possibility. 'But the fact that I was not able to get a hearing from Hitler for my views on the necessary measures and that Göring only visited me twice in my Channel command post, and then only addressed me very briefly in connection with *Sealion* (the code name for the operation) is for me the undoubted proof that Hitler merely played with the idea.'

It was, without doubt, the most serious decision of Hitler's life. His army advisers were optimistic, his naval advisers pessimistic. Admiral Gladich confided to Otto Bechtle that an invasion attempt could easily cost the lives of 100,000 men (the French campaign had cost 60,000) and still be unsuccessful – Hitler's prestige would crumble, and that might mean the end of the Nazi Party and the end of the war. Invasion was the only chance for Hitler to win the war; it was also the only chance for Hitler to lose power.

There were no modern precedents by which to judge the matter. General de Gaulle, who had witnessed the German methods of close co-operation between tanks and aircraft, judged that the Channel was an anti-tank ditch so formidable that it would fatally separate these two components; he believed a successful invasion was hardly possible.[1] Opinion in the Royal Navy generally was that blockade was a more serious threat than an invasion, although raids were always possible. But Admiral Ramsay, commanding at Dover, believed invasion to be a possibility and fifth-columnists to be a fact (de Gaulle thought the fifth-column much exaggerated, mostly panic

---

[1] Given, through an intermediary, to the French Institute in London on 28 June. The author made notes of what de Gaulle's views were, but is not aware if they were ever published.

rumours spread by the cowardly). Churchill spent the
summer intermittently planning a whole series of
invasions of his own, all impractical, and actually carried
out one of them, which failed; he can hardly have been
obsessed by anybody else's invasion.[2] Dowding, believing
the strength of the Luftwaffe to be greater than it was,
thought that only careful and precise handling of his
forces could prevent the preliminary conditions for an
invasion from being established.

The British public, deluged with scare stories of para-
chutists and fifth-columnists and denied even their own
signposts, unaware that Hitler's plans for the French
campaign had not envisaged a total collapse of France
and that consequently no preparations for invading England had been made, assumed that the Germans were
most thoroughly ready; but did not in their bones believe
that they would come, although government measures
made it seem likely. Particularly drastic (to an Englishman) had been the suspension of habeas corpus and the
consequent imprisonment without trial of many people,
mostly refugees from Hitler, as a precaution against the
off-chance that one or two of them might be potential
traitors. This contrasted oddly with the firmness of Elizabeth I in refusing demands to take similar sweeping
measures against a suspected but hypothetical Catholic
fifth-column, even when the Armada was actually in the
Channel.

Possibly it was these very measures (which to Hitler
must have appeared a vain beating of the air) and the fair
guess that might be made at the state of mind of the
people behind them, that decided him to make the actual
preparations for a landing in England; in spite of defiant

[2] *The Central Blue*, p. 302, by Sir John Slessor. The assault on Dakar
took place on 23 September, 1940, while the Battle of Britain was at its
height.

speeches and the expected doggedness of the British people, resistance might not continue very long. A series of blows by the Luftwaffe might make the difficult business of an invasion a mere formality, or might avoid the necessity for it altogether by inducing the British leaders to conclude hostilities on terms relatively lenient. If this was so, and some such thoughts do seem to lie behind Operational Directive No. 16, then the parallel with 1588 is exact – for the Spanish Armada, too, was largely an imposing bluff, intended not to conquer England but to force Elizabeth to change her policy.[3] Both in 1588 and in 1940, this was wishful thinking of the most dangerous kind, for it resulted in a confusion of aims. The unfortunate striking force, in both cases inadequate to its task, was unable to concentrate on the preliminary tactical condition – the defeat of the enemy force barring the way; instead it was dissipated on invasion measures and strategic bluff. Everything had to be done at once, instead of in due order. Whatever chance the Germans may have had of carrying out a successful invasion in 1940, and it must have been very slim, was denied them by the probably well-founded intuition of their leader.

But certainly Hitler hoped for, and even promised his people, a victory; to impose his will on the British and to force them out of the war; this, at least, he calculated on achieving – by a mixture of bombing, bluff and blarney, with invasion boats in the background.

Although Great Britain had been stripped of her Allies and her army virtually disarmed, her weakness was momentary only; potentially, the Island Empire was at least as strong as Greater Germany. British bombers now

---

[3] See *Spanish Calendar*, Vol. IV (HMSO), particularly document 253, the King's instructions to the Duke of Parma, in case he should be able to effect a landing in England; the document to be returned, unread, if it should not be possible.

ranged almost every night over Occupied Europe and the Reich, a portent of what the future might hold. What they might be able to do in the event of invasion was the factor most difficult to evaluate. To some of the Luftwaffe leaders, judging by RAF attacks on their airfields and on targets in Germany itself, Bomber Command appeared a negligible quantity compared to their own force – and with this view some British Admirals most heartily agreed.[4] There were few successes, many failures. But the causes of failure were temporary and some at least did not apply where invasion targets were concerned.

Squadron Leader R. J. Oxley, who is now a Group Captain, with the DSO, OBE and DFC, was then a Hampden pilot in 50 Squadron of No. 5 Bomber Group. He had begun his operational tour on 19 June with a trip to Hamburg; it was a Sunday, and it seemed to him all wrong to commit a hostile act on that day. His attitude was typical of the atmosphere:

'We were mostly young men, with a very lethal cargo, so there was a tight political control over us; thinking was dominated at this time by the SEMO (Self-Evident Military Objective) and the MOPA (Military Objective Previously Attacked). For instance, one night, it was 29 June, I had to bomb a particular warehouse in a particular street in Hamburg – that and nothing else. If I couldn't find it, I had to bring the bombs back. We had no flares or target markers to help us then, we were constantly enjoined not to kill civilians, and this tended to hinder initiative. On this occasion our take-off was delayed until 3½ hours after everyone else had gone, and when we came to the coast it was nearly dawn, much too late to go inland, so I went to Sylt instead of Hamburg. Flak came up at us from

[4] See *Gedanken zum Zweiten Weltkrieg*, by Generalfeldmarschall A. Kesselring, and *Max Horton and the Western Approaches*, by Rear-Admiral W. S. Chalmers.

the seaplane base at List (which had been bombed before, so it was a MOPA), but I decided to attack the Hindenburg Dam, which carried the railway line to the island across the mudflats, as it was obviously a SEMA and miles from a house anyway. When I returned and reported what I had done, I was put under arrest by the Station Commander; he thought I ought to have brought my bombs back.' The official report recorded that the bombs were jettisoned in the sea; it was intended that Hitler should not have the least excuse to retaliate on the British civil population – until Bomber Command could hit back hard.

What puzzled Oxley at that time were the reports of the more experienced men. They rarely claimed to have hit the target, the bombs had either just overshot or just undershot it; and Oxley wondered how they managed it, because he usually failed to find the target at all, particularly when it was in the Ruhr and shrouded by industrial haze. Bland answers were returned to his questions – 'Ah, if you get up high, you can see through the smoke.' He tried that – and could see nothing. Next he tried coming down low, picking up an autobahn, following it along to the intersection which led off to the city in which his target was located – and was then usually blinded by searchlights on the outskirts. On one occasion he was following the Dortmund–Ems Canal at low level and passing a cottage with a light in the window, when one of his gunners started to pour a hail of bullets into it; that was plain murder, and Oxley climbed up out of range. Generally, there was no theory of bombing, each pilot experimented with his own methods and learned a little; there was no radio beam, such as the Germans had, nor the elaborate target-finding methods and devices which Bomber Command developed a few years later. But there was one other reason why successes were rare.

'The fact is,' said Oxley, 'we didn't believe in what we were doing. We were not convinced of the importance of what we did, not when sent off to an oil refinery at that stage of the war. Later on, when we had the methods and the equipment, we did believe; we believed we were winning the war. For the invasion barges, too – we were convinced – we felt the nights simply weren't long enough.'

Apart from attacks on German invasion preparations, the one other satisfying business at that time was mine-laying, known as 'Gardening', because each harbour in the North Sea and Baltic had a vegetable code name, such as 'Onion'. It was satisfying, because the pilots knew it was effective; it sank ships or it delayed them while the channels were swept. 'Very accurate, more precise than dive-bombing,' was Oxley's opinion, an opinion shared by the German mine-laying pilots, who used the same methods. From a bomber flying by night over a darkened countryside few, if any, landmarks are visible; but a coast-line is as clear as a silhouette.

On 21 July, while the Channel Battle was rising to a climax, Oxley was out interfering with the Swedish iron ore traffic to Germany, a stealthy, hazardous, but satisfying task. He crossed the North Sea in daylight, fired at only from the northern tip of Sylt, at dusk, as he entered Denmark. By 11.30 he was over the target area – the Baltic between Denmark and Sweden. On the one side, in Occupied Denmark, was the blackout, with tracer coming up at him from the darkness – on the other side, in neutral Sweden, the towns and villages were brilliantly illuminated and when he flew low over the coast, he could see the street lights, civilization, and even people waving up at the darkened British bomber. Then the timed run to the navigational channel, so engrossed in the job that for the moment the hazards were, so to speak, filed away, ready to be taken out and considered later – when the mine had gone down from 600 feet into its allotted place. In the long run, the mine-layers (on both sides) sank more ships than did the daylight attacks, hectic though these were at times.

There was a lull in the Channel Battle from the last week of July to the end of the first week in August: there were no more ship targets in the Channel for the Luftwaffe to attack or for the RAF to protect, and attacks on inland targets were forbidden except for single aircraft flown by picked crews in cloudy weather or by night. The British had withdrawn the target, produced the lull, and were using it to good effect to improve their defences before the full strength of the Luftwaffe came at them. This in no way suited the Germans and prevented them from continuing the second part of the 2 July directive, which was to gain and maintain air superiority – that is, to cripple the enemy fighter force, so that it would be unable to interfere with the bombers when they came over in numbers. To do this it was necessary to bring on a series of fighter combats in circumstances favourable to the Germans. Therefore, the 109s were sent to roam over the Channel and south-east England in large formations, freed from any hampering commitment to guard bombers, also to use height and the sun as they liked in order to have every advantage on their side; theoretically, it was admirable. In practice, Dowding kept his fighters on the ground and German intentions were frustrated. Galland, who led his gruppe frequently over England during this phase, recalled that no matter what they did, the Germans could produce no reaction. They therefore sent over the *lockvögel* – a few bombers acting as decoy ducks for the fighters waiting in ambush high above – but there was no result. 'Schweinerei!' said Galland, 'but still they didn't come!'

The lull lasted until 8 August, when the British again presented the Germans with a target which the Luftwaffe was allowed to attack and which it was worthwhile for the RAF to defend; they thereby brought on a series of air battles so intense that some people thought the main assault had really started. The date is still sometimes given as the beginning of the Battle of Britain and a Hurricane pilot, Squadron Leader J. R. A. Peel, who retired as a Group Captain and now runs a farm, is claimed to be the pilot who fired the first shot for the RAF.

The British had refused to accept the verdict of 25 July, but they had realized that they could no longer merely pass through the Straits – the Straits of Dover would have to be 'forced'. They adopted the following measures: the convoy would pass through the Straits in darkness, thus avoiding close-range air attack and possibly detection; the escort would consist of *Hunt*-class destroyers, which had a more adequate AA armament than the trawlers and occasional destroyers used previously; barrage balloons would be flown from small vessels hurriedly converted to this purpose, to prevent stuka attacks being pressed home; and there would be full co-operation from Fighter Command in place of the token protection which had so irritated the Royal Navy by its implication that the defence of shipping had somehow no connection with the defence of the country. So when the twenty-five merchant ships of Convoy CW9 sailed from the Thames Estuary on the evening of 7 August, it was a combined operation. Dowding was committed to its full protection; it was this which brought on the air battles of 8 August, which went some way to justify his reluctance to engage fully under these conditions.

A convoy had already been sailed in the opposite

direction under cover of night, starting from Falmouth on 5 August; by day it had lain in various harbours under the protection of the AA guns. As the ships were mostly sailing 'light' they were not of the same order of importance as the colliers of CW9, heavily laden with part of the 40,000 tons of seaborne coal and coke which was required every week to keep industry going in the south. This successful night sailing promised well for CW9.

Radar was the most closely guarded of British secrets, and it would probably have disconcerted the men sailing with the convoy to know that the Germans had a radar set, with a range of seventy-five miles, emplaced on the French side of the Straits for the primary purpose of watching shipping movements; consequently, the night passage availed them nothing. The Germans had plenty of time to set a trap, which they duly snapped shut in the early hours of 8 August. An E-boat flotilla, the noise of their engines masked by German aircraft, crossed over from France and took up an ambush position ahead of the convoy and beside the swept channel through which it must come. 'They ravaged it like wolves from Beachy Head to the Nab Tower,' said Captain J. H. Potts of the *Betswood*, who by the end of the war held the Channel 'Blue Riband' for 120 wartime passages of the Straits. Three ships went down and two were damaged; a collision in the hectic confusion of the night action had accounted for one in each category.

At dawn on 8 August, although two destroyers had come out from Portsmouth to help, there was no convoy – merely little groups of ships scattered beyond hope of reassembly from Shoreham to the Nab. At about 10 A.M. the stukas of Richthofen's Corps, escorted by the 109s of *Jagdgeschwader* 27 from Cherbourg, made their first attack. The first squadron to intercept, No. 145 led by Peel, interfered with the bombing so much that it was ineffective. One of his flight commanders, now Group Captain R. G. Dutton, DSO, DFC, said, 'Convoys were the most profitable hunting ground of any! The stukas were so tightly packed and so numerous that provided one could get in to them before they dived to attack it was virtually impossible to fail to knock a couple or so down. They were easy meat, but the trouble was that unless the 109s or 110s could be fully engaged it was virtual suicide to wait long enough to confirm the kills – some blew up, but some did not!'

The vulnerability of the stuka to the British eight-gun fighters, and the difficulty of escorting it, was indeed worrying the German fighter pilots. That morning Werner Andres, who led a gruppe of JG 27, was off duty and did not take part in the first attack. He received a direct order, by telephone, to take part in the next, and his protest – that his machine was in pieces undergoing an engine overhaul – was over-ridden. The mechanics hurriedly began to reassemble the engine, but it was not ready even by the time the second wave of attack, which had struck at about 12.45, was returning. They reported, 'All ships sunk except six.'

Captain Potts had been underneath that attack, which took place off the east side of the Isle of Wight. 'The stukas were nerve-wracking – they broke the crockery and cracked the steam pipes. The effect was that the scene changed from a perfectly flat sea to a typhoon.' The *Betswood* steamed through untouched, as she did throughout the war, the sea around her littered with wrecks. Two armed yachts and four armed trawlers were sent by Portsmouth Command to their assistance; one of the former, the *Wilna*, lying in St Helens Roads, made for Dunnose, passing on the way only one empty lifeboat, riddled with bullets, and a Dutch wheelhouse, complete with bell. She was off Dunnose in company with an armed trawler when the third wave of attack came in at about 5 P.M.

Before the stukas and fighters took off for the third time that day, they received the order, 'The convoy must be completely destroyed.' 'Rubbish!' snapped Andres to the other pilots. 'Why won't they let those few ships get away? Even supposing the English are very stupid, they will guess by now that any assembly reported by their radar must be going to attack the convoy again; and that'll mean heavy losses for us.' He suspected that a desire on someone's part for a mention in the communiqués lay behind the order which meant sending out a force of single-engined aircraft to make a long flight over water against a fully-alerted enemy. With an invasion due in the near future, when every stuka would be needed, it seemed pointless to sacrifice them for so little gain. They should, he thought, anyway be confined to the Dover area where the distance over water was less than twenty miles instead of more than sixty as at Cherbourg.

Werner Andres, who is now the Mayor of Kirn, a country town between the Moselle and the Rhine, was thirty at the time; as he said, 'a very old daddy' to be a fighter pilot. His gruppe had been formed the previous January; apart from himself and six other pilots, it consisted of boys just out of the training schools. Their only formation flying experience was in the basic rotte of two machines; they were not proficient in the staffel formation of twelve, and they had had no tactical training. Hardly any were National Socialists, because when pupils finished their political schooling in the *Napolas* they were asked if they wanted to go into the armed forces or into the armed SS. About ten per cent opted for the *Waffen* SS (which in its own way was an élite formation), thus getting rid of most of the convinced Nazis; those who joined the Luft-waffe did so because they were eager to fly. The young pilots were often vocal in their criticism of the excessive pressing home of propaganda points which they had experienced in the *Napolas*. 'Even your piss-pot,' as they elegantly expressed it, 'could be connected in some way with National Socialist philosophy.'

As his number two in the third attack of the day Andres took the most inexperienced of the young pilots. His job would be to fly in loose formation with Andres, the number one, and watch his tail all the time; *Katchmarek*, a faithful old servant who'll do anything you tell him, was a term often applied to the 'steady old plodder', the number two.

When the formation arrived off the Isle of Wight, Andres had to swivel his head a good deal, doing the *Katchmarek*'s job for him, in addition to his own. The feat they had to attempt was to peel off with the stukas and go down with them, so that the fighters were still in attendance when the Ju. 87s pulled out at the bottom of their dive – a favourite time for the British fighters to fasten on to them. As Andres turned over on his back to go down in the dive, he cast one final look at his *Katchmarek*, saw him in his proper place, thought 'All right, then,' and went plunging down. Trying to stay with the clumsy dive-bombers when flying a high-speed fighter is an ordeal requiring great concentration, and Andres had now no time to look behind – that was the number two's job.

When the stukas flattened out and pulled up from their attack, Andres was still with them – but instead of his *Katchmarek* there was a Spitfire sitting on his tail, banging away at him. While trying to throw it off, the radiator of his 109 was hit and damaged, and although he escaped the engine was overheating; about halfway between the Isle of Wight and Cherbourg, it stopped. Andres found himself swimming in the water, no dinghy, only an old

Mae West, and thirty miles from land in both directions; he had made his point about single-engined aircraft.

The main target of the stukas had been the six rescue ships, not one of which escaped damage. Off Dunnose the *Wilna* and the *Kingston*-class trawler lay stopped, the former with her mast down, riddled by fragments, and with three dead and six wounded men aboard out of her tiny ship's company. The trawler was in a far worse state, wreathed in steam, with most of her crew dead, wounded or scalded. There was no other ship visible on the sea.

Although in mid-July a 'Churchill Order' had directed that ambulance seaplanes of the German Air/Sea Rescue service should be shot down,[5] British attempts to establish a similar system for picking up pilots of both sides from the Channel had not been anything more than an improvisation; and so it was that on this day Pilot Officer 'Nobby' Clarke, still pressing for a transfer to fighters, and still flying unarmed aircraft on tedious duties from Gosport, was ordered to direct the rescue ships (now themselves in need of help) to any survivors. Squadron Leader Carpenter, his CO, told him to use his own aircraft, a Roc. This was a fighter version of the stuka, very similar to the Defiant, including the four-gun turret – except that this had been removed from Clarke's aircraft. Carpenter told him that the ships had been stuka-ed and that there were plenty of 109s around. Clarke replied, 'Oh well, nice to have known you, sir,' and walked out to the machine, secretly pleased that it was he who had been chosen to go, vanity, as he said, being a bold conqueror of nerves. Fifteen minutes later he was airborne and heading across Spithead for the Isle of Wight.

'Half a dozen miles south of the island I found the

---

[5] See *Their Finest Hour*, by W. S. Churchill, p. 284. The reason there given is that the rescued German pilots might 'bomb our civilian population again'.

wreckage,' he wrote afterwards. 'It stretched in every direction. Tables, chairs, timber, hatches, spars, empty lifebelts, chests of drawers – debris of every sort. And coke – vast rafts of it, grey-black against the dark blue of the sea, damping the waves to gently heaving mounds. And there were patches of oil, too, silver-grey in the sun – spreading from already sunken ships as great gobs of it rose to the surface to feed each ever-widening pool. There were ships in various positions of death throes. One, seemingly normal from a distance, I found to be an empty shell of red-glowing coal – the shimmering heat lifted my Roc in the manner of a vicious Cu. Nim. cloud. The steel masts had crumbled into the inferno, the decks and sides showed bright red through the slashes caused by bomb splinters, the bridge structure had mostly collapsed.

'There were others, too. One, upside down, showed a barnacle-encrusted bottom and part of its enormous propeller, which looked like a giant shark swimming past a half-tide rock. I saw another ship, seemingly undamaged, rear into the classical vertical position before it slid under, and yet another, which was burning furiously the whole time I was there, was still floating when I left three hours later. But my job was to search for survivors and although I flew around at nil feet scrutinizing every ship and every piece of wreckage I could not find a solitary human being – and neither could I see any of the so-called rescue ships.

'Then, after half an hour's circling, a *three*-star Very cartridge exploded right under my nose – so close that it almost hit the engine. I whipped over in a steep turn and there, held afloat by a strange sort of Mae West and wearing a *black* helmet was – well, to my mind it could only be a German pilot; he was certainly not British in that rig-out. He waved frantically as I roared around him and I had that momentary qualm; should I do something about a Jerry or carry on looking for our own fellows?

Then common decency took charge and I tried to fix the position of this solitary survivor by cross-bearings from the shore – now about twelve miles distant. Then I set off to look for a rescue ship. I found her twenty minutes later, steaming at speed from somewhere up Channel – grey-painted, of indeterminate class, with the nomenclature T68 on her sides. In relief I headed straight for her and received a shattering welcome from the trigger-happy navy.

'I sheered away from the shell-bursts and cursed their ignorance at not recognizing an aircraft of their own Fleet Air Arm. I had no time to waste, so I circled to their stern and made another run at nil feet directly towards her backsides – a particularly vulnerable position for most naval ships. She twisted in an attempt to bring her guns to bear, but I turned with her – throttling back, lowering the flaps and opening the hood – and as I flew past her starboard side, level with the cluster of ducking men on the bridge, I waggled two fingers in the uncomplimentary fashion of Englishmen. Winston Churchill had not then made the sign famous, but my recognition was achieved all the same . . .'

Clarke picked up a message-streamer, wrote, 'Bloke in drink: follow me,' and dropped it, weighted with a hunk of lead, on to the deck of T68. After all, they had shot at him first. He flew slowly back to the German pilot, who was waving feebly, and circled to mark the spot.

'While T68 was picking up the pilot I recommended my search and found a body (dead or alive?) in a water-logged lifeboat and an overjoyed man on a Carley Float who waved vigorously. By this time T68 was following me around like a hungry dog behind a butcher. Something, perhaps intuition, sent me further out. Thirty miles south I saw the dot of a small boat and edged towards it cautiously. It was an RAF launch, badly damaged – her ensign hoisted inverted in the universal distress signal. From 2,000 feet there was no sign of T68 – and the bleak aspects of the naked horizon, the white horses which were beginning to appear as the wind increased, the brassy sky overhead, all made me wonder what I could do to help. I waggled my wings encouragingly and sped homewards. A tug from Portsmouth found the launch before nightfall; there had been eight men on board, most of them injured. That was the end of my first Air/Sea Rescue patrol and it certainly showed up our inefficiency compared with the Germans.'

Andres was in mid-Channel for two hours before being picked up by one of the thirty-odd Heinkel 59 seaplanes which the Germans were using for this work; they could land alongside the survivor and they carried a doctor.

The Germans believed that they had sunk thirteen ships and damaged fifteen, by air attack alone. On the British side, at the time and in the years since then, the figures have varied a good deal because there were a number of confusing factors. The actual losses by air attack appear to have been four merchant ships sunk and six damaged (some of them beyond repair), plus six rescue ships damaged; apart from this, three merchant ships were sunk and two damaged in the E-boat action. In all, twenty-two ships became casualties in the Channel between 3 A.M. and 5.30 P.M. on 8 August.[6] At the time, the loss of two ships by air attack was admitted.

The total aircraft losses, in all actions around the British Isles that day, were also amended later:

The Aeroplane (aviation weekly, publishing the Air Ministry claim, 1940): 60 German aircraft and 16 British fighters.

[6] These figures were kindly supplied by the Admiralty to the author, the names of all the ships concerned being given. It is, of course, thoroughly inadvisable when operations are actually in progress to give the enemy an accurate and reliable picture of the results he has achieved.

The Defence of the United Kingdom by Basil Collier (HMSO, 1957): 28 German aircraft and 20 British fighters.

The Luftwaffe claimed to have shot down 43 Spitfires and Hurricanes. Their own records are now incomplete, partly because many of them were lost in the great Dresden fire raid of 1945 and partly because much of what remained was captured by the Allies and dispersed. Thus it is not always clear whether the figures for losses are those 'by enemy action' only or whether they also include accidents incurred in operations, sometimes a not inconsiderable figure, particularly in bad weather. However, it seems that the German losses off the Isle of Wight on 8 August amounted to fourteen aircraft – eight Ju. 87s, five Bf. 109s and one Bf. 110. Notwithstanding the damage inflicted on the ships, the loss of virtually a complete stuka staffel in one day – nearly ten per cent of the force – was obviously too high a rate to be borne for long. But their losses in single-engined fighters, only a quarter that suffered by the British, was good arithmetic; if they could maintain it, the British fighter force would be destroyed before the German, and air superiority would have been won. Although they sometimes lost sight of it in pursuing the destruction of other targets, attractive from the political view or from pure opportunity, it was this which was throughout the battle the background of all German plans: the destruction of the British fighter force by their own fighter force. The methods varied but the principle was the same – to enforce battle on the British and to ensure that the British engaged at a disadvantage.

As regards place, and disregarding tactics, the location most favourable to the Germans was France – but the British could not be induced to fight over there; the next most favourable location was over the Channel, which would close over the fallen without regard for nationality;

the least favourable location was over England, where all damaged aircraft and pilots who baled out would come down in enemy territory. The importance of this, statistically, may be seen in the battle casualties of 54 Squadron in their first year of operation – 3 September, 1939 to 3 September, 1940 – which amounted to 13 pilots and 31 aircraft. Had they been fighting throughout over enemy territory, as the Germans were forced to do, they would have lost nearly as many pilots as they did aircraft; that is, at least twice as many. In short, a fighter force on the offensive is likely to have at least double the number of pilot casualties as a defensive force. In fact, it is likely to be higher, because a number of aircraft will only be damaged and make forced landings; if they come down over their own country the pilot will be in action again the same day and the machine very shortly afterwards. If operating over enemy territory, both will be lost. Additionally, the British radar, reporting and control system would be working at full efficiency against inland penetrations, whereas over the Channel and in coastal areas it was less efficient and gave a shorter warning time. How, in these conditions, were the Germans to gain air superiority?

For various reasons they thought they could do it; three air fleets were assembled round the British Isles in a gigantic arc stretching from Norway to western France; they were ready now, and waiting only for favourable weather. It was patchy for several days, but on 11 August there were signs of impending change. For the first time the attacking forces included Junkers 88s, now in service in numbers and a very different proposition from the Ju. 87s. Portland harbour was heavily raided; attacks were made against east coast convoys, there being nothing of importance in the Channel; the Germans lost 28 aircraft; and they thought they saw signs that some of the defending pilots were operationally inexperienced. The day represented an expansion of the policy previously employed – not a new policy – but on 12 August there was an almost total departure in type of target, as well as in weight of attack, from anything which had occurred previously. On that day a wide range of different targets along the whole of the south-east coast of England came under almost simultaneous attack.

PHASE II:
Ports and Aerodromes

4
The Battle Begins
12 August

In early August, shortly after Fink had completed his task
on the Channel coast, Kesselring called at his headquarters and mentioned that an important conference was
to be held next day, 'because we are planning to put the
whole thing on a different basis'. For a moment Fink
thought that he was being taken off operations and the
job given to someone else; however, he recalled, 'At this
meeting the actual Battle of Britain was planned and
initiated. Previously, we had not been allowed to fly over
England – we were not to attack anything on land, even
if conditions were most favourable, because Hitler was
still hoping it would not come to total war with England
and that he would be able to obtain a peaceful solution.
Now, at this meeting, it was planned how to attack the
RAF, particularly their airfields.'

Ever since the Norwegian campaign, *Luftflotte* 5
(Generaloberst Stumpf) had been based in Norway and
Denmark; during the Channel Battle two much larger
fleets had been established in Occupied France, Belgium
and Holland – *Luftflotte* 2 (Generalfeldmarschall Kesselring) and *Luftflotte* 3 (Generalfeldmarschall Sperrle).
Their strength in serviceable aircraft (i.e. two-thirds of
the total) was approximately:

Bombers – 860	Single-engined fighters – 650
Stukas – 250	Twin-engined fighters – 200
Reconnaissance aircraft – 80	

On paper, this was a formidable force; in the air, against
defences of the British calibre, the stukas and the twin-
engined fighters had proved a liability rather than an asset

and the use to which the former were largely assigned was that of diversionary strikes at coastal targets. Additionally, the bombers were too lightly armed to raid unescorted; and as 650 fighters could not possibly escort 860 bombers, but less than half that number, the remainder were virtually 'unemployed'. Some way had to be found of using them, otherwise half the striking force of the Luftwaffe would have to stay on the ground until such time as the fighters achieved air superiority. This question was therefore an important factor in the planning, and was to become more important as the weeks went by and revealed that, even so, the RAF had been underestimated. Of all the Luftwaffe's 'evader' bombers, only the new Junkers 88 might still be classified as such; it was not faster than the fighters, but it was fast and, with some height advantage, might well manage to get away.

The issue, therefore, would be balanced on a very narrow thread; if the RAF became progressively weaker, then the Luftwaffe could make its attacks progressively stronger; it would not be the same force which was making them but a much larger force. If, however, Fighter Command could decimate the German fighter force, then the number of bombers which could be escorted would fall in proportion and the attacks would become gradually weaker.

The Germans calculated that the British would have about 675 single-engined fighters serviceable. It was a good estimate. There were some 400 Hurricanes, 200 Spitfires and several squadrons of Defiants (which hardly counted). In short, 200 modern fighters and 400 obsolescent fighters; the British, in consequence, planned to engage the 109s with their Spitfires, so that the Hurricanes could take on the bombers. The bulk of these machines were in south-east England in No. 11 Group, commanded by a New Zealander, Air Vice-Marshal Keith Park. On his right flank, in south-western England, was Air Vice-Marshal Sir Quintin Brand's No. 10 Group; on his left flank, guarding the east coast and the Midlands, Air Vice-Marshal T. L. Leigh-Mallory's No. 12 Group; covering the north-east coast was No. 13 Group, commanded by Air Vice-Marshal R. E. Saul. No. 10 Group had only recently been set up, during the westward extension of the British defences caused by the fall of France; in the second week of August they took over from No. 11 Group responsibility for the Middle Wallop Sector.

The limiting factor on the British side was pilots and not aircraft; had another 100 pilots been available, there were sufficient machines for them. The production problem had already been solved; partly because of the planned expansion programme controlled by Air Marshal Sir Wilfrid Freeman, partly by the impact of Lord Beaverbrook's personality, and partly because of the crisis atmosphere after Dunkirk. There was a shortage of AA guns, particularly of the lighter type most useful for airfield defence; and here the limiting factor was production – but a number of substitutes were found. This, then, was the force which the Germans had to destroy if they were to win the battle. It was to be found largely in the air, but it was dependent on airfields and aircraft factories for its existence, and for its efficiency on the radar stations, located along the coast, and the Sector Operations Rooms, located at the main base airfield in each Sector. The controlling headquarters for the whole force was deep underground and beyond the reach of bombers.

It was a problem quite unlike any other which the Germans had previously faced – fast, well-armed fighters which could not be evaded, a long-range radar warning of the bombers' approach, a radio control system to direct the fighters on to the bombers before they even reached the target, and no possibility of going forward effectively by leaps and bounds, with the tanks driving on to take advantage of the confusion created by the raids before the effect evaporated. Nevertheless, the advance 'by leaps and bounds' was the solution adopted, because the Luftwaffe was limited by a technical factor – the short range of their only effective fighter, the Messerschmitt 109. There was not the slightest possibility of unleashing an air attack which could surge at once over the whole of the United Kingdom, striking at the most vital parts of the British war machine, and at the same time confusing the defence by coming in simultaneously from all points of the compass.

The German plan has been summarized, by a German staff officer, at a time when all documents were available, as follows:

Luftflotten 2 and 3 were detailed to gain air superiority in the area of southern England by operating against –

(a) Enemy aircraft, specifically fighters, in the air and on the ground;

(b) Main harbours and wharf storage facilities;

(c) The ground organization of the RAF in the area of London.

'It was the task of *Luftflotte* 5 to tie down defences in the area of Newcastle by attacking aerodromes.

'To complete the task of putting the enemy fighter defences out of action in the area of southern England, the Government hoped that four days would be sufficient. Once this goal had been reached, it was intended to extend the air offensive by means of day attacks over the line King's Lynn–Leicester, in sections northwards, until the whole of England was covered.

'Four weeks after the beginning of the scheduled attack against the British Isles, which was supposed to begin with "Adler-Tag" ("Eagle Day" – the opening date of the attack by three air fleets), the actual invasion was intended to take place. The preparations for the crossing had to be completed by 20 September. The plan was: to cross in various places along the south and south-east coast with the 6th and 9th Armies, the main landing front to be between Dover and the Isle of Wight. The code name for the landing operation was "Seelöwe" (Sealion).'[1]

It was thought that Fighter Command would concentrate on southern England; if they did, it would allow some of the bombers for which no escort was available to be used against the Midlands and the North. Apart from any damage caused, it would tend to force the enemy commander to shift his squadrons about unnecessarily. But Dowding was not that sort of man. He hardly changed his dispositions at all, but met the problem by rotating his squadrons – keeping the bulk of them in the south and, as they became weakened and inefficient through tiredness and losses, moved them to rest in the other areas where they would meet, not the deadly 109s, but easy victims in the shape of unescorted bombers. When rested and up to strength again, they returned south to replace another tired squadron. This process continued throughout the battle. A weakness of the German plan was that it made no allowance for this factor; if the battle could be quickly won, it might not matter much, but if it went on for any length of time the German pilots and aircrews would become operationally tired and therefore inefficient.

The actual selection of targets was made by OKL (*Oberkommando der Luftwaffe*), that is, Göring's head-quarters, and forwarded daily to Kesselring, Sperrle and

[1] This study, which will be referred to again, was produced by Major O. W. Bechtle in April, 1944, after he had been permitted unlimited access to the documents for a period of some months; as many of the records did not survive the war, the study is of some importance, particularly in view of the fact that Bechtle himself had flown in the Battle of Britain.

Stumpf, the three air fleet commanders, for action on the following day. The Germans appreciated that part of the efficiency of the defence depended on the radar stations, although quite how important these were they could not guess. The position of the tall radar towers, standing on cliffs and hills at various parts of the coast, could not be hidden; but how were they to be attacked? It will be recalled that a gruppe of the *Immelmann Stukageschwader* had dive-bombed the transmitters of Warsaw Radio Station without the least success; the structure was flexible and offered no large areas of flat surface to blast. The key point was probably the engine rooms and, thought the Germans, these were probably underground. All the south coast radar stations were to be attacked, but the Germans did not expect to achieve very much by this; they would be guided by results, as to whether or not the attacks should continue.

The Germans also appreciated that the British system of radio control of their fighters postulated operations rooms and radio transmitters – the latter could be pin-pointed, but where were the former? They were in fact at the main fighter aerodromes, the Sector Stations, but there was no reason why they should be and every reason why they should not. A main aerodrome, with full base facilities for handling fighters, was an obvious target, liable to attack, and therefore not the place for an operations room – except on grounds of administrative convenience. It is possible to take the bearing of a transmitter, but not of an operations room, which is connected to it by landline and may be any number of miles away. Therefore, because they did not know where they were, it was impossible for the Germans knowingly to attack a Sector Station; but because the operations rooms were at the main aerodromes, mainly around

London, they did in due course come under attack and a number were knocked out.[2]

As far as the airfields themselves were concerned, the Germans intended to attack all those which appeared to be operational, regardless of whether they housed squadrons of Fighter Command, Bomber Command or Coastal Command, because they could not be quite sure which was which, but above all because any fully-equipped aerodrome could handle fighters if necessary. As to the results to be expected from attacking airfields, there was not a great deal of evidence available. The Poles had certainly managed to continue to operate their fighter force, despite the destruction of their peace-time bases, by using camouflaged emergency landing fields. On the British side, Dowding had initiated tests before the war which showed that aircraft on the ground, particularly if dispersed and protected by bays of raised earth, were most unprofitable targets for bombers. On the other hand, photographs brought back by German reconnaissance machines showed that, on a number of aerodromes on the south coast being used by other commands, there were no protective bays and the aircraft were not even dispersed – they were lined up in front of the hangars inviting attack. It was apparent that some of the British, in spite of Dunkirk, simply did not realize what they were in for.

A curious omission from the German target list was that of the aircraft factories producing fighters. Some, including those producing most of the aero engines, were out of range of escorted bombers, but two of the most important were in southern England: Hawkers and Supermarines. Their importance could not be precisely estimated by the Germans and the effect of bombing on

---

[2] This so-called 'Battle of the Sector Stations' was thus, from the German point of view, nothing of the sort; the fact has not emerged in the British official histories.

factories was also a matter of guesswork, but in fact the
target offered was an inviting one.

On the other hand one category of target – main
harbours and wharf storage facilities – had nothing whatever to do with the problem of beating down an enemy
fighter force operating over its own country behind land
defences not yet overcome; it was a blockade measure
and reflected the view in some quarters in Germany that
Britain could only be forced out of the war by strangula-
tion of her seaborne trade – which was exactly the view of
the Admiralty and, in particular, of the Commander-in-
Chief, Admiral Forbes. But, at this time, it was a disper-
sion of effort from the primary task of defeating Fighter
Command, although in so far as naval harbours were
concerned it might perhaps help in the problem of
invasion. If the Royal Navy was to be kept out of the
Channel by night as well as by day, it would be necessary
to force the destroyers, not only out of Dover, but out of
Chatham, Harwich, Portsmouth, Portland and Plymouth
as well.

In short, the targets laid down for the three air fleets
represented three separate policies – the destruction of
Fighter Command, invasion and blockade. Further, the
time laid down for the destruction of the fighter defences
in southern England – four days – was markedly optimistic; it was not in accordance with the reports of the pilots
fighting on the Channel coast nor of their commander,
Osterkamp. But if it could have been carried out in that
time, the rest might well have followed. The first air
campaign in history was about to begin, and whatever
course it followed, a great many Englishmen were going
to die; for the first time for eight centuries, the foreigner
was in a position to carry war into the heart of England.

The scheduled attack by the forces of all three air fleets,
converging simultaneously on the British Isles in an
overwhelming series of blows, was planned to take place

after 10 August on the first date when the weather was suitable for such a combined and intricate operation; when it came, it was to be called 'Eagle Day'. In fact, this operation did not take place until 15 August, by which date part of the force had already been loosed in a series of attacks, some of which had gone badly wrong, on 13 August – but which, the Germans decided, were sufficiently heavy to constitute 'Eagle Day'. On 12 August, however, the weather had been sufficiently good to allow an overture to the delayed main attack and as the targets were the same as those laid down in the directive, the main phase of the Battle of Britain may be considered to have begun on the 12th.

The targets attacked on 12 August were the three forward fighter airfields of Manston, Lympne and Hawkinge, six radar stations in Kent, Sussex and the Isle of Wight, the naval harbour at Portsmouth and a convoy in the Thames Estuary.

The first German attack went in against Lympne airfield at nine in the morning; it was attacked again in the evening. At 10.30 radar stations near Eastbourne and Hastings were bombed; the latter was bombed again in the evening, when another radar station near Dover was attacked for the first time. None of the radar stations was badly damaged. At mid-day came a complex attack on the Portsmouth area, dive-bombers picking targets on both the Portsmouth and the Gosport sides of the naval harbour, while another formation attacked the radar station at Ventnor in the Isle of Wight. The Portsmouth defences disposed of some eighty guns of various calibres; but there were in harbour the cruiser *Manchester*, the monitor *Erebus*, the French gunnery battleship *Courbet*, and a number of British and French destroyers and light craft, all of which carried AA guns. The gunfire appeared absolutely continuous and the dive-bombers came screeching down into it, two or three at any one time diving down in follow-my-leader style while the rest waited above to peel off and the leaders were already rocketing upwards again from the pall of smoke and dust rising above the cranes and buildings. It was an impressive display of determination and valour, for few targets hitherto attacked by the Luftwaffe had put up such a reception as this.

The basic reaction to this démarche by the Luftwaffe was, strangely enough, surprise. One witness saw what he thought must be at least fifty aircraft wheeling overhead – 'Must be ours – too many to be Jerries.' Another had seen first of all a large aircraft very low, probably a Ju. 88 pulling out of its dive – 'Can't be a Jerry – must be one of ours.'

Behind Portsmouth harbour and stretching for about five miles from east to west is a hill several hundred feet high – Portsdown. I was cycling with friends through Fareham. We stopped a moment to watch the dive-bombers; then we all rode hell-for-leather up the hill. 'One of the stukas attracted my attention,' I wrote that evening. 'It was falling swiftly, rocking from side to side, twisting, jerking – there was an awful finality about it which made it clear I was seeing for the first time an aircraft shot down.'

It was a Ju. 88A-I of 8/KG 51 flown by Oberleutnant Wildermuth, although I did not learn his name or unit until more than forty years had passed.

As we raced upwards four dive-bombers came flying towards us, passing directly over the four barrels of a nearby AA battery, which did not fire. 'I was near some houses at the time, where people were crowded outside to watch the spectacle – they were shouting out insults at the gunners and the RAF. There were no fighters at all.'

Portsmouth was a Gun Area, over which fighters were not supposed to operate, but Dunkirk had left an impression, among those in contact with the navy and survivors of the BEF, which propaganda served only to irritate; the comment in Portsmouth on the Heinkel brought down at Southwick a month previously had been, 'It took ten of the RAF to shoot down one German.' As far as the navy were concerned, Fighter Command was very much on trial at that moment. And at that moment the Luftwaffe had been occupying the sky over Portsmouth uninterruptedly for fifteen minutes.

Three more Ju. 88s, black crosses bold and clear, passed over my head, some of them heavily fired at, their wings rocking in the bursts; bombs slammed into the fields and smoke poured up. 'I realize now that I was not a very good witness that day,' I wrote. 'I was in the open and very excited, with everything happening very fast; indeed I couldn't tell bomb explosions from gunfire. But one learned quickly, in a matter of days only.'

From the top of the hill I looked down from 500 feet across Portsmouth harbour to the Isle of Wight. Six fires were burning in the city, each one a bright red glow rising and falling, expanding and contracting, sending up columns of smoke to the height of the balloons. One was the Harbour Station, burnt out completely, some were in the dockyard. From the Gosport side two more, and from the Isle of Wight, from the wrecked Ventnor radar station, another two – and a single aircraft going down past the smoke in a long slant, jinking. Then the first British fighter appeared, a single Hurricane flying east towards Tangmere or Westhampnett. 'Notably dispersed and ineffective', was the German comment of the day on Fighter Command's efforts; 'inaccurate and often late' their comment on the AA fire.

At that time *Jagdgeschwader* 53, based on Guernsey,

usually provided the escort to dive-bombers attacking targets in the Portsmouth area. Leutnant Erich Bodendiek, now the editor of *Jagerblatt*, a magazine read by fighter pilots and those interested in the subject, was then a 109 pilot in this unit. 'On this day we had to escort Ju. 87s to Portsmouth,' he said. 'They flew over Guernsey first, we took off when we saw them and joined up as escort. But sometimes we were in the air twenty minutes before the bombers came! They flew at about 2,000 metres (about 6,000 feet), very slowly; we were 100 kph faster and had to turn and weave, so it was quite easy to lose them. At Portsmouth we saw fires and heavy flak. No use to dive with the stukas, so we shot at the balloons instead. At the coast there were fighters, as always. We met them there so often that we suspected that there was a telephone connection between Guernsey and England; our airfield commander was on good terms with the Dame of Sark, but he could find out nothing, and we couldn't discover the cable. We also escorted Ju. 87s to Plymouth, and we sometimes flew so low that some pilots bent their prop. tips on the water, but we still found fighters at the coast.'

In short, what was happening in coastal areas on this day and during the subsequent weeks, was that the German fighter escorts, much larger than the numbers sent up early to oppose them, were able to 'hold the ring' for the bombers; so that fighter interference with the actual bombing was negligible. Nevertheless, the spectacle of 12 August over Portsmouth was never repeated – the brassy impudence of the bombers in apparently unchallenged occupation of the sky over the whole area for some twenty minutes.

As the raid was ending 'Nobby' Clarke took off from Gosport in his unarmed Skua dive-bomber and flew east towards Littlehampton, where a Spitfire was supposed to have come down in the sea. He found it – one wheel floating in a patch of oil, with no sign of the pilot. Climbing to 3,000 feet and heading for home, he saw a tiny dot approaching him from inland, pretty obviously a British fighter. 'I prepared to dodge his opening fire,' wrote Clarke, 'for it was amazing how few pilots recognized the Skua or Roc. During Air/Sea Rescue patrols I was inspected, and sometimes fired on, by Hurricanes, Spitfires, Blenheims, naval ships and coastal batteries. This one made a nice change – it was a 109. As he started to dive at me I half-rolled and lowered the flaps which, in a Skua, were also the diving brakes. Then I held her in a vertical dive – vertical, not just steep. Hardly anything could dive so slowly as the Skua with flaps down and no aircraft could pull out so easily and at such low level.

'Looking back up the fuselage I felt a sudden emptiness in my stomach as the never-to-be-forgotten squat squareness of a white-nosed 109 slid into view. He was depressing his nose, trying to lay off deflection, but his estimate of my speed – which was actually less than 300 mph – was, as always happened, at least 100 mph too fast. With blazing guns he flashed past, no doubt frantically heaving back on his stick to avoid hitting the drink. I began to ease out of my dive at 300 feet, flattened out at 50 feet without any "squash" whatever, lifted those wonderful flaps, and continued on my way home keeping a wary eye open for the frustrated Hun. But he had had enough. These schweinhund English pigs obviously did not fight fairly.' Among the German claims that day was listed a Morane, which may well have been Clarke's Skua, last seen at 300 feet, going down vertically.

At almost exactly the same moment, in a fight going on over the convoy a hundred miles away, Galland was hanging on to a Hurricane from 12,000 feet down to 4,500 feet, from which height he watched it go in, trailing dark smoke, to make a belly landing between Margate and Broadstairs; there was no witness to countersign his victory report, so his claim was not allowed.

Colin Gray, flying with 54 Squadron, had already had a fight in the morning, the first of six sorties this day, and had chased a 109 back to France, putting it on to the beach at Cap Gris Nez. With the rest of the squadron he was at Manston when the telephone rang in the dispersal hut about an hour later. 'Hornet Squadron scramble.' As they climbed up over Dover they saw high above a formation of Fink's Dorniers coming in, protected by two or three times the number of fighters. 56 Squadron were at their forward aerodrome, Rochford near Southend, having returned from a sortie in which no contact was made. Geoffrey Page was amusing himself by dropping dollops of strawberry jam on to wasps which were buzzing round like dive-bombers, exclaiming, whenever he brought one down, 'Bang! Bang! Jolly good!'

'We pull his leg and say he'll come to a sticky end, like the wasps,' Constable Maxwell recorded. 'Then – flap! Gracie leads the Squadron with Page number two and I number three. We are ordered off to Manston, Angels 15.' The Hurricanes came climbing up along the Estuary, but the bombers had already reached Manston, their vastly superior escort keeping the Spitfires of 54 Squadron engaged so that they could not interfere with the bombing. Even as the 109s came streaming down on 54 Squadron, the Spitfires of 65 Squadron were taxi-ing out at Manston and forming up in squadron formation for take-off. They also were based at Hornchurch and one of their flight commanders, Jeffrey Quill, had been Supermarine test pilot until a few weeks before. After leaving the RAF in 1936 he had taken over the testing of the prototype Spitfire and then worked on the later marks; when the Battle of Britain was impending he went to see Keith

Park to ask if he would have him in 11 Group, and had joined 65 Squadron on 5 August.

The twelve Spitfires of the Squadron were now lined up in vics of three with their engines running, so that it was not possible to hear outside noises; directly behind Quill was a hangar. Then, surprisingly, he heard a noise, a kind of soft woomph! behind him, turned his head – and saw the hangar sailing upwards in bits and pieces. The overshoots from the sticks of bombs exploded among the Spitfires as they went racing, tail up, across the grass. An enormous cloud of black smoke billowed up from behind one of them, the blast overpowering the fighter's slipstream and stopping the propeller. The pilot, Flying Officer Wigg, got out in a hurry and made for shelter.

Quill had shoved his throttle forward, and gone screaming out over the boundary and into a turn; looking down and to the side, he saw great clouds of black smoke erupting from Manston and clods of earth sailing upwards. Out of the smoke shot Spitfires, in ones and twos. They were barely airborne when a pack of 109s came roaring down on them. But the German leader had miscalculated – he was going much too fast, so that the Messerschmitts overshot and lost their initial advantage. A confused dogfight began and between them the two Spitfire squadrons engaged the bulk of the escort, leaving the returning bombers almost undefended to the attack of the Hurricanes of 56 Squadron, climbing hard over Herne Bay as the Dorniers began to turn out to the north over the Estuary.

'It is a wonderful sight,' wrote Constable Maxwell. 'A huge black mass in three vics of nine each. An exhilarating moment; there is no chance of missing them. We go into echelon right and come at them from the port side, but before we reach them they have passed us and we are astern, and Gracie goes flat out at them, diving slightly below them – and then up, up, up. I see Page thumbing his nose at me.' The Hurricanes were too low, still climbing, and with insufficient speed to put in a fast attack from the quarter. Still climbing, they flew straight into the fire of Fink's well-drilled crews.

'The formation of the Dorniers is super. No Hendon display was better. Close and tight, their fire control is perfect – streaks of tracer in two-second bursts converge on Gracie. He breaks away, Page and I attack. Suddenly a 109 passes on my left, quite close; he is painted yellow and going fast, straight at Page. I give him a long deflection shot; he jinks violently and breaks away downwards, and I see a parachute – it may be Page, it may be the 109.'

Barry Sutton, coming in on Page's left, opened fire on the Dorniers from 150 yards; then he saw Page going down steeply towards the sea, a plume of black smoke coming from his Hurricane, hit by the converging fire of the rear-gunners. 'I was quite certain he wouldn't get out; it looked as though the whole thing was too final.'

'Everything blew up,' said Page. 'I was in a cone of fire, controlled by a gunnery officer, I think; I saw the "electric light bulbs" going by, I went on firing at a Dornier, then I was hit by the cross-fire. I simply went pummmmmmpfff! The Hurricane had two wing tanks and a header tank above the engine, and it was this that blew up. I kicked the stick as she was rolling over and just went out. I was burned on hands and face, my trousers were completely blown off, also one shoe, and I had a bullet hole in one leg. I got out at about 15,000 and fell to about 14,000 before, with my burned hands, I was able to pull the ripcord. It was cold then; I had a long fall, perhaps ten or fifteen minutes, before I would hit the sea.'

When Page last saw Sutton, he also was going down, hit by the bombers' cross-fire. 'I kept my sights on one

Dornier and gave him a long burst,' said Sutton, 'but before I could see the results, my machine shuddered and clouds of glycol filled the cockpit; I had stopped one in the radiator and shoved the nose down so suddenly that I was thrown forwards against the pull of the straps, barking my shins and breaking my pipe.' The glycol covered the windscreen and Sutton's goggles, so he throttled back, pushed up the goggles and tried to see round the corners of the windscreen. He drifted in to Manston, unable properly to see what was in front – if he had been able to, he would never have attempted to land there – and touched down safely.

An army officer came running up to him, shouting, 'Did you see them?' Thinking he meant German bombers, Sutton snapped back, 'Why the hell do you think I'm here?' The young officer immediately looked terribly pleased. Glancing round, Sutton saw now that, within a few minutes of the bombing, this officer and his men had marked out with yellow flags the only serviceable part of the aerodrome left, most of it being a mass of wreckage, bomb craters, and white chalk dust. Sutton had not the heart to say that he had seen none of this, and that his landing in the marked lane was pure chance.

A few miles away, Al Deere of 54 Squadron, flying low down after destroying a 109, heard the Hornchurch controller calling, 'All Hornet aircraft to land at home base. I repeat, home base.' Looking to his right, Deere saw the reason – mushrooms of smoke drifting across Manston's ruined surface. Meanwhile, suspended high above Herne Bay, Geoffrey Page was slowly drifting down towards the sea on his parachute.

'When I hit the water I found it hard to knock off the parachute harness. My burned hands only fumbled at it, but I did get it off. The Mae West then had no self-inflating bottle, just a tube down which you had to blow, like a balloon. But it had been ruined by the fire; when I blew – all that came out were bubbles. As I came up on a swell I could see the English coast, so for a few minutes I tried to swim to it. I was very cold, partly from shock, and I thought, "This is the moment you've waited for." My mother had given me a silver brandy flask which I carried in my left breast pocket, and it was full. Often enough in the mess, when the bar was shut, the chaps would try to persuade me to open it, saying I could easily fill it again next day; I'd always managed to resist their arguments.

'I turned over on my back and it took perhaps five minutes fumbling with the pocket to get the flask out. Then I held the flask between my wrists while I tried to get the top off it with my teeth; at the moment I succeeded a wave knocked the flask from the grasp of my wrists, and it sank.' Then the upperworks of a Trinity House vessel appeared. The crew saw him and sent over a small boat to investigate. 'They were not very enthusiastic,' he recalled. 'They asked me what nationality I was. I used a number of words not in the English dictionary, and they took me aboard.'

Page was in hospital for some time and received treatment for his burns at East Grinstead, where many other Battle of Britain pilots, including Richard Hillary, were to join him. He flew again during the Normandy invasion.

The German radio programme in English began to put out a running commentary of results: the first report was at 1 A.M. – 'Our aircraft are attacking the naval dockyard at Portsmouth. The fight is still in progress.' News flash succeeded news flash. At 3.45 P.M. – 'Our raiders approached Portsmouth over Spithead, dividing into three groups. One bombed the munitions and mines depot of Priddy's Hard; the second attacked the dockyard; the third the storage tanks (at Gosport).' By evening – 'Seventy-one British planes have been destroyed. We have lost seventeen.' The announcer had a particularly alert audience in the target areas, because here at last was a chance to check the accuracy of German broadcasts against observed facts. Jeffrey Quill, tuned in at Hornchurch, learned that his squadron had been destroyed on the ground. I, with the fires burning in front of me, was listening to the German account of the Portsmouth raid. The BBC report, when the Corporation finally condescended to broadcast it, with British phlegm implied that, not only had nothing happened, but that nothing ever would happen, if they had anything to do with it. The enemy had been 'beaten off', 'a number of bombs had been dropped', 'casualties were not numerous, having regard to the number of bombs dropped'. Three Ju. 87s had been shot down over Portsmouth. In sum, the German radio was broadcasting the excited accounts of the pilots immediately they landed and the British radio, after a long pause to consider how much might safely be released, had found a formula which said nothing, gave nothing away, and tended to irritate people actually in the target areas, who had had exciting and sometimes shattering experiences.

My father, a Surgeon-Commander, RN, had been present at the Naval Barracks when one formation of stukas dive-bombed it; a friend of his, standing on the steps of the mess, had watched a Ju. 88 let go two bombs, one of which had struck the road and blown him backwards through the door; he himself had had to establish definitely all absence of life in an underground shelter, crowded with ratings, which had taken a direct hit. Most of the men had been eviscerated and a horrible acid smell clung to the ruins. But, although the barracks and the dockyard presented a somewhat battered appearance, the damage was neither widespread nor vital.

In the late afternoon I visited the Gosport side of the

harbour. 'The bombing had been good but not quite good enough; probably the AA fire had distracted the bombers just sufficiently. The oil storage tanks had certainly been attacked, as the Germans reported, but all the bombs had been near misses; huge mounds of earth had been ploughed up, railings, trees and a pair of goalposts had been blown down, an RAF Balloon Barrage site was in ruins, the balloon gone, the winch lorry battered, the crew's shelter destroyed and some of the bodies lying outside, under sacking. And in a ruined house, a cap still hanging placidly from its hook above the rubble. Guns began to fire and a stream of bursts in a steady, extending line appeared above the harbour – Jerry checking up on what he'd really done. I went home rather depressed, probably the result of the let-down after the excitement of the morning. The fires in Portsmouth were still burning as darkness fell.'

Luftflotten 2 and 3 had lost twenty-five aircraft between them, and they believed that they had shot down seventy – forty-six Spitfires, twenty-three Hurricanes and one Morane. They were mistaking Hurricanes for Spitfires, as well as over-estimating the numbers shot down. The results of the attacks on radar stations appeared to them to be disappointing – 'bombs in the target area, but results not observed' reported most of the pilots. In one case, however, two direct hits were claimed, plus the collapse of a mast; and the reports of the attack at Ventnor were encouraging – sheets of flame, fires and smoke. It had in fact been knocked out, and for ten days there was a gap in the radar chain.

5
Eagle Day
13 August

The Germans were becoming impatient: it was late in the year for invasion; late in the year for air operations; the days were slipping by. They had studied the meteorological records and they knew that in September the weather over England was poor and unreliable; September was only a few weeks away. On 13 August there was cloud for much of the day over most of southern England, but nevertheless they launched two attacks against it, one in the morning and one in the afternoon, along a front of 200 miles from Portsmouth to the North Foreland. Some of the targets were on the coast but a number were aerodromes some distance inland, and although only two of the three air fleets were involved, the operations were on a sufficient scale to warrant the description of 'Eagle Day'. Consequently, by German reckoning, 13 August marks the beginning of the Battle of Britain.

In the east, the whole of *Kampfgeschwader* 2, led by Fink personally, was to attack Eastchurch aerodrome and Chatham dockyard. In the centre, KG 54 was to raid Odiham aerodrome and the Royal Aircraft Factory at Farnborough. In the west, *Stukageschwader* 77 was to make a diversionary feint at Portland. All these formations were to be escorted by fighters.

At dawn Johannes Fink led his Dorniers up from their base at Arras; three gruppen of twenty-seven aircraft each, one led by Paul Weitkus, with Fink in the additional HQ flight of three machines. As they circled and took up formation, they had already been plotted by the British radar. In the cold light of early morning they flew out

towards Pas de Calais, the grey waters of the Channel
before them. The escort, which was to join on to them
here, consisted of the 110s of one-legged Joachim Huth's
Geschwader. Above the assembly point they saw the
Messerschmitts, which began to dive and climb around
them in a peculiar way. There was no radio link from
Geschwader to Geschwader, and Fink had to assume that
this was their way of showing that they were ready; the
Dorniers bored on across the Channel, nosing through a
lot of thin cloud which grew steadily thicker as they
crossed the English coast.

There was no longer any sign of the escorting 110s.
Fink was surprised that they seemed to have lost him in
the clouds, but he kept on for the target. After the French
campaign he had remedied some of the defensive
deficiencies of the Dornier by having extra machine-guns
built into them; the rear-gunner now controlled two
quarter guns as well, which had the additional advantage
of solving partly the reloading problem, often acute in an
emergency. It was these, combined with a high standard
of training, which had made a shambles of 56 Squadron's
attack the previous day. Escort or no escort, Fink thought
he would manage it somehow.

Paul Weitkus, leading the twenty-seven bombers of II
Gruppe, had seen the Messerschmitts pull up and turn
away before the coast was reached. To his own formation
he had passed the code letters 'AA' (*angriff ausführen*:
carry on). Unknown to all of them, and because of the
bad weather, Kesselring's headquarters had already
passed the message 'AB' (attack cancelled). This had
been taken in by the leader of the 110s, but was not
received by the long-range radio sets installed in the
machines of Fink and Weitkus – because the former,
unknown to Fink, was out of action, while the W/T
operator in Weitkus's machine was suffering from 'flu and

a high temperature, and had simply failed to take in the message. What Huth had been trying to tell them with his curious manoeuvres was that the operation was cancelled. So the Geschwader, seventy-four twin-motor bombers, ploughed on through increasingly thick cloud towards Eastchurch, unescorted.

Park had already begun to scramble his squadrons to intercept them – 151 from North Weald, 74 (the 'Tigers') from Hornchurch, 257 from Northolt, 64 from Kenley, 111 ('Treble-one') from Hawkinge. As yet KG 2 was only a mass of 'blips' on the radar screens, there was no indication of its objective. Some of the fighters were sent to patrol a convoy in the Estuary, in case that should be the target, and others were sent to cover the forward airfields of Manston and Hawkinge, both damaged on the preceding day and both of them now serviceable again. The sweating ground crews, covered in chalk dust, had just finished filling in the bomb craters; they now regarded each one as a personal insult.

Fink, droning on over Kent, could not see the target because it was obscured by cloud, but knew that they must be somewhere near it and gave the order for the whole Geschwader to shake out into loose kette formation of three aircraft and to go down through the clouds. As some of the pilots were inexperienced, he added a few words of encouragement, to the effect that they had practised this manoeuvre with him, and they ought to be able to do it now. Then they put their noses down and went into the opaque white mist of the clouds, able to see their own wingtips and dimly beyond that the shape of the bomber next to them. The cloud below began to show a more solid darkness and suddenly there were only wisps of vapour driving past their cabins; directly below was the dull green of the fields – the Eastchurch aerodrome, two squadrons of aircraft lined up wingtip to wingtip. No attempt at dispersal, no sign that anyone had yet realized that the German air force was on the other side of the Channel. Roaring over the aerodrome in formations of three, and somewhat scattered by their descent through the clouds, the Dorniers released their bombs on the airfield, the dust, confusion and smoke making it impossible for the leaders to assess the effect, except that everything was on the target. Eastchurch was in fact heavily damaged and put completely out of action; although a Coastal Command station, it housed two squadrons of fighters. When Fink flew over they were stationary, but when Weitkus emerged in his turn from the clouds, some of them seemed to be taking off.

Squadron Leader J. M. Thompson, leading 111 Squadron's Hurricanes under the cloud base, which he estimated as 8/8ths at 4,000 feet, was being directed by his controller on to the bombers; he sighted them as they were bombing Eastchurch and intercepted as they were leaving it. 'We shot down five – there were aircraft going down in flames everywhere. The rest escaped by diving into cloud, which was just thick enough to hide them. We had no losses ourselves.' Two other squadrons – 'Sailor' Malan's No. 74 and 'Teddy' Donaldson's No. 151 – also intercepted as the Dorniers were dodging in and out of the clouds.

II *Gruppe*, led by Paul Weitkus, were blazing away at balloons on the way out, some of the gasbags falling away, collapsing and dripping flame; then fighters got among them – Weitkus survived several fighter attacks by going into cloud, but his gruppe had losses. Fink found himself under attack, but the cloud had scattered both the bombers and the fighters and most of his opponents came at him singly; he took to flying just above or just under the cloud, dodging into it whenever a Spitfire or Hurricane appeared. But the Geschwader had lost six bombers in

all, the first time that it had lost heavily. A lot of Fink's
friends had been killed unnecessarily and when he landed,
still gripped by the excitement of the battle, he was in a
most unaccustomed state of rage. He went straight to the
telephone and got on to Kesselring, shouting down the
line exactly what he thought about the staff – what was
the idea of sending out bombers unprotected, and so on.
This was unlike Fink, who is a quiet, gentle man, but
Kesselring was unable to get a word in edgeways and was
reduced to saying, 'All right, all right, I'll come over
personally.'

Then the story of the last-minute cancellation of the
raid became clear. A bad bit of staff work, thought Fink.
And an inauspicious opening to 'Eagle Day'. The Luftwaffe had little experience of handling large-scale co-
ordinated air operations, because in their previous tactical
rôle they had been geared to supplying help in 'penny
packets' whenever and wherever the army called for it.
All the same, Fink's attack was one of the most successful
of the day; elsewhere there were some outright failures.
They were meeting a co-ordinated defence against which
the rough-and-ready methods of the past were no longer
good enough; each attack required careful planning.

The raids on Odiham and Farnborough were successful
and in the west an error occurred which was the reverse
of that in the east – the fighters, vulnerable 110s, arrived
off Portland without their bombers and suffered the loss
of five aircraft without having achieved anything at all.
On the other hand, the defence was still engaging with
small numbers, possibly because the Observer Corps
tended to become confused when there were many aircraft about, particularly when the sky was not clear.

The plan for the afternoon was: *Luftflotte* 2, in the east,
to attack three aerodromes, including the forward fighter

field at Rochford near Southend and the Coastal Command station at Detling near Maidstone; *Luftflotte* 3, in the west, to attack Southampton (alternative target Poole) and the aerodromes of Andover and Middle Wallop, the latter being a Sector Station newly transferred to 10 Group. The attack on Southampton came in first.

Shortly before it began I went into Portsmouth to view the damage done to the dockyard area twenty-four hours before; the cloud layer had thickened since the morning and covered most of the sky. 'I was heading for the dockyard main gates, when the sirens sounded. A scurrying and scampering started, people fading to shelter and a marked progression away from the direction of the dockyard got under way; it was headed by a horse-drawn van, soon overtaken by cars, with pedestrians hurrying along in the rear. The horse broke into a gallop. When I came to the railway bridge, there was a crowd sheltering under it and a queue at the bus stop, mostly women, in a flap. A Wren, standing undecided by her bicycle, made up her mind and rode away. The Hard, normally busy with traffic from the dockyard, the ferries and the station, was eerie; not a footfall, not a sound. The effect was enhanced by the broken windows, the wrecked station and burned-out trains lying inside it. Dead ahead, the Commodore's flag was still flying from HMS *Victory* which, in her full Trafalgar warpaint and dismantled topmasts, looked strikingly out of place amid the gashes caused by the dive-bombing. Then the harsh beat of German engines – rrrhmm-rrrhmm – a big formation coming; the bang of a single gun; frightened faces at the entrance to a packed surface shelter, outside which a grim old Surgeon-Commander was standing, and a couple of trolleybus men lounging idly, chatting.

'The bombers were coming on, invisible above the clouds, in an apparently never-ending stream and directly

overhead. The scene became suddenly vivid. I saw every
oil mark in the road, all the petty details that are there
but you never notice normally. But the bombers went on,
obviously to Southampton. Minutes later, a violent explosion in the dockyard, roar of German engines, and
absolutely continuous bursts of machine-gunning overhead, nothing visible, but a lot of gunners ripping off
short bursts; and all the noise going east, away from
Southampton. Then, under the clouds, a Ju. 88 streaking
across from the west, going like a bat out of hell. Four
AA bursts above it, then six under, very close – and the
high rattle of machine-guns – it went through them all,
then steep-turned out to sea. Close behind it, two more
Ju. 88s, racing over the harbour.

'At that, a pandemonium of fire broke out. Absolute
terror among the birds; the seagulls and sparrows went
berserk. Machine-guns emplaced on tall buildings let go
at hopeless ranges; the two bombers were dusting up the
balloons with repeated short bursts. Sharp cracking noises
from the walls of buildings behind my back, soft thumps
around me. Something went past my head into the
harbour mud, another struck the pavement and spun
against my shoe. Shell splinters. I didn't dare turn and
face them, rather get it in the back of the head than the
face. A subaltern standing beside a truck grinned ruefully
at me; no point in running now. After, I felt amazingly
happy, as though I had just come into a substantial legacy
and the world was a good place to be in. The all-clear
went and people began to come out of shelters and to
stream off the harbour ferry. I marked an austere Captain, RN, and an extremely snooty Wren, stiff upper lip,
if you like; that is, until the sirens went again.

'The Captain beat at least six Sub-Lieutenants to the
dockyard gates in a burst of power that was simply
amazing and the Wren was off like a long-dog. The mass

of people just off the ferry went filing by, not in a panic but hurrying as if there was some point in moving, the tin hats perched on some of the women's heads bobbing up and down in rhythm with their haste; you could feel their tension, and feel it relax too, as nothing happened. The only shelters available were of brick and on the surface, a death trap if bombs were dropped. When the second siren went, I was told, two old men on bikes, with the whole of Guildhall Square to manoeuvre in, managed to collide with each other.'

The targets attacked at Southampton were in the 'blockade' category; a cold storage building sent up a column of smoke day and night for two weeks, melted butter flowed knee-high. Captain Potts, whose ship was in the docks at the time, passed the building and saw an extraordinary sight: the rats were evacuating. 'It was a procession of rats, crossing the road; young, healthy rats first; then the old, the maimed and the sick, plodding after.'

The other attacks came in two hours later, at 5 P.M. Andover aerodrome was badly damaged, the more important Middle Wallop escaped comparatively lightly, and Detling was dive-bombed by a gruppe of Ju. 87s which laid flat some of the hangars, workshops and quarters – it housed the Ansons of 500 (County of Kent) Squadron, which had an anti-invasion rôle.

In the late afternoon 56 Squadron were scrambled from Rochford to meet the raid directed against it, but the bombers were baffled by the cloud and were unable to find the aerodrome. South of the estuary, Constable Maxwell saw them – about twenty Ju. 88s, in wide formation, going south, and diving slightly. When attacked, they jettisoned in the neighbourhood of Canterbury. 'We cross the bombers' slipstream,' wrote Maxwell. 'It annoys me to an astonishing degree that Germans are using

British air. It is my first real feeling that Germans are trespassing.' High above the Hurricanes was the usual large pack of 109s. 'My eyes are glued on the 109s above and as soon as I see them starting down on us, I break away and up, hard. The 109s hurtle past and then up. The bombers are out of sight. Straight above are about forty 109s and one Hurricane. The whole sight is so commonplace and natural. Forty-odd aircraft are wheeling aimlessly, slowly, like so many plovers on a windy day. Yet it is a fight for life.'

So ended 'Eagle Day'. A thousand fighter sorties, by 109s and 110s, had been flown over England; and 485 bomber sorties, some of them by night. *Luftflotten* 2 and 3 had lost seventeen bombers, nine 110s and six 109s. Fighter Command had lost thirteen aircraft and seven pilots.

For Dover and other towns on the Straits, a new experience had just begun – heavy shells from batteries set up by the Germans to protect the flanks of their invasion armada fell at various points in Kent on 12 August and again on the 13th. The guns were newly installed and these were ranging shots; as they were firing at extreme elevation, the accuracy was not very great. The Channel convoys, from which the main weight of the air attack had now been lifted, ran the gauntlet of the shellfire several times weekly, but it was rare for damage to be done.

On 14 August the weather was again cloudy. *Luftflotte* 3 made use of it to send over bombers in small groups throughout the day and some damage was done to Middle Wallop and other RAF stations. Over the Straits of Dover *Luftflotte* 2 mounted an elaborate operation designed to keep Manston out of use by repeated attack. While Galland's fighters provided close escort to a stuka gruppe between Folkestone and Dover – a 'decoy duck' mission which drew to them the bulk of the British fighters – a staffel of 110s converted to light bombers employed the cloud cover to pass across the Straits unchallenged and then to carry out a shallow-dive attack on the battered aerodrome.

Manston was used by Spitfires and Hurricanes only as an advanced base during the daytime, where they could rest, refuel and rearm; its code name was 'Charlie 3' and when it was first bombed most of the pilots sincerely hoped that they had seen the last of 'Charlie 3' – it was much too exposed for their liking and it had nothing to recommend it, operationally, except convenience for convoy patrol. Fighters taking off from there on an interception would find themselves climbing laboriously at 150 mph directly under the packs of incoming 109s; they soon abandoned this practice, which was tantamount to suicide, and gained height instead by flying *away* from the coast towards London. They might just as well have taken off in the first place from their base aerodromes on the outskirts of London, and gained height in the opposite direction – towards the enemy instead of away from him. There were, however, political reasons why Manston should not be abandoned, as indeed there had been for keeping the Channel convoys sailing. In Kent, twenty miles from the German Army, there was a feeling of 'invasion impending' which was not to be found elsewhere. The visible abandonment of the Channel and an evacuation of Manston might have had repercussions on morale; therefore ships had to be sailed through the Channel, 'light or lame', to prove that it was still English, and fighter squadrons using Manston were told to fly low over Margate and Ramsgate on their way in to land, in order that the population could identify them – 'Look, there are our Spitfires.' Tactically wrong, it was morally the right decision. There may have been wider implications, because representatives of the world's press had been crowding into Dover since mid-July to report the battles – and world opinion had mostly written off England. Alone, she could not resist the power of German arms; she would come to terms or she would be conquered. They were there to report and photograph the event for their papers.[1]

One squadron only was permanently based at Manston. This was 600 (City of London) Squadron, a unit of the Royal Auxiliary Air Force equipped with Blenheim night fighters. They had not yet recovered from an attack delivered against German troops on the opening day of the battle in Holland when, out of the six machines of 'B' Flight, one only had returned, and the CO had been lost. On 14 August the ground crews were working on the machines in the open, far from any shelter. One of them, Trevor Tarr, who is now Manager of the Technical Publications Department of Napiers, saw the 110s diving in and ran to some sandbags, where he lay down. The bombers roared into a hail of fire from light AA guns and an affair known as 'Cookey's Sheep-Shooter' – four Vickers K guns, for use in aircraft, on a ground mounting made by the squadron's armourers.

Almost instantly, a shell blew the tail off a 110 at about 600 feet. Tarr saw the rear-gunner come clean out of the aircraft and his parachute open. The tail fell into an

---

[1] Among the masses of news photographers at Dover the representative of the local paper was significantly absent; on learning that, if his man was to take photographs, a permit would have to be applied for, the proprietor replied, in effect, that if a lot of —— foreigners could take photographs freely in the area covered by his newspaper while he could not unless humble application was made, then they knew what they could do with their permit. And no photographs were taken by that newspaper. This attitude is probably a better guide to actual morale in Dover at the time than any fears the Government may have entertained.

orchard and the gunner landed on the concrete in front of
the hangars; through the gouts of flame and the billowing
smoke from exploding bombs, Tarr could see the German
staggering about, his hand pressed to his head, obviously
hurt. One of the RAF men scrambled to his feet, ran
across the open ground, reached the German, and
dragged him away to shelter. Another 110 had crashed
actually on the aerodrome, but the crew were dead. The
airfield was cratered again and four hangars destroyed, in
addition to the workshops damaged on the 12th. The
indignity of being sprayed like rabbits, unable to throw
even a spanner back at the enemy, had not yet embittered
the ground crews; a number of them that evening made
enquiries about the wounded German gunner. It seemed
that he wanted to be moved to a shelter, he was muttering
something about a 'Big Lick tonight'. Everyone took the
hint, but in fact the 'Big Lick' was due, not for that night,
but for the morrow in daylight.

Meanwhile the pilots of JG 26 had had the difficult task
of protecting the 'decoy ducks', which had attracted
several British squadrons. At about 1.30 P.M. Galland
recalled that he came down on a Hurricane which was
attacking a Ju. 87. 'I had to fire from a long distance,
because the Ju. 87 was in great danger. The Hurricane
dived, went into cloud, then pulled up through the cloud
– and at this moment I killed him.' Another Hurricane
attacked Galland, whose number two picked it off his tail.
At this time Galland was racing his friendly rival, Mölders, for the title of top-scorer.

'The first-rate chaps always had something – and it was
usually bloody good eyesight,' said Wing Commander
Blake, whose coldly calculating temperament was similar
to Galland's. Neither believed in the 'cheerful old Charlie'
technique of optimistically spraying the enemy at long
range ('Fire when you see the rivets' was Blake's idea),

and both believed in preparation, in thinking everything out beforehand. The technical problems involved in shooting accurately from a high-speed fighter, often not a good gun-platform because it was vibrating with the speed of a dive, were very difficult. It was, said Brian Kingcome, rather like having to stand in the back of a fast-driven vehicle bumping along a road, and shooting out of it at pheasants rocketing across from one side or the other. Tracer ammunition was not much use, because it could be misleading – although some pilots found other uses for it; loaded at the start of a belt it might intimidate a rear-gunner and loaded near the end would give warning that the ammunition was almost used up. For aiming purposes, the British pilots were unanimous in preferring De Wilde incendiary ammunition; the flashes of its strikes were unmistakable. Many of them, particularly the good shots, took issue with Dowding in his insistence that their eight guns should be aligned to converge their fire at a distance greater than 400 yards; in their view, this was an unreal-istically long range – 250 yards was more like it, better still, 200. Even then, that was only the opening range, to correct the aim with a sighting shot; the kill should be made when 'you could see the rivets'.

Galland, like Mannock of the RFC in the first world war, had only one good eye, the other having been damaged in a crash, but he was a superlative shot. However, he opposed the ideas of Mölders and Udet which were for a concentration of armament in the nose – a cannon firing through the spinner and two machine-guns firing through the propeller, as in the 109s of the time. 'That's a good idea for a very good shot,' he commented. 'But the average pilot is not so good, he needs something like a shotgun. And the Spitfire was a real shotgun. So, when it was fighter against fighter, if you tried to shoot down the enemy while turning, the Spitfire was better.

Also, you had a better gunsight, not fixed like ours, which calculated the deflection angle automatically, whereas we had to do our own calculations. I invented a card game, to test the pilots' allowances for deflection; invariably, it was not enough.' To put the matter in proportion, however, Blake's comment on the Germans was that, 'They were very, very good shots.'

Galland's list of the essential qualities of a fighter pilot reads as follows:

(a) *Very good eyesight* (so that you see the enemy before he sees you),
(b) *Very rapid reaction* (so that you can take advantage of this),
(c) *Very good shot* (without which the other qualities are wasted),
(d) *Very great self-confidence.*

To a certain extent very good eyesight is a trick of scanning and focusing so that you can see in three dimensions in the air, instead of merely looking and seeing nothing. The self-confidence, he thought, was partly good nerves but also partly the ability to make your calculations, very rapidly, beforehand. The list, apart from this last item, is generally agreed; but, on the British side, only Wing Commander Blake made it – and then by stating the reverse. 'LMF (Lack of Moral Fibre) was basically lack of confidence. I had bags of confidence, I felt I could get out of a sticky jam.'

Among a number of fighter pilots there were usually to be found one or two who would find an excuse to go home; when a formation had broken up in the dog-fight, there was no possibility of making an unwilling pilot engage, and little chance of checking up on him. This was what the RAF called Lack of Moral Fibre.[2] But, as Blake

[2] See *Nine Lives*, by Al Deere, and *Fly for Your Life* by Larry Forrester.

suggested, it was probably basic lack of self-confidence. 'Dave' Glaser, of 65 Squadron, put it this way: 'You had to go in wholeheartedly; it was like rugger – if you hesitated because you thought you might get hurt, you probably would be hurt.' The German word for their fighters summed it up perfectly – *Jäger*, or hunter.

'What made war tolerable – exciting – even pleasurable,' said Barry Sutton, 'was this. It was as if you went out for a day's sport with friends from a pleasant country house in which you had the privilege to live. We had our private jokes, a language of our own, superimposed on the general slang, and that created a feeling of separateness, of snobbishness, if you like. We never thought of the wider issues, we were wrapped up in our own life. You never heard politics discussed; we read only the newspapers, or if a book, then it was a novel. We talked mostly about aeroplanes, although not so much shop as today. I think we were affected by the past history of the squadron; we had in the mess mementoes of Ball and McCudden, I think Ball's tunic and logbook, and certainly I had read about 56 Squadron when I was a schoolboy. We were wilder than pilots today, drank more, enjoyed ourselves more. We didn't doubt that we would win. At the start, I don't know if we were all as anxious to get to grips with the enemy as we made out but when the battle really began, I never saw anyone show he was frightened, although probably they were. "Frightened" is a bad word – we were keyed up, tensed. The moment of running to the aeroplane was the worst – the nearer you got to it, the less you thought about what was going to happen. Strapping in was a nervous moment; and then climbing – in those bright, clear skies – lumbering along, trying to get height.'

The underlying truth is that the man who was fitted to be a fighter pilot experienced the boundless superiority of being not as other men. The vehicle which he controlled was enormously powerful – it could span the breadth of England in half an hour; in all England there were only a few hundred such machines – those who flew them were highly privileged; they were a flying gun-platform – and at this point in history the fate of England depended on the picked men who handled them. Spitfire and Hurricane, they were sword and buckler to the few hundred champions who were to ride up and engage the enemy in the public arena of the sky. The dog-fights of the first world war had been a ritual, deciding nothing; but this battle, the one now being fought out over southern England, would decide everything.

6

The Greatest Day of All

15 August

On the morning of 15 August, on a ring of airfields stretching from Norway in the north, through Denmark, Holland, Belgium and northern France to Brittany in the west, the world's largest air force was being prepared for the great attack. Heinkels, Junkers and Dorniers were being bombed up on the captured aerodromes, Messerschmitts were being armed and fuelled on the grass airfields of Pas de Calais, the Cherbourg peninsula, the Channel Islands – a gigantic organization, three air fleets, about to strike at last the decisive, concentric blow which was to overwhelm the Royal Air Force and drive it from the skies. 801 bomber and dive-bomber sorties, 1,149 fighter sorties – in one day. A few days ago it would have seemed enough, and more than enough. But now Göring and his senior commanders had doubts. While the giant machine they had set in motion began to send off its swarms of bombers and fighters to England, they were in conference.

A potentially very serious situation was developing. From the start of large-scale operations, a few days previously, they had employed the well-tried method of giving bomber formations the absolute minimum of protection from close escort fighters and had used the maximum possible number of fighters in the 'free-hunt' – or 'fighter sweep' rôle. These were in the target area, but not tied to the bombers in any way. Free-hunting fighters were efficient fighters; masters of height, time and position, they had, despite radar, an advantage over the British fighters rising slowly from below, dazzled by the glare of the sun and the sky whenever they looked up; and the Germans had moreover almost always the advantage of numbers – not absolute numbers, but of numbers at the time and place of the battle, for it was of their own choosing. But fighters committed to the task of weaving slowly around and above the bombers had lost the fighter's supreme advantage – surprise, and initially, because they were throttled well back in order to stay with the bombers, they were at an actual disadvantage. An effective RAF defence could enforce on the Germans a vicious circle: heavy losses among the bombers, therefore more close escorts, therefore fewer free-hunting groups, therefore a lower toll taken of the enemy fighters, therefore more of them available to attack the bombers, and therefore heavier losses still among the bombers. The conference decided that the chosen targets must now be limited more strictly to Royal Air Force installations and they admitted reluctantly that increased escort would have to be given.

Major Bechtle, summing up the conference, wrote: 'Already, during the first few days of this kind of air war, it had become obvious that, because of the numerous, stubbornly-fighting British fighters, supplemented by the volunteer pilots of those nations which had been defeated by Germany, the operations of the bomber and dive-bomber units were made so much more difficult that, in order to give them sufficient protection, it was in most cases necessary to give them double or treble the strength of escort previously planned.'

Throughout the 15th, from about 11.30 A.M. until the evening, attacks were coming in continuously along a front of more than 500 miles, from Northumberland in the north to Dorset in the west; the northern attack was soon spent, but in the evening the bombers surged up to the outskirts of London. Apart from a feint at Portland, the raids were concentrated on airfields and aircraft factories. In the south and south-east the bombers were escorted by the short-ranged 109s, in the north-east only by the long-ranged 110s, or not at all – the distances involved were far too great for the single-seaters to cover. It was thought that the British, in their desire to guard London, would probably have few fighter squadrons so far north.

Two attacks came in against the north-east in quick succession – the first directed at the Tyne-Tees area, the second in the vicinity of the Humber, both in the area of 13 Group. The first British squadron airborne was No. 72, from Acklington near Newcastle, led by Flight Lieutenant Edward Graham; the same unit which had met Klein's staffel of the *Löwengeschwader* off the Firth of Forth the previous December. Once again, their opponents were to be KG 26, and once again Desmond Sheen was flying one of the Spitfires.

Radar had picked up the enemy bombers when they were still far out over the North Sea; as 72 Squadron climbed steadily out to sea, their controller passed to them the picture as seen on the radar screens – ten bandits at 12–15,000 feet. A few minutes later, he amended that – thirty bandits. And just after, another amendment – fifty bandits. As the radar picture, which was then notoriously inaccurate as to numbers and height, showed an increasingly large formation, so more squadrons were scrambled – No. 605 from Drem, No. 41 from Catterick, No. 79 Acklington, No. 607 from Usworth. But it was 72 Squadron which first sighted the enemy – an enormous broadfront formation led by the bulk of the *Löwengeschwader* in their Heinkel 111s, followed by Junkers 88s, with a mass of Messerschmitt 110s of *Zerstörergeschwader* 76 bringing up the rear. At least a hundred and fifty of them, thought Sheen, opposed at this moment by only twelve fighters. Excited sighting reports were passed among the British pilots, but there was utter silence from Graham, their leader. 'Have you seen them?' someone called. Then Graham replied, with his usual slight stutter, 'Of c-course I c-can s-see the b-bastards – I'm just tt-trying to-to w-work out w-what to d-do!'

He decided to attack from the starboard flank, each man to take his own target. As the Spitfires came whining in, the mass formation began to heave – some of the squadrons jettisoning in the sea and wheeling round for home, the 110s breaking away to go into a defensive circle, followed by a squadron of Ju. 88s which also began to chase each other's tails. Into this circle went Sheen, closing to 200 yards and firing at a Ju. 88 which was carrying under its belly either a large bomb or an auxiliary petrol tank. There was no time to see what it was; as Sheen fired, so the bomber blew up directly in front of his windscreen, the Spitfire going straight through the smoke and the rain of debris. When he pulled himself together after the shock, the rest of the Ju. 88s were in a dive which took them to sea-level and back to Norway.

Sheel pulled back on the stick and went up towards the 110s circling above; as he climbed, so their leader dived out of the circle at him. Sheen fired, the 110's port engine began to burn, but it came on unswervingly; possibly the pilot was dead. Sheen shoved the stick forward and the German flashed just over his head; he looked round – there were no aircraft in sight. A commonplace of air fighting, due to the high speeds, the limited vision out of a fighter, and the difficulty of seeing scattered, individual aircraft in a vast expanse of sky and sea, it is still surprising the first time it happens to a pilot.

Shortly afterwards, the shaken German formation, split into two groups, crossed the coast and was intercepted on the way in and on the way out by other squadrons; the bombs fell haphazardly near Sunderland. Eight bombers and seven 110s were shot down, entirely without loss to the RAF.

While these running battles were being fought, the second German raid was approaching the Humber. Radar indicated six aircraft, then thirty – actually it was the whole of *Kampfgeschwader* 30, the Ju. 88 equipped unit which had been paired with KG 26 during the shipping strikes early in the war. Their fast bombers, using cloud and ignoring losses, pressed on to the Bomber Command aerodrome at Driffield and badly damaged it. This was in the area of Leigh-Mallory's 12 Group.

A month previously Squadron Leader W. A. J. Satchell, who had been flying Defiants ('most unfunny') with the ill-fated 141 Squadron, had been appointed to form the first squadron manned by Polish pilots, No. 302. Satchell, who retired as a Group Captain and now breeds Orkneyinga Dachshunds in Gloucestershire, was completely taken aback. In his first night in the mess, standing in the centre of a crowd of pilots babbling away happily in Polish, German, Russian, Czech, French and pidgin-English, he wondered how he was going to control them. Most had got out of France without even a toothbrush, in some cases without footwear, but every man had either a rifle, or revolver, or machine-gun – and ammunition to go with it. They were fine fighting material and experienced pilots; all they needed was to learn the modern techniques associated with flaps and retractable undercarriages. They had to unlearn almost everything they had been taught about approaches and tended to confront him with a 'Me very old pilot' – meaning, what's good for a P. 11 is good for a Hurricane. A number of Hurricanes were 'bent' in the process, but by 7 August they had their full establishment of eighteen Hurricanes, had been formally inspected by General Sikorski and afterwards invited to the theatre in Hull by the RAF officers who thought it would be a nice gesture to introduce the lonely Poles to the girls. It turned out, however, that the Poles already knew the girls and would be only too glad to introduce the British officers.

On the morning of 15 August, considering that the squadron was in all respects fitted for operations, Satchell, from their base at Leconfield, north of the Humber and just south of Driffield, rang up Leigh-Mallory to ask permission to go into action. It was agreed that he might take out a flight to patrol a convoy off Withernsea.

The flight took off, passing about twelve miles south of Driffield, at the same time as KG 30 were crossing the North Sea, bound for Driffield and Bridlington. The flight was led by Satchell, who had 2,000 hours in his logbook; learning to fly in 1930, he had been a fighter pilot in Bristol fighters (a two-seater dating from the first world war), then in Siskins and Bulldogs, with a spell in Coastal Command on flying boats. There was another experienced British pilot, Flight Lieutenant Farmer, and four experienced Polish pilots who had flown already in two campaigns. Between them they had three or four times the flying experience of any normal unit, in which Pilot Officers would have only about 300–400 hours. They took station over the convoy but within half an hour the Church Fenton controller ordered them to return to base and land; he repeated this order several times, each time sounding more agitated, but giving no reason for it. As far as he was concerned, Satchell's flight was not fully operational, and therefore presumably hardly trained.

Satchell obeyed the order and as he was taxi-ing in at Leconfield, he saw a number of Poles pointing frantically upwards. He looked round and saw to the east, just gaining height after their devastating attack on Driffield, some fifteen to twenty Ju. 88s of KG 30. He had been in a perfect position to intercept, and they must have caused the unescorted bombers heavy losses, but it was now far too late; although the Hurricanes took off again, they were low on petrol and the Germans had had too good a start. As it was, KG 30 had lost eight bombers out of the two groups into which they had split, 12 Group had lost no fighters.

12 and 13 Groups, together with the AA defence, had accounted for twenty-three German bombers and two-seater fighters without any loss to themselves; the forces which they had engaged represented nearly the whole of *Luftflotte* 5 which was numerically the weakest of the three air fleets. On the debit side, about a dozen British bombers had been destroyed or badly damaged on the ground at Driffield, but that did not affect the operations of Fighter Command. It had been made decisively clear that long-range operations could not be carried out by the Luftwaffe without prohibitive losses, because the bombers could not protect themselves and because the only long-range fighter the Germans had could not defend the bombers, and indeed could not even defend itself. In short, the greater part of the British Isles was out of range of German attack in daylight. The only part which could be attacked was the south-east, because it was within the range of the 109. The Germans were in the position of a boxer who may not move beyond a chalk-marked circle on the floor of the ring, while his opponent could retreat beyond it whenever he wished.

But within that chalk-marked circle the German boxer could deliver cruel blows. He packed a much heavier punch than his opponent. Numerically, he had an absolute superiority in numbers in the south-east, precisely because Dowding had justifiably posted a considerable part of his fighter force to guard the north – the force which had just dealt so roughly with the bombers and fighters of *Luft-flotte* 5. Furthermore, because the initiative was his, he had time to mass fighters in large formations, which his opponent could not do, the effective warning time being too short. The British radar could detect the German formations at an early stage, as they were forming up over northern France; long before 'someone blew the whistle and they all came trundling off' the British knew that an attack was imminent. But the radar picture was not a television picture – it did not show whether the formations were bombers or only fighters, or even a feint attack by stukas; nor did it show the objective of the raiders – that would not become clear until the Germans were actually over England and were being tracked by the Observer Corps posts. Additionally, the radar being so vague and frequently inaccurate as to the actual numbers of the enemy, surprise could often be achieved. It was necessary to guess at the intentions of the enemy, to take snap decisions (and hope that a reasonable proportion would be right), and almost always to engage with only one or two squadrons at a time.

The results became immediately clear as, at the same time as *Luftflotte* 5's aircraft were approaching the east coast, a stuka gruppe, escorted by the 'hunting packs', the *Jagdgruppen* of *Jagdgeschwader* 26, roared in from the Channel to dive-bomb Hawkinge and Lympne once more. Al Deere of 54 Squadron, which was scrambled from Manston to oppose them, wrote: 'It was an impressive yet frustrating sight as the dive-bombers, in perfect echelon formation, swept towards the airfield and peeled off the attack. A mere handful of Spitfires altered the picture very little as, virtually lost in the maze of 109s, they strove to interfere.'[1]

---

[1] *Nine Lives*, by G./Capt. A. C. Deere (Hodder & Stoughton, 1959).

Galland, leading III *Gruppe* as close escort, did not have to fire a shot. Then, having seen the stukas well on the way home, he assembled his 'hunting pack' at 15,000 feet in mid-Channel for a sweep against British fighters. Under him a Spitfire squadron, possibly No. 54, were reassembling, and he led his gruppe down on them in a surprise attack. Pieces fell off the first Spitfire he attacked, then it caught fire; he went after another and scored a good many hits, but it escaped by turning tightly inside the faster 109s.

A few hours later the process was repeated at Martlesham Heath, in Suffolk, a coastal aerodrome in the North Weald Sector; it was dive-bombed without effective opposition, the 109s holding off the British squadrons as they came in singly. At the same time there was a high-level attack by Dorniers on Rochester aerodrome, which housed two aircraft factories, the most important being the Short factory, just about to go into production of the Stirling four-engined heavy bomber ('the first of the ours'); the first seven Stirlings had just been completed. The factory had been built, very rapidly, in 1938 to produce the strategic weapon which would enable Bomber Command to lay in ruins the industrial centres of Germany.

Eighteen Dorniers, twin-engined medium bombers, came in over the airfield and the factory in arrowhead formation from the south-east, without a fighter being visible or a gun being fired; their bomb-doors opened and a pattern consisting of hundreds of 100-lb bombs whistled across the landing area and straddled the factory building, the bombers turning away successively to the north as their load was released.

Mr W. Capps, a foreman, heard the warning hooter blow, saw the black crosses on the wings, the bomb-doors open, the bombs tumbling out – until that moment, he

had thought they were bound for London; then he dived
for a shelter. He was at the south side of the aerodrome,
but Mr R. T. Fryer and Mr H. G. Bramwells were at the
north side, a stone's throw from the factory buildings. Mr
Fryer, who was chief clerk of the cashier's office, was
running down the steps at the entrance to a shelter, when
the bombs arrived; earth-shock and blast at close range
lifted him into the air and dropped him in a heap at the
bottom. Mr Bramwells was already inside a shelter (like
all the others it was partly above ground) when the shock
waves struck it, and 'the air seemed to split asunder'. A
man packed up at the far end in darkness amid a crowd
of others began to call, 'Let us out, let us out!' Then there
was a muffled gasp; someone had hit him.

When they stumbled up, there was nothing to see
except smoke, the whole airfield was wreathed in it; but
quite distinctly, they could hear oxygen bottles exploding
in the heat of the flames. Some of them began to grope
their way forward to the bell shelter, a conical metal affair
for emergency use by two or three men, which was inside
the factory; it was like a pepperpot, riddled by splinters.
Of the two men inside, one was dead, the other injured.
They were the only casualties, although hundreds of men
had been sheltering all around the factory. The bombs
had landed directly on the works or overshot a little to
the north, where there was a dogtrack. Released grey-
hounds, some of them with wounds, began to pass the
factory gates, leaving spots of blood on the Rochester
road.

The bombers were now turning out to the north, over
the Thames Estuary, with 54 Squadron's Spitfires coming
down on them; Colin Gray tackled one, hit it, chased it
and over Dover was engaged by the escort – a new lot of
109s with yellow-painted wingtips.

Mr D. Robins, driving back to Rochester from London,

saw a great pall of smoke hanging over the aerodrome; he was assistant secretary to the chief accountant and his home was nearby, somewhere under the smoke. As he drove on, he could see that the flames were coming from the factory.

The inflammable Finished Parts Store, built of wood, the key portion of the factory, was burning; there were stored thousands of items essential to the production run of the Stirling. Elsewhere, the damage was not great. The roof was holed like a colander by the entry of upwards of a hundred small bombs which had damaged beyond repair some half-dozen aircraft in the final stages of erection, but rows of mainplanes, seven complete fuselages, the machine tools and even the wooden jigs were undamaged. What could not be remedied was the loss of the finished parts, which would have to be made again; in consequence, the production of the Stirling was set back for more than a year. Eighteen Dorniers, carrying 100-lb bombs, had cost the RAF nearly two hundred giant four-engined bombers; the destruction of the cities of Germany had not been averted, but it had at least been delayed.

About an hour after the bombing of Rochester and Martlesham, at about 5 P.M., other raiders began to come in, headed for Eastchurch, Tangmere, Andover and Worthy Down; Eastchurch was bombed heavily, Worthy Down was hit, but instead of Andover, Middle Wallop was bombed – as it was a Sector Station and hits were scored on hangars and aircraft on the ground, the error was all to the good, from the German point of view. The fighter pilots were making sortie after sortie – 54 Squadron were airborne six times this day, Al Deere being shot down in flames after chasing a Messerschmitt back over the Channel and being attacked in turn; he escaped by parachute. In very similar circumstances, and in the same area, Galland claimed his third victory of the day. His

Jagdgruppe had no escort mission in the afternoon; instead they were flying the more satisfactory and aggressive 'free hunt' in the area in which British fighters were being vectored on to bombers. Over Folkestone he so riddled a Spitfire that the parts flying off it endangered his own aircraft; the British fighter went into a spin, trailing smoke, and crashed into the sea. Seven minutes later, having reassembled his pilots after the dog-fight, he saw a single Spitfire in mid-Channel; he thought it was from the squadron which they had just engaged and that it must have followed them. Galland and his number two went down on it; after Galland had fired, it half-rolled on to its back and flew on upside down. As Galland broke away, his number two came in, firing, but said after that it was done for already; the Spitfire rolled right way up, then dived into the sea.

The targets for the waves of attack which followed at about 7 P.M. and shortly after were the Sector Stations of Biggin Hill and Kenley and the aerodrome of Redhill, all in the same area, just south of London. These raids were preceded by an elaborate diversion against Portland, designed to draw up fighters an hour before, so that many would be in the south-west and anyway short of fuel when the genuine attacks crossed the coast in the south and south-east. The feint was made by the *Stukageschwader Immelmann*, with fighter escort; as usual they flew from their base at Angers to a forward airfield near Dinard for the operation. Bruno Dilley flew on some five or six similar missions from mid-August onwards; the stukas, the 'Fire Brigade of the Luftwaffe', which had led the assault of the *Wehrmacht* in Poland, Norway and France, had by now been clearly revealed as too vulnerable for serious operations against England; they were restricted to coastal targets or feints, and not very often used. The pilots were not very pleased to risk their lives for so little.

'It was not very exciting,' said Dilley, who led a staffel of Ju. 87s to Portland that day. 'There were no ships in the Channel and not many fighters; the targets were not very important.'

They crossed out over the French coast, flying in loose formation of vics of three; as they neared Portland, they changed to defensive formation of vics stepped up in echelon; and just before the target, went into echelon in line. They were at 6,000 feet now, and the Bill of Portland was beginning to slide into view through the small window set in the floor of the pilot's cockpit; when the target showed there, it was time to dive. There were two ways of starting the dive – the simple method of just pushing the stick forward, or the more elaborate and graceful 'peel-off'. The leader half-rolled on to his back, pulled the stick into his stomach, so that the nose fell below the horizon, then reversed the movement as the engine cowling neared the vertical and he was looking straight down along the nose at the target; the rest of the staffel duplicating his movements in succession and diving in a long, stepped-up line, making their final aiming corrections through a ring-sight in front of the pilot. At heights of between 900 and 1,500 feet they released their bombs, beginning the pull-out at once, but not zooming into the heavy AA fire which was coming up at them, as they would have done if opposition had been ineffectual. Dilley released his bomb, went straight down to sea-level and stayed there, twisting and turning on his way out, to throw off the gunners' aim. Among the 'unexciting targets' they bombed that day was a car park on Portland Bill, the naval base.

His staffel suffered no losses. Their usual opponents were the fighters from Warmwell aerodrome near Weymouth, but they appeared not to press the attacks. Dilley assumed that, as soon as the British saw that the attackers

STUKA FORMATIONS

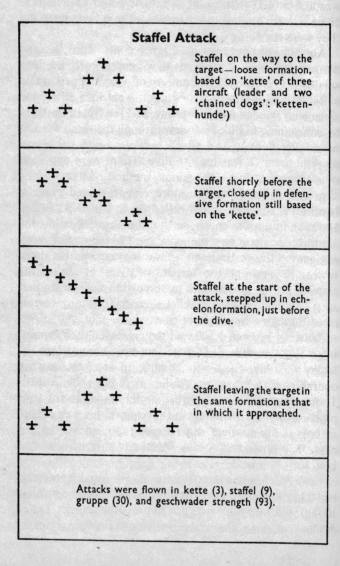

Staffel Attack

Staffel on the way to the target—loose formation, based on 'kette' of three aircraft (leader and two 'chained dogs': 'kettenhunde')

Staffel shortly before the target, closed up in defensive formation still based on the 'kette'.

Staffel at the start of the attack, stepped up in echelon formation, just before the dive.

Staffel leaving the target in the same formation as that in which it approached.

Attacks were flown in kette (3), staffel (9), gruppe (30), and geschwader strength (93).

did not intend to go inland, they recognized that the raid was a feint and that the main attack would very shortly come in elsewhere, and that therefore even as a diversion they were not being very successful.

Air Vice-Marshal Park was certainly alive to the danger, inherent in the confused radar picture, that his small force might uncover important areas in pursuit of will-of-the-wisp attacks. 'As I had barely enough fighter squadrons to defend the most vital targets, I had normally to concentrate on what I judged at the time to be the main enemy bomber target, and purposely to ignore diversions by German fighter formations or even small bomb raids.'

In this case, the main enemy bomber target was a hundred miles away – at Redhill, Biggin Hill and Kenley. Here, as in the Winchester area, there was a complex of aerodromes most confusing to the German pilots and navigators – and none of these targets was bombed. Instead of Biggin Hill, its satellite of West Malling was hit and put out of action for several days; instead of Redhill and Kenley, Croydon was attacked and a number of important aircraft factories badly damaged.

Croydon was also the base of Squadron Leader Thompson's 111 Squadron and of No. 1 (Canadian) Squadron, led by Squadron Leader E. A. McNab, which was not yet operational. Only that afternoon, McNab had flown with Thompson and another British pilot, in order to gain practical fighting experience; they had sighted two Dorniers going home over the Thames Estuary; and after a chase Thompson had got one and McNab the other – the best sort of introduction to air fighting. When the raid came in on Croydon the Canadians were away at Northolt but 111 Squadron were patrolling their base at about 10,000 feet.

The raid came in at comparatively low level and there

was no warning. Thompson looked down and saw them
2,000 feet below, already streaking in for the airport. M
H. G. Robinson, an old soldier who had been a traffic
hand at Croydon in its airline days and was now on duty
with the RAF Crash Crew, was standing beside the
vehicle when a metallic voice on the Tannoy bellowed,
'Take cover!' – and simultaneously the first raider, a
Messerschmitt 110 converted to the fighter-bomber rôle,
was roaring in and the first bomb was dropping away from
it, looking from head-on exactly like a big black football.
He went straight into the nearest shelter and from there
listened to the thud of bombs bursting on the hangars and
the airport. 'C' hangar caught fire and some forty or fifty
training aircraft which were inside were reduced to molten
skeletons in a few minutes; behind this, camouflaged to
resemble a row of houses, were the Rollason aircraft and
engine factory and another factory making components
for aircraft. Both were seriously damaged and about
eighty people were killed or badly wounded.

At almost the exact moment of the attack, Mrs Norah
Robinson, visiting friends in the same Croydon street as
that in which she and her husband lived, had been talking
about the raids and of how lucky London had been so far.
With a roar, a squadron of aircraft passed low overhead,
going in to the airport from the same direction as that in
which airlines from the Continent had approached; looking up, she was horrified to see that they had black crosses
on their wings. She was hardly conscious of the noise, but
the pall of smoke rising above the rooftops from the
direction of the airport made clear what had happened.

Her first thought was to find out what had happened to
her husband, but the roads leading to the airport were
thronged, 'like Epsom Derby Day', with sightseers. This
was the first London suburb to be bombed, there was
novelty as well as excitement, and a certain amount of

technical curiosity. So she telephoned the airport, to be answered with, 'What's it to do with you?' An apology followed her explanation, but the operator had no news of the dead and wounded. Her husband did not in fact come home until three o'clock the following morning; whistling cheerfully and apparently covered from head to foot in chalk (actually foam), he rode up on his cycle after many hours spent fighting the fires.

From 10,000 feet, Squadron Leader Thompson had seen the raiders – about fifteen Messerschmitt 110s – starting to dive on Croydon from about 8,000 feet. He had taken his Hurricanes straight down on them and the whole raid had gone to deck level very fast. But the Germans were just in front when they reached the airport and his first shot was at a 110 that was rising up vertically in front of his nose, after bombing. He fired, saw pieces come off the port engine, then broke away quickly; it was subsequently found to have force-landed near Croydon. After breaking away, he next remembered shooting at a 109; until he saw it, he had had no idea that the 110s had an escort. The single-seater was diving along a main road beside the airport; Thompson came down on top of it from behind, and the two fighters screamed along the line of the street almost at chimney-level, the Hurricane banging away briefly with its eight guns – too late. Thompson realized that he was probably raking the rooftops as well as the 109. Then, because it was fairly suicidal to fly for more than a few seconds in a straight line during a dog-fight, he broke away quickly.

All over the area to the south of London were scattered other British squadrons, some of them returning from a chase of the tail-ends of the other raids. Squadron Leader Worrall was leading the Hurricanes of 32 Squadron back from Selsey Bill and Flight Lieutenant R. W. Oxspring was south of Croydon with the Spitfires of 66 Squadron.

Oxspring, now a Wing Commander and still serving, had the then unusual number of 400 hours on Spitfires because 66 Squadron were the first to be equipped with the type. Oxspring knew nothing of the raid until the Kenley controller's voice cracked over the R/T, telling them that 110s had attacked Croydon at low level and were now nipping out right down on the deck. 'They've just left Croydon, chaps! Can you catch 'em?'

Oxspring turned on to the course he was given, pushed the stick forward, and led the Spitfires in a screaming dive down to the ground near Redhill. Then he sighted the 110s against the skyline ahead – going flat-out for the coast, with their throttles through the 'gate' and black smoke trailing from their over-revving engines. Slowly, much too slowly, the Spitfires began to close the distance. Oxspring gave the 'Tally Ho!' call, and the course of the escaping raiders. This new procedure was designed to off-set the time-lag between a radar or Observer Corps sighting and instructions being given to squadrons already airborne. The lag was only a matter of minutes, but those minutes were vital at speeds like these.

A controller picked up the 'Tally Ho!' and Oxspring could hear him vectoring Hurricanes into the path of the escaping Germans. Halfway to the coast the Hurricanes intercepted, the Messerschmitts broke away to try to avoid them – and the Spitfires came screaming into the fight with throttles fully open. At about 2,000 feet a mass of aircraft unravelled across the sky, the Germans out-numbered nearly two to one. Oxspring and another pilot fastened on to a 110 until it came down; afterwards, they thought they had got them all. This was not so, but nevertheless the 110s were roughly handled.

Meanwhile, the Hurricanes of 'Baron' Worrall's 32 Squadron were involved in the Croydon area with a 'circus' of Bf. 110s, Ju. 88s, and Do. 17s; raiders were streaming back to the coast both from the attack on Croydon and from two waves of attack on the unfortunate West Malling – the sky south of London was full of scattered dog-fights. Some of the bombers were still queueing up to attack and Worrall took his pilots into the middle of them, while most of the 109s idly wheeled above. 'They were not helpful to their bombers,' he said. 'You just waded in and did what you liked; they were killed off like frogs. It was the most murderous thing I'd taken part in.'

The Luftwaffe that day had been at its peak – never was it able to make such an effort again, nearly 2,000 sorties in one day. And never again was it to sustain such losses – 73 bombers and fighters. Although there was to be another 'great day' precisely a month later, on 15 September, the effort the Germans were capable of making steadily declined. And as it did so, the efficiency of Fighter Command also declined. The British and German air forces were fighting each other to a standstill. It was to be a question of who would be the first to give way.

7

Alas, Poor Hollywood!

16 August

'Then an air battle developed, and away up in the blue the glistening shapes of friend and foe could be seen twisting and turning . . . tracer streaks and vapour trails wove fantastic patterns against the blue sky, and the shrieks and whines of diving aircraft added sound to a scene hitherto undreamt of, even by writers of "Air Ace" fiction. It was a grand sight, tragic no doubt, but nevertheless a scene more spectacular and stirring than any film studio could produce.'[1]

The public on both sides were regaled with sound and fury; Test Match scores of aircraft shot down and crushing blows daily delivered against the stubborn island. In a small-scale combat, pilots tended if anything to underestimate what they had done; in increasingly large, scattered and confused dog-fights an optimistically large margin of error developed, partly as a result of the confusion and partly from the general excitement. The careful checking systems used by both sides to prevent a repetition of the exaggerated claims made in the first world war (one aircraft actually shot down to every three claimed) went by the board; the fighters were making sortie after sortie, there was no time to sift the reports or cross-question the pilots. One aircraft, fired at by three pilots, might be claimed by all three and awarded to all three, separately and individually; a bomber, streaming smoke from one engine and losing height might be claimed as definitely destroyed – but often enough got home all the same; in the whirling chaos of the dog-fight, in which the wise man

---

[1] *I Had a Row with a German*, by T. P. Gleave (Macmillan, 1941).

never flew for more than a few seconds in a straight line,
a pilot might fire at an enemy machine, break away, catch
a glimpse of a similar machine falling, and believe it to be
the one he had fired at; and particularly with the 109,
which had a standardized evasion procedure of diving
away vertically, throttle fully forward and smoke streaming from the exhausts, was it only too easy to believe that
a victory had been scored, when the enemy had been
merely frightened. But the root causes were optimism and
excitement.

On 15 August Fighter Command shot down 73 of the
enemy and claimed 182. The Germans shot down 34
British fighters, a number of British bombers on operations over their own territory, and destroyed on the
ground a number of aircraft of various types, in addition
to dealing several heavy blows at the British aircraft
industry. They claimed as shot down or destroyed on the
ground 143 British bombers and fighters.

'We knew that the claims were too high,' said Al Deere.
'In August and September the experienced pilots were
too tired to shoot anything down; and the inexperienced
pilots couldn't – so who was doing it? There were some
false claims – and we knew, in the squadrons, who was
making them – but a lot of it was inexperience. Early on,
in July, when the Dunkirk-experienced pilots were fighting, the claims were much more accurate; the inexperienced pilots didn't really know what was happening.'

The fact was equally obvious to those who stood out in
the open underneath the air battles and watched them;
even those who took shelter had some guide in the fact
that, despite the claims that Kent, for instance, was 'knee-
deep in German aircraft', a crashed aeroplane was a
rarity, and a landmark which drew excited crowds. By
the same token, the Air Ministry knew perfectly well
that the totals were wrong and it may appear in retrospect

that the provisional nature of the claims should have been stressed; the Prime Minister, who was disturbed by the discrepancies, nevertheless refused facilities for investigation to those members of the American press who were also sceptical, and from the general morale point of view he may well have been right. There was a debit side, however, for in the coastal areas where it was obvious that the Germans were able to do pretty well what they liked and the propaganda claims of boundless RAF superiority were daily proved false, the glaring discrepancy between fact and fiction sometimes created anger, particularly on the heels of a successful raid.

The same anger was felt by the German pilots when their own propaganda machine, and sometimes their own staff officers, suggested that England was finished and the RAF had hardly any fighters left. That did not accord with their experience. 'We thought that the propaganda about England being unprepared was wrong, and it annoyed us,' said Galland. 'We found the English well prepared and our job was not an easy one. We were not hopeful of victory.'

In both cases it was 'soft-centre' propaganda, the implication that it was all just too easy, which caused the irritation. That such an attitude was ever struck at all is surprising, because both war leaders were either advocates or exponents of the opposite propaganda policy. Churchill had just promised the British people nothing but 'blood, toil, tears, and sweat', which he had described as a short and popular programme, while Hitler, whose real genius lay in his abilities as a psychologist and propagandist, had ably analysed in *Mein Kampf* the faults of German propaganda and the superiority of British in the first world war, and reached the same conclusion.

But the German under-estimate of their opponent was not entirely propaganda. They had no such check, as the

British had, on the claims of their fighter pilots; nor on those of their bomber crews. They knew for certain only their own losses. These were considerable, but if the enemy's were higher, particularly of fighters, then victory was still possible. Fighter losses were the vital point. Bomber losses were probably offset by damage done on the ground, but in any case there were plenty of bombers, more than the fighters could escort. Therefore, a statement of total aircraft losses was meaningless; the key point was the ability of the German fighter force to cause more casualties to the British fighter force than they themselves suffered. To this had to be added the proviso that German fighter losses were absolute losses – the planes and the pilots came down over England, and they stayed there; the British fighter losses had to be subdivided into – pilots dead or seriously wounded, pilots slightly wounded or escaped unhurt by parachute or forced-landing. The number of fighters lost in fact meant nothing – because the production problem had been solved. The pilot problem had not, and it was a shortage of pilots and not of machines which was the real weak point of Fighter Command.

In detail, the Germans could not possibly know this. They were forced to estimate in general terms. The Luftwaffe staff therefore produced, as a guide to future plans, an estimate of the situation of Fighter Command as a result of the battles which had taken place between 1 July and 15 August. The starting point, the number of fighters available on 1 July, was basically correct – 900 in all, 600 operational at any one time. Production they estimated at 270–300 aircraft – correct a few months earlier, it was too low now that the British were producing at crisis-rate. Battle losses, based on the unchecked claims of their own pilots, they put at 574 – which was much too high. The figure for losses by accidents and by other causes was estimated at 196. They reached the conclusion that by 16 August Fighter Command had been reduced to a total strength of only 430 fighters, of which some 300 would be available for operations at any one time. This was the basis of their plans for the continuation of the battle.

The actual position which confronted them, however, was that Fighter Command possessed 570 Hurricanes and Spitfires; adding the other, less efficient types, the total was 672 first-line aircraft. In reserve, for immediate issue as replacements, were 235 Hurricanes and Spitfires.

Unaware of the real situation, the Luftwaffe continued its attacks in much the same form for another week, by which time it was obvious that something drastic would have to be done, if air superiority over southern England was to be attained. There was no policy for the escort of bombers by fighters because up till now the fighter had been regarded as a purely defensive aircraft for the protection of Germany against enemy bombers. The methods used varied therefore in accordance with the ideas of the various fighter leaders. Some of the fighter units, such as JG 26 in their protection of the stukas attacking Hawkinge and Lympne on the 15th, had been most effective; others, notably those operating inland to just south of London, had failed almost completely. The problem was in fact a difficult one to which there was no absolutely satisfactory solution; the RAF were to discover this when they in turn found themselves in the wretched rôle of flying escort to bombers operating against northern France in 1941. When an air force goes on to the offensive its fighters, paradoxically, are on the defensive – tied to the bombers, sitting targets to be shot at. Many RAF pilots enjoyed the Battle of Britain; they did not relish nearly so much their offensive rôle during the following summer, in which their losses were twice as high as those of the Germans.

Consequently, when the bomber crews complained about their losses and the blame was put on the fighter pilots, the latter reacted furiously; they felt that they were doing their best, that their difficulties were not understood and, in particular, that the demands of the bomber crews for more and more close escort were unrealistic. 'The bomber crews' ideal was that the fighters should be tied to them with string,' said Galland. He went on, 'At this time Göring visited us, and insulted us for about an hour.' What happened on that occasion became a legend in the Luftwaffe. Among the witnesses present, whose accounts add substantially to Galland's own (he has also described it in his book, *The First and the Last*), were Johannes Fink and Paul Weitkus, the bomber leaders, and Carl Viek, who was chief of staff to the JAFU 2.

The fighter commanders had stood rigidly, under formal military discipline, while Göring abused them in front of the other officers. 'Göring was roaring like a bull,' recalled Viek. The heavy losses of the bombers had been due entirely to their cowardice and ineptitude. 'You've got the best fighter aircraft in the world!' bawled Göring. 'What more do you want?'

Galland clicked his heels and said, quietly, formally, as if making a perfectly routine request – 'Spitfires, Herr Reichsmarschall.'

There was a shattering silence, which no indignant protest or loss of control could have achieved. Göring went pale with fury, screwed up his face as if to make some blasting retort, then abruptly turned on his heel and stamped away. Of course, Galland did not mean a word of it – he much preferred the 109 for 'hunting' work, although it was true that the slightly slower and definitely more manoeuvrable Spitfire would have been a better aircraft for close escort tasks.

* * *

During the eight days following 15 August attacks were launched in force on two days, the 16th and the 18th, the targets on each day being seven aerodromes and one radar station. The apparent lack of success against radar stations had discouraged the Germans; believing them to be difficult targets, which they were, these were the last attacks to be made on the radar chain. It would certainly have paid them to continue.

On the morning of 16 August, with 1,720 German aircraft about to come over, the staff of Shorts turned up for work at the bombed Rochester factory. But it was not business as usual; far from it. On 15 August many of the men were either lukewarm about the Minister of Information's war, or openly sceptical of it. On 16 August it was *their* war, and they got down to it. And during the lunch hour they spent a good deal of their free time piling earth around the expensive but hitherto neglected shelters with which the company had provided them. It is doubtful if as much as fifty per cent of the population had been in favour of war from the beginning; Dunkirk had sharply increased the percentage; but only actual attack produced enthusiasm. Consequently, when it was decided to disperse the factory this was done in record time; little more than two weeks after the bombing the machine tools and thousands of other items had been moved in local lorries and in RAF 'Queen Mary' trailers to two places in the west – a large railway shed at Swindon and a half-finished factory building at South Marston. From these factories, eventually, 353 Stirling bombers were built – with the machine tools which the German bombs had been insufficiently powerful to destroy. Thus, unpredicted by the prophets and unrehearsed by the planners, began the policy of dispersal; used by the enemy, it was to make the attacks of the four-motor bombers against the German aircraft industry almost totally ineffective. But while the other aircraft factories in southern England remained concentrated the Germans had a chance, which was never to recur, of striking at the start of the battle a blow against British fighter production serious enough to be felt. They chose instead to attack them when the battle was nearly over and the results had minimal effect; they lacked also bombs sufficiently powerful to destroy the machine tools which, rather than the actual structure, were the source of production.

At about mid-day the Luftwaffe began to pour in over Kent, the main target being West Malling. Bronislaw Malinowski, now flying Hurricanes from Kenley, went into his first action in the Battle of Britain. He never saw the enemy until he was hit and his engine stopped; the squadron had been 'bounced' from above by 109s. He promptly baled out and landed in a field near Ashford hospital. Although there were some farm workers about, a few did not seem keen to approach him at first, possibly because they thought he might be an armed parachutist.

The bomber force consisted of the Dornier 17s of *Kampfgeschwader* 76, based on Cormeilles-en-Vexin. Piloting the staffel kapitan's machine in 9 *Staffel* was Oberleutnant Rudolf Lamberty, who is now the manager of a shop in Trier, the old Roman city on the Moselle. At the moment when they were intercepted by the Hurricanes of 111 Squadron they were, he recalled, 'in a *Valhalla* flying south of the Thames Estuary in a westerly direction before the target'. A *Valhalla* was the name given to any large escorted formation, at least seventy bombers and perhaps two or three times that number of fighters; in short, an impressive 'Ride of the Valkyries' thundering in over Kent. According to Squadron Leader Thompson's logbook, his squadron went into the *Valhalla* over the Tonbridge area (Lamberty had lost his logbook, and was relying only on memory).

They scrambled from Hawkinge and cut across in front of the massive German formation. Attack from the rear was unprofitable, not only on account of the gunners, but because the Dornier had self-sealing tanks double-wrapped in rubber and virtually bullet-proof, together with air-cooled engines which, being less delicate than the water-cooled type, could take a good deal of punishment and still keep turning over. But an attack from head on could be deadly, because a really good burst through the unprotected nose could disable the entire crew, who were concentrated there.

'The fighters came in front and from the side and attacked head on,' recalled Lamberty, who thought the *Valhalla* idea altogether too cumbersome; the British pilots, of whose abilities he had a high opinion, were often able to come in from the side and pick off a number of the bombers as they went through and before the escort could interfere. Although the 'aces' on the German side had far higher scores than the top British pilots, Lamberty's impression was that the average standard of performance of the British was better than the German average – and that was what mattered to him.

For Squadron Leader Thompson the interception posed a number of delicate problems of judgement; he had to cut across the bows of the *Valhalla* with sufficient space in hand to turn and then dive at them head on – the combined speeds being between 400 and 500 mph. On this occasion he managed to put in an exactly accurate attack, turning in just in front of the noses of the leading Dorniers, the rest of his squadron turning inside him, the inner machines throttled back, the outer machines at full throttle, then hurtling at the Dorniers all together. But one of his pilots, on the inside of the turn, did not throttle back sufficiently and surged ahead of the squadron. It was a flight commander, Flight Lieutenant Henry Ferris,

DFC. Lamberty, about a thousand yards away at the rear of the *Valhalla*, watched in horror as he collided head on with one of the leading bombers.

There was a violent explosion and then the sky was filled with small pieces of wreckage which came fluttering back and falling through the bomber formation on their way to the ground 15,000 feet below. 'They were torn to pieces,' said Lamberty. 'The biggest pieces I saw were wings – and all the bits were going straight down. The crew of the German plane neither returned nor were they reported as prisoners of war, and we didn't see a single parachute.'

The flight commander was killed and one other pilot had to bale out, but 111 Squadron claimed four bombers shot down.

At West Malling, and indeed at many of the other aerodromes, the interruptions to, or loss of, the main meal caused by mid-day raids was a much greater irritant than the actual bombs; they thought the Germans did it on purpose to annoy them and there was a good deal of 'bloody-mindedness' among the Erks. But there was a perfectly good tactical reason for it.

As the bombers were returning from West Malling another large force was approaching from the south towards the Isle of Wight. With the sun at its zenith, above and behind them, wave after wave of dive-bombers began to attack a complex of targets in the Portsmouth area while their fighters held the ring – the naval aerodrome at Lee-on-Solent and the Coastal Command aerodrome at Gosport, both to the west of Portsmouth, the radar station at Ventnor to the south, and the Sector Station at Tangmere to the east. All these attacks went in simultaneously; in particular, the aerodromes of Gosport and Lee-on-Solent are only a few miles apart and the dive-bombers were peeling off above them both at the

same time. Up to that moment peacetime routine had continued undisturbed, unruffled even by the dive-bombing of
Portsmouth harbour five days before. The aircraft were
in the main either packed inside the hangars or drawn
up neatly on the tarmac, and for close-range AA defence
one or two old Lewis guns pointed skywards from
circular emplacements. The violent bang of a gun firing
from an army battery and the rising shriek of dive-
bombers on the way down abruptly ended this idyll for
ever.

'Nobby' Clarke was having lunch in the mess at Gosport. He should not have been, because everyone else
was in shelter, but air raid warnings so seldom meant
anything that he simply had not bothered. It was the
whine of aircraft diving directly above the mess roof
which sent him curiously to the entrance. He was just in
time to see a Ju. 87, half invisible in the blinding noonday
glare, coming directly at him, the bomb falling away when
the stuka was still 1,000 feet up. He covered the sixty
yards to the nearest shelter at a hot pace and was
scrambling down the steps when the bomb exploded,
blowing him on to a number of officers who were peering
up to see what was happening.

Three miles to the north, at the back of Portsmouth
harbour and sufficiently detached to have a perfect view,
I was reading an American flying magazine of the lurid
type popular in England because it was so much more
exciting than life. On this occasion, life beat the lurid
magazine – which went flying into a corner while I
scooped up my camera from the table and dashed into the
garden. Directly south a staffel of Ju. 88s were literally
falling out of the sky on to Gosport, one or two actually
coming in partly on their backs (presumably having overshot), in their pull-out appearing to bounce on invisible
springs and go whirling up into the heights again. Another

stream of twin-engined dive-bombers were ripping down on to Lee-on-Solent. The earth shook with the explosions and smoke was rising in clouds from both aerodromes, shooting up from the bomb bursts and then drifting away; what did not drift away but poured up continually was a pall of white smoke from the aircraft blazing in the hangars. I had time to take two photographs (into sun, but they showed the tall columns of two simultaneous bomb bursts, showing that what I saw were indeed Ju. 88s), then the dive-bombers were gone and only the smoke, with a fierce red glow at its base, and the shell bursts dispersing with the wind, showed that they had ever been there.

Then there was a howling, echoing roar, a sudden metallic rattle of machine-gun fire, and a balloon over Portsmouth flamed red; slowly, very slowly, it dropped, collapsing and leaving a long black irregular smear against the sky. Some 109 of the wide-ranging escort, quite invisible in the glare, had taken a parting shot before going home.

Apart from these, which were probably from JG 53, Erich Bodendiek's unit, other hunting packs were ranging the area to pounce on the slowly climbing British fighters and it was in a combat with one of these that Flight Lieutenant J. B. Nicolson gained the only Battle of Britain VC for Fighter Command. Mr Eric Shaw, stationed that afternoon with a unit of the Royal Engineers just outside Southampton on the Romsey road, saw a dog-fight going on over the northern part of the city. From the general mix-up two planes stood out: one was spinning slowly and burning; the other appeared to have shot it down. The burning plane, which was British, crashed two miles away to a chorus of delighted cheers from people who thought it must be German. Shaw then saw a man on a parachute about to come down a few fields away, so he ran towards where he thought the airman would land, but when the pilot was down to about 300–400 feet from the ground, he heard two or three shots fired. Some 'coon', he thought, had opened up with a rifle at the helpless man. He did not see him afterwards, but heard that it was Nicolson.

The official story is that Nicolson's machine was set on fire over Gosport by a 110 and that he stayed in the burning fighter until he had shot the enemy down; while landing by parachute, badly burned, he was shot at and again wounded by a member of the Local Defence Volunteers (as the Home Guard were then known). They could now justifiably claim, in addition to a good 'bag' of unwary motorists, one fighter pilot VC, confirmed.

Of the three aerodromes simultaneously attacked, Tangmere was the most important as it controlled three fighter squadrons, Nos. 43, 601 and 145, the latter flying from the nearby satellite field of Westhampnett. Tangmere's immunity during the first few days of aerodrome attacks had produced a theory that the Germans were leaving it alone because they wanted it themselves. The formal Tannoy warning, 'All persons not on operational duty take cover,' had sounded so many times that they were bored by it. This time, there was a real note of urgency in the voice that said, 'Take cover, take cover.' To one AC1 in particular that tone meant, 'This is it.' And it was.

'Magnificent bombing', he called it. 'They were all Ju. 88s, and they all had a particular target, apparently. They got all the hangars, all the buildings round the square – cookhouse, NAAFI, and so on – and knocked off the corner of the officers' mess. Immediately afterwards, the impression was that the airfield had changed its physical shape in a great cloud of smoke and dust. For instance, you could now see a barrack block which before would have been hidden by a hangar or other building.'

Fourteen aircraft had been destroyed or damaged on the ground but most of the fighters were airborne in time and subsequently a number of captured German aircrews were brought in; it was felt that their bearing was arrogant and they were forced to help clear up the mess they had made at Tangmere. If they were indeed arrogant, after the shock of being shot down, it says a great deal for their courage that they could still put a bold face on it.

Until that day the WAAFs at Tangmere had been treated with slight contempt; it took three of them to do the job of two men and anyway it was felt that war was a man's job. But no one could have been calmer than those girls; in the dust and confusion, with the dead still being carried away, they organized meals from five old field kitchens and in spite of the destruction of the cookhouse all the men were fed. After that, no one despised WAAFs again.

At Lee-on-Solent the two main hangars burned throughout the afternoon, with smoke pouring up and the occasional crash of a fallen beam – the mass of aircraft inside long ago reduced to molten metal. On the dirt- and rubble-covered tarmac outside there were no longer any lines of neatly regimented aeroplanes, but simply a collection of almost comical wreckage; not a single machine was intact. Some were burnt out, others piled in heaps; in one place an Albacore, torpedo slung under its belly, stood nose to nose with a Roc, as though engaged in argument, and another Albacore was the resting, or nesting, place for a Skua, which was perched on top of it. At Gosport also hangars were still burning, but the attack there had caused destruction less complete.

Had the Germans been able to follow up with tanks, they would have found confusion, of which advantage

might have been taken, and a certain amount of stunned
surprise among men who had just seen their friends killed
and wounded, but no observable panic at all. Indeed,
grisly stories were being passed around with a relish not
altogether surprising to those who know what the Sunday
reading matter of the English usually is; a human hand, it
was said, had been found by a Lee householder in his
fishpond.

The first newspaper report was entirely accurate, so far
as it went: 'Two houses on a marine parade on the SE
coast were demolished.' At least one bomb had indeed
missed Lee-on-Solent aerodrome, causing this damage;
all the others were on the target. The BBC reported:
'Damage on the ground was slight, and only a few civilians
were killed.'

During the day aerodromes at Harwell and Farnborough were also attacked and in the evening Ju. 88s
destroyed forty-six training aircraft in the hangars at Brize
Norton. At 4.45 P.M. 56 Squadron were told to take off
and orbit their base of North Weald at 10,000 feet, but
before they had reached 5,000 were vectored to Chelms-
ford. 'Forty bandits approaching from the SE.' They went
into cloud. 'Seventy bandits approaching from the SE.'
Just before they came out of cloud this was hastily
amended to '*Many* bandits approaching . . .' and as they
burst into the sun at 6,000 feet, so Constable Maxwell
recalled, 'There straight overhead is a veritable armada.
They seem to go up in layers and layers. There being full
twelve of us, we go up and up.'

Maxwell, Barry Sutton and Sergeant Higginson, one of
the best pilots in the squadron, were together. Higginson,
a Welshman and a fine rugger player, had once had the
distinction of being sent off when playing against the
Welsh Guards. 'It was a very dirty game indeed,' recalled
Sutton, 'and old Taffy gave the Welsh hooker a Roland

for his Oliver, but was caught and sent off.' They reached the bomber before the escort had time to come down and Maxwell and Higginson picked one each and chased them out of the formation. Maxwell came up from below the Dornier he was pursuing, opening fire at 250 yards and closing right in to ten yards, but it was jinking and he failed to hit. 'I turn hard right and he turns hard left. I again get on his tail and rain bullets at him. For a heavy bomber he does staggering aerobatics – a stall-turn, steep turns and a half-roll. I fire off 2,000 rounds from twenty-five yards but do not appear to do him much damage. He half-rolls, but I am going too fast and overshoot; and he goes down past another Hurricane and then vertically into the clouds.'

Meanwhile Sutton had attacked two fighters, which he thought were Heinkel 113s,[2] and sent one into the rain-clouds trailing smoke; following the other and losing it, he saw a sudden red glow through the clouds. For a moment he thought it was the sun breaking through, the gleam was so intense – but it was below and not above. Then, coming through underneath the cloud, he saw on the muddy foreshore at Whitstable the half-submerged, shattered and smoking remains of an aeroplane; the glow he had seen must have been from the flash of the detonation as it hit the beach and exploded. Circling

[2] The Heinkel 113 did not go into production and only a few dozen prototypes existed. Nevertheless they were frequently reported during the Battle of Britain, probably because the British aeronautical press publicized them – 'This new fighter is the best the Luftwaffe has yet had,' wrote one solemn scribe. The aeronautical press were also responsible for pilots reporting bombers as Do. 215s – Maxwell thought this was the type he had attacked. In fact, the standard Dornier bomber of 1940 was the Do. 17. The Do. 215 was a reconnaissance version, faster, lighter, carrying cameras instead of bombs, but visually identical. Less understandable 'gaffes' were the description of the Bf. 110 as a formidable aircraft and the Hurricane as faster than the Bf. 109. The contemporary files are a veritable mine of misinformation.

Whitstable, he caught sight of another aeroplane – a Hurricane – down in a field just inland; it was burning, and behind it were the long skid marks showing that it had made a belly landing. Flying a few feet above it, he saw that it was Higginson's machine.

Higginson returned to the aerodrome that evening. He had brought down the Dornier at Whitstable at the cost of some bullets in his engine; as he was coming in to make a forced-landing, the Hurricane had burst into flames, so he had forced it down on to the ground at well over a hundred miles an hour, hence the length of the skid marks.

On 17 August there was, comparatively, a lull. 'Ju. 88s had given Portsmouth a hammering several days previously and our aerodrome at Gosport had been attacked by Ju. 87s – leaving shattered or burnt-out hangars, buildings and aircraft,' wrote Clarke. 'As a result we were decidedly nervy when informed that a formation of thirty-plus Ju. 88s were headed in our direction. A 10/10ths cloud sheet covered the sky at about 6,000 feet, and soon we could hear the rumble of aircraft flying above it. Our protection then appeared in the form of a single Hurricane clawing upwards at maximum boost – one could imagine the controller insisting "The bandits are now above you at Angels 8. Buster! Buster!" and the lonely pilot caning hell out of his engine in an endeavour to reach the invisible enemy before they started bombing. Up, up he went – one against so many; there was not one of us who did not feel sorry for him. Thousands of pairs of eyes must have been watching this solitary defender of our faith – even the ack-ack was silenced in deference to his presence! The gigantic stage had been set, the audience assembled, the curtain raised . . .

'The Hurricane disappeared into the cloud. For perhaps a minute we could hear nothing except the drone-drone of the Ju. 88s and the harsh roar of the straining Merlin. Then, suddenly, machine-gun fire – rat-tat-tat-tat-tat! rat-tat-tat! followed, very briefly, by a burst – b-r-r-r-ump! – from our eight-gun fighter. He only managed one shot! Rat-tat-tat! Rat-tat-tat! answered the Jerries; and then silence. Drone-drone, drone-drone went the bombers unconcernedly.

'A screaming engine warned us what to expect. The Hurricane appeared out of the cloud, diving vertically and leaving a trail of black smoke. Higher and higher rose the blue note until the pitch was unbearable; then – wumph! the waters of the Solent silenced it for ever.

'And the pilot? In the awful quietness which followed we could almost hear the flutter of the parachute as it appeared from the cloud. The drone-drone disappeared inland – they were not attacking us after all – but that poor solitary pilot dangled before his audience for a good five minutes until he too landed in the Solent, to be picked up unharmed. He had done his best against bitter odds – but what must he have felt like on the way down after his meagre fifteen-second battle with the dreaded Hun?'

8
'So Few'
18–23 August

'Never in the field of human conflict was so much owed by so many to so few.'

(Prime Minister, House of Commons, 20 August)

On 17 August the Minister of Information, in a broadcast, informed the country that the Luftwaffe had been defeated. On the same day the Air Ministry, in response to a request by Dowding, decided that a number of volunteers from Bomber and Army Co-operation squadrons should be transferred to Fighter Command, that the reservoir of trained Allied pilots[1] should be drawn on, and that the courses at the fighter operational training units should be reduced from four weeks to two. These pilots reached the squadrons with ten to twenty hours on Spitfires or Hurricanes; some had never fired their guns, and some did not know even how the reflector sight worked.[2] On 18 August the next great wave of attack began.

The first operation, which came in between 1 P.M. and 2 P.M., was directed solely at fighter airfields, two of them sector stations, situated in a small area just south of London. They were Kenley, Biggin Hill, Croydon and West Malling. The second operation, which took place in the afternoon, was aimed at three Coastal Command and naval airfields and one radar station, situated in a small

[1] 302 (Polish) Squadron had already been formed; 303 (Polish) and 310 (Czech) Squadrons were to be formed; other Allied pilots, including French and Belgians, were attached to British squadrons.
[2] See *Nine Lives*, by G./Capt. A. C. Deere, pp. 130–1.

area on the borders of Sussex and Hampshire. They were Gosport, Thorney Island, Ford and the Poling radar station. In each case, therefore, the front of attack was about thirty miles long and the assaults were interconnected in order to throw the maximum strain on the defenders. In some cases a single target was itself to be the object of several waves of attack, closely timed so as to interlock and cause maximum confusion. The staff work was therefore intricate and the times at which bombers took off and were joined by their fighter escort after forming up had to be precisely adhered to. In the evening there was to be a third operation directed against North Weald and other aerodromes to the east of London.

At 1.35 P.M. precisely, Oberleutnant Lamberty, piloting the leading Dornier of 9 *Staffel* of KG 76, was to be over Biggin Hill at zero feet, after a low-level run in from the Seaford Gap near Beachy Head. The aerodrome was to be already cloaked in two clouds of dust and confusion, the first delivered at 1.25 P.M. by a gruppe of Dorniers, bombing from high level with fighter protection, the second delivered at 1.30 P.M. by a gruppe of Ju. 88s at high level. *Staffel* 9 were low-level attack specialists and their follow-up to the two high-level waves, which should destroy, blind or confuse the close-range AA, was expected to be the coup de grâce.

Lamberty, who had been an army officer, had transferred to the Luftwaffe on its formation, inspired largely by the fact that an uncle had been a fighter pilot in the first world war; he had been brought up on much the same diet of Albatros and SE 5 as had most of his opponents. As *Fliegerführer* (or captain) of the leading aircraft, he took them across the Channel at wave-top height, underneath the radar, in three vics of threes; as the English coast loomed ahead the nine Dorniers roared over a patrol vessel lying a few miles out, which fired at them. Their gunners replied, without visible result, then Beachy Head was in front and above them; they went straight through a cleft in the tall cliffs, crossing into England actually below clifftop height, then zoomed up over the edge and down again to zero altitude.

Beside Lamberty in the nose sat Hauptmann Roth, the Staffel Kapitan; below, in the lower gun position, was the flight mechanic, Oberfeldwebel Geier; behind Lamberty and Roth were Feldwebel Eberhard, the radio operator, and Hauptmann Peters, who had no function to perform in the aircraft – for him it was simply an acclimatization trip. He would gain experience of how this low-level work was done. Firing directly ahead was a 2 cm heavy machine-gun, which was fixed and operated by the pilot; to one side was a movable machine-gun operated from the observer's seat, occupied by Roth; Geier manned a single gun firing below and to the rear; above in the radio operator's cabin were three machine-guns, covering various arcs to the rear. The bomb-load was the regulation one (for a Dornier) of twenty 50-kg (100-lb) bombs. At less than ten feet they bored on for Biggin Hill.

It was precisely this type of low-level attack which the RAF controllers, who knew the deficiencies of the system better than anyone else, most feared; throughout the battle they dreaded the day the Germans would try it in force. It would create maximum confusion. The high-level attacks on this day, as on most others, were picked up fairly early, while the bombers were still orbiting over France and being joined by the fighters. With practice, and they were getting it, it was possible to keep the defending fighters on the ground until the very last minute – which meant that they could stay in action until the very last minute, because fuel shortage was as much a British problem as a German one. They had to be scrambled about twenty minutes in advance of a raid, because it took that time for them to get up to 109 height. If sent later, they were liable to be 'bounced'; if later still, they might be caught on the ground. In all, a very fine judgement was required, to balance all these factors to maximum effect.

On this day, watching the raids being plotted in the Operations Room at Biggin Hill, was the Station Commander, Group Captain R. Grice. The plotting board was not the usual table but an upright glass screen, on which it was easier for the controller to read off the vectors. On it was a map of southern England on which a group of WAAFs, with headphones on, marked the rapidly altering positions of the incoming enemy, according to the information being fed to them by telephone. Thus the controller could see at a glance what the position was. Their own fighters were not shown, because none had yet been ordered off. No one there, on his own initiative, could order the fighters to take off. That order came from headquarters, No. 11 Group, which controlled Biggin Hill and five other Sector Stations. At a similar Operations Room at 11 Group, the strategic decisions were taken for all the Sector Stations. The danger of the raid was assessed, then the number of fighters which could be spared to meet it, then orders were passed by telephone to this or that Sector Station for so many squadrons to take off, to intercept or to patrol.

Once airborne, it was the controller's task to bring about an interception, bearing in mind that as long as they were still climbing he had to keep them away from the enemy and try to bring them eventually into a position in which they had both height and sun in their favour; to help him pass the orders he had deputies, known as 'Ops Bs'. The AA defences were integrated into the system and an Army Liaison Officer was present in the Operations Room. Two days previously, Squadron Leader

Worrall had handed over 32 Squadron to Michael Cross-
ley and had become Senior Controller at Biggin Hill.
Another controller was Roger Frankland and one of the
Ops Bs, who became a controller during the battle, was
Bill Igoe; now retired, as Wing Commander and Squad-
ron Leader respectively, they are both in business in
London.

It was now obvious that some of the incoming raids
which the girls were plotting were headed directly for
Biggin Hill. 'There was excitement,' said Igoe, 'but I
never saw people work more efficiently than during raids;
on the contrary, under pressure you got a higher rather
than a lower performance. But, unlike civilians, we knew
exactly when we were in danger and when we were not.'
The danger was now becoming acute; the two high-level
raids – the gruppe of Dorniers followed at a distance by
the gruppe of Ju. 88s – were now only about ten minutes
flying time away. And still no order from Group for the
Spitfires of 610 Squadron and the Hurricanes of 32
Squadron to take off. On his own responsibility, Group
Captain Grice gave the order. The engines were started,
the pilots closed the canopies, and within a few minutes
the fighters were racing over the grass and rocketing up
over the boundary, undercarriages retracting.

Still some miles to the south, undetected by the radar,
9 *Staffel* were flying at zero altitude over Sussex. As the
ground screamed past underneath, the grass flattened
behind them by the racing propellers, what struck Lamberty most were the large fields prepared with anti-landing
obstacles; apart from that there was no sign of prepared
defence against troops. South of East Grinstead, directly
in their path, was what appeared to him to be a sort of
castle, with people standing outside it on a lawn; presumably a large country house. 'At first,' he said, 'they looked
interested in us – then, seeing black crosses, they ran into

the house. But first, they made sure what kind of plane it was.'

As the ground went past below like a roller map, Lamberty saw what he judged to be a Home Guard camp, consisting of many tents, at which his gunners fired brief bursts from out of the racing Dorniers. It must have been a Regular Army camp, for the Home Guard lived at home.

At that moment, which must have been approximately 1.30 P.M., Section Officer Pamela Beecroft, Cypher Officer at Biggin Hill, was in her office, catching up with work she had been unable to attend to because an alarm during the morning had kept her down in the shelter for an hour or so, although nothing had happened. She is now married to D. Hamilton Grice, DFC, then a pilot in 32 Squadron who had been shot down and wounded over Harwich a few days previously. Another alarm was sounded, and she started to return to the shelter. In the Operations Room the WAAFs at the plotting screen were putting on their steel helmets. Pamela Beecroft walked to the shelter entrance, saw an airman running over the grass towards it – and then the first bomb exploded, catching the man while he was still in the open. She had a momentary glimpse of the bombers; she thought there were about eight or nine of them.

Lamberty, in the leading Dornier, saw a fighter station, from which fighters were taking off, a mile or so away on the port side; possibly Redhill, he thought, possibly Kenley. At low level, navigation was extremely difficult; what they expected to see, as a guide for the final run-in, were the plumes of smoke and dust rising from Biggin Hill after the two high-level attacks which should just have taken place.

Then straight in front of them, suddenly and without

warning, loomed the camouflaged roofs of aircraft hangars – and beyond them, planes on the ground apparently at refuelling points. It was Kenley. And it was quite untouched.

Lamberty released all bombs at once, on to those first hangars, then screamed at low level straight across the airfield, hoping to get clear in time, before the light AA woke up. Directly in front, at the far side of the field, he could see what appeared to be mushroom sites for small-calibre flak. The Dornier went thundering across the field towards them, the other eight bombers following behind, and billows of smoke shot up from the bomb explosions.

'Halfway across the airfield, all hell broke loose,' recalled Lamberty. The Bofors guns in the mushroom sites began to crack away with bursts of five shells at a time, and with equally startling suddenness, 'a damn carpet of some kind of rockets were being shot up on the north side; they had small parachutes from which wire hung down. I pulled back on my stick and went up; we were wary of a weapon like that.'

These were PAC (Parachute and Cable) rockets, a cheap, improvised weapon produced to offset the shortage of guns. Roaring upwards, he collided with one of the wire cables, which cut a gash in the leading edge of one wing but caused no significant damage. Still climbing to get above the tiny parachutes drifting in front of him, he passed directly over the two Bofors gun positions; inside the Dornier, they could hear the guns firing, see the vivid muzzle flashes leaping up at them, and feel the pressure as they fired rocking the aircraft. At 150 feet they blew a hole in his port wing, puncturing the fuel tank and putting that engine out of action.

Lamberty feathered the port propeller, slammed open the starboard throttle, and went over the boundary, turning to starboard and still hoping to get out of it. Then

two or three Hurricanes of 111 Squadron came down on
him. Lamberty never actually saw them, he was too busy
trying to handle the crippled bomber. What he did see,
looking straight ahead, were dust spurts leaping up from
the ground where the first fighter's bullets were kicking
up the earth; the pilot had probably come down on him
too fast and overshot. Then there was a noise, inside the
Dornier, as of a handful of peas being rattled against a
window pane. 'That,' said Lamberty, 'was the second
fighter attacking – which was for good. The left side of
the plane was all afire and we could feel the heat. So there
was no other possibility but to land.' He glanced round
quickly for a suitable field.

Behind him, over Kenley, the other eight Dorniers had
run into the same curtain of fire; most dropped their
bombs at once, a few made two deliberate run-ins,
dropping part of their load each time. One Dornier went
straight down and crashed, others turned away, riddled,
and began to limp for home; and another Dornier reared
up over the airfield, the pilot dead with a bullet through
the heart, and the crew struggling to get him out of the
pilot's seat.

Putting the nose down, Lamberty turned away towards
a field just about long enough to allow him to flatten out,
touch down, and skid to a standstill with the wheels up;
but it would be a near thing. Cutting it very fine, he
brought the bomber in over the hedge, the starboard fin
actually brushing through the branches of a tree. With
flame and smoke streaming from its port engine, the
bomber levelled out just above the ground; as it did so,
the men of a Home Guard detachment were firing at it
with rifles, getting away 180 rounds. Lamberty knew
nothing of this and it is likely that all the shots passed well
astern of him. With the stick back in his stomach, he held
the burning Dornier a few feet up until it stalled. As he

touched down, the bomber rocked violently, bouncing across the field at high speed, the front perspex panels shattering and a cloud of dust coming into the nose. It lurched to a stop, shrouded in smoke and flame from the blazing port wing.

Strapped into his seat, hardly able to breathe in the sudden blast of heat and billowing dust and smoke, Lamberty knocked off his harness and because there was a solid sheet of flame at his back tried to get out through the nose. The panels were too small for him to squeeze through and the frames were steel too strong to bend. He began to panic at the thought of being roasted alive.

Looking around frantically for a way out through the rear, he saw that someone had jettisoned the escape hatch but that he would first have to crawl over the radio operator's seat, now crumpled and glowing with heat. Either that or be burned to death. With the last strength in him he scrambled over to the hatch, being forced to drag himself up only by grasping with his hands the molten metal. He slithered down to the ground on the starboard side, feeling unaccountably weak; there was no pain yet in his burned hands or face, but he felt on the point of collapse and was swaying from side to side.

Some of the Home Guards now ran up, pointing shotguns and rifles at him, 'excited and yet also a bit fearful'. They hung back, merely covering him with their weapons, while Lamberty patted with burned hands, from which all the skin had come away, at the smouldering sleeves of his tunic.

He saw Hauptmann Roth standing a few yards away, the skin hanging in shreds from his face, hands and wrists, and arguing with the Home Guard, telling them to point their guns in some other direction instead of at him. At that moment there arrived over Biggin Hill airfield, which lay about half a mile away, the first gruppe of high-level

bombers which should have opened the attack; a torrent
of bombs came tumbling down at least twenty minutes
too late, and splinters shrieked and moaned through the
air. Everyone dropped flat, Home Guards and the two
Germans, and they stayed with their noses to the ground
until the bombers turned away. They had been seriously
delayed, while connecting with their fighter escort over
France. Inside the shelter, Pamela Beecroft put her hands
over her ears to blot out the noise; the shuddering of the
walls raised clouds of dust, but she knew everyone there
and felt, How can they die?

The Home Guards took the two wounded airmen into
a street, presumably Biggin village, which led to the
aerodrome gates. Curious civilians crowded round, saying
the first thing which came into their heads, 'Are you glad
it's all over for you?' Lamberty and Roth were not, and
said so, as tactfully as they could. 'I'm sorry to have to
stop flying for some time,' was all Lamberty would admit
to. They wanted to rid themselves of their parachutes but
with crippled hands could not undo the harness. One man
understood, and when he undid the parachutes, Lamberty
hinted that what he now had was 'good silk for making
shirts'. What he needed above all was a cigarette. When
the man took out of Lamberty's pocket the cigarettes
which he managed to indicate were there, there was a
gasp of astonishment – English cigarettes! (which he had
bought in Guernsey the previous week).

Almost at once Eberhard, the radio operator, was led
into the street from its other end; he was almost unhurt,
just a few scratches on his hands. All three were then
taken by car to Station Sick Quarters, Biggin Hill, where
all the casualties, wounded English and wounded Germans, were ranged in the order of severity of their
injuries. 'When it was my turn I got excellent treatment,'
recalled Lamberty, who possessed ever afterwards a high

opinion of the British medical profession. 'There were two doctors and one spoke good German. He put a cup of tea before me, with a straw through which to drink it – because I couldn't hold the cup. I couldn't eat at all, my mouth was burned inside, but they thought it was because I didn't like the food, so they brought me other types of food. Some officers came and asked who had shot me down – guns or fighters? (It was certainly not the Home Guard, although just possibly they may have hit the machine.) The officers tried a little interrogation, but saw we were not able to stand it.'

Lamberty still retains, as a souvenir of his last flight in the Battle of Britain, the RAF form of admission to Station Sick Quarters, which shows that he was transferred next day to Kent County Hospital, Farnborough, and a cutting from a contemporary British newspaper containing a photograph of the crashed Dornier and the caption:

'This is the plane that made British air history – the bomber shot down with rifle fire by Home Guards in South London.'

While in hospital, where the treatment for burns was so good that the scars on his hands are now hardly visible, he was able to work out with the other members of the crew what had really happened in the last few moments of the crash. When it landed, only Hauptmann Roth and himself were in it. Geier, the flight mechanic, and Hauptmann Peters, the passenger who had come along for the experience, had jumped at not more than 150 feet; the evidence lay in their injuries – no burns, but severe fractures of the skull and thigh. Their parachutes had not fully opened, and they had had no hope that they would; but they had preferred to jump rather than burn. Feldwebel Eberhard, however, had virtually no injuries at all

– no burns, no fractures, merely abrasions to both hands; it was this which bore out his otherwise incredible story.

With the Dornier at about 150 feet and losing height, he had thrown off her rear escape hatch, got out on to the back of the fuselage, his legs towards the tail, and hanging on to the cockpit with one hand, had pulled the ripcord of his parachute. It had bellied out behind him, tearing him loose from his grip – hence the cuts on his hands – and he had swung just once under it, from the horizontal to the vertical, when he had crashed into a fence. The speed of the aircraft would have been about 100 mph, the exact height impossible to guess, but certainly low enough to put Eberhard's effort in the World Record class.

After the war, Lamberty was able to reconstruct the fate of 9 *Staffel*. Out of nine Dorniers, one was a total loss, all killed, somewhere near Kenley or Biggin Hill; there was his own, with all wounded and prisoner; two more crashed into the Channel on the way back, the crews being rescued by motor launches; three force-landed in France not far from the coast; one aircraft got back to base with a dead pilot on board; and one landed intact, with no casualties.

Probably the most extraordinary occurrence of the whole disastrous day took place in the aircraft which had had the pilot killed directly over Kenley. Oberfeldwebel Illg, the flight mechanic, grabbed the stick with one hand to put the machine's nose down again and keep it from stalling, while with the other he tried to get the dead man out of his seat; with help from one of the others, he managed it. He then took over the controls, although he was not a qualified pilot, and turned the bomber round towards France, heading south through the area where the Biggin Hill fighters were delightedly picking off the scattered bombers, survived an attack at the cost of a few bullet holes, and landed safely at Cormeilles-en-Vexin with the wheels down. Awarded the Knight's Cross, he was shot down near London a week afterwards and taken prisoner.

The raid had been an almost complete fiasco, but the fact that it did not catch the squadrons on the ground in spite of that was due entirely to the moral courage of the Station Commander. When Group finally telephoned the order to scramble, Grice replied, 'You're too bloody late, the airfield's been bombed and we got twelve down.'

The damage at Biggin Hill consisted mainly of cratering of the field. At Kenley the damage, however, had been serious. Six Hurricanes destroyed on the ground, only one hangar left standing, and the Operations Room put out of action; this was transferred to an emergency centre in a butcher's shop in Caterham, which was able to control only two squadrons in place of the three previously handled. West Malling and Croydon had also been damaged again.

The afternoon raids in the Portsmouth area were preceded at 1.30 P.M. by a warning sign in the sky – ruler-straight, a white vapour trail came burrowing across the blue from France. At its point, it was as thin as a pencil and as sharply defined, but its mile-long tail was billowy and blown out by the high winds in the heights. It was a beautiful sunny day with only a few scattered cirrus clouds, perfect for photographic reconnaissance. At Gosport, dispersal had not yet taken place; in the undamaged hangars were many aircraft.

A few hours later I wrote in the diary I was keeping: 'A short but sharp bombing of Gosport aerodrome has just taken place. At least a dozen Ju. 88s literally fell out of the skies, surrounded by shrapnel bursts and smoke, on to the aerodrome, pulling out just above the treetops, the flash of exploding bombs clearly visible and shaking the crockery in the kitchen. At any one time there seemed to be at least four or five of the big twin-motor bombers going down at the aerodrome; they plunged on to it with a horrible vicious certainty, tearing through the yellow flame of bursting shells. A high-level bomber is just a shining silver piece of machinery, but you feel there's a man controlling a stuka and that he can pick any target he chooses. Then the bombers were gone, leaving fading puffs of smoke drifting in the sky.'

I then took out a notebook, sat down at a table in the garden and jotted down the sequence of events almost as rapidly as they occurred: 'Just after the dive-bombing, two Ju. 88s high up and flying west, followed a few minutes later by a flight of Hurricanes. Lull, then – sound only – cannon and machine-gun fire up top; then, there they are – three or four fighters diving on the Portchester balloons – one balloon going down, slowly, glowing red and orange, with a black plume of smoke above it. Funny how balloons wriggle down like worms, so slowly, twisting and writhing from side to side. Like sharks, the Messerschmitts rolling and plunging among them . . . another balloon going down over the dockyard, trickling down the sky like a fiery blob of water running in slow motion down a window pane . . . pop-pop-pop of cannon and rattle of machine-guns . . . Cams Manor balloon going down in front 200 yards away, like a blackened and blazing parachute as it hits the ground . . . can count six smoke columns in the sky, personally saw four balloons go down in flames, no 109s fell, no Junkers down that I could see. Three more black streaks over Gosport, with a little glow of fire at the ends, moving slowly downward; with the usual noisy death music. "This is what comes of Duff Cooper boasting last night," remarks a neighbour.'

The 109s were from JG 2, the new Richthofen Geschwader, and were free-hunting in the target area, led by a rising star of the Luftwaffe, Helmut Wick, whose log survived. He had attacked the balloons because he was bored; there were no RAF fighters around. At the time I did not know that there was a new 'Richthofen Circus', let alone that they were based on the French coast opposite Portsmouth and Southampton, and I had never heard of Helmut Wick. But I had noticed that, contrary to the boastful propaganda being put out by press and radio, the Luftwaffe could do more or less what it liked on our sector of the front.

'I was in a shelter alongside the north hangar through-out this attack,' wrote Clarke. 'It was hectic that time! When we came out the hangar was blazing but I organized some blokes to try and get the aircraft out – mostly Skuas, Rocs, Battles and Queen Bees. We managed to save some. All communications with Pompey were cut off by the bombing and I volunteered to fly across in a Queen Bee with messages. I landed on the rifle range behind the AA School buildings at Eastney and was nearly arrested by an indignant Pongo who had spent three months putting up anti-landing posts! I landed between them – just.'

Thorney Island and Ford received much the same sort of treatment and the Poling radar station was very badly damaged and put out of action. There was another gap in the radar chain. In addition, the previous raid on the damaged Ventnor station had set back the efforts to repair it.

But in contrast to the notable success in this area, the evening attacks against the eastern aerodromes failed almost completely, possibly because 110s were used in large numbers. Colin Gray, flying with 54 Squadron, was in action three times during the day. During the morning six of them came across a lone 110 over the Estuary; it was sighted by George Gribble, but Gray was nearer to it and arrived first. He fired all his ammunition into it from behind; both engines caught fire, pieces fell off, and the holes in it were clearly visible. 'That slowed him down a bit.' Consequently the other Spitfires now diving on to it overshot. 'Murderous,' said Gray.

At 12.40 they took off to meet a tougher enemy – 109s over Dover. At 5 P.M. they were ordered to patrol Manston, and were vectored to Harwich to meet the force bound for North Weald – 'a colossal raid', Gray said. The bombers lost their fighters when coming through cloud and all the squadrons engaged, which included No. 56 and No. 151 from North Weald, had a successful time. Gray picked a 110 which pulled up in front of him. He fired at that moment, probably hitting the pilot, for the big two-seater fell away in a stall turn and went straight down from 15,000 feet without any attempt to pull out; Gray, following behind, was still at 5,000 feet when he saw it go straight in. 'It was as quick as that. After this scrap they weren't so free with their 110s.'

These were the main attacks. There were others, one on Manston which was continually being raided; German bombers and fighters returning from inland were inclined to spend what they had left on the battered aerodrome, and 109s and 110s hung around waiting to catch Spitfires or Hurricanes in the circuit, when with flaps and under-carriage down, they were virtually helpless. A section of 65 Squadron, led by Flying Officer ('the good') Wigg, was attacked in this way; Wigg landed, unaware that anything had happened to the two other Spitfires until the columns of smoke rising from the crashes were pointed out to him. They were caught so often when taking off or landing that the rumour of spies transmitting messages to the enemy went round the camps; some people felt they knew who the spies were. However, as we know, the area was under radar observation from Wissant, thirty miles away, and all R/T conversations between controllers and pilots were being monitored at the same place; in good weather visual observation would have been possible. Trouble, when it came, was very sudden.

Trevor Tarr had just completed a forty-eight-hour task on one of three Blenheims which was standing in a triple bay, and was waiting for the 'all clear' to sound before he ran up the engines, when without much interest he noticed six fighters, which looked like Hurricanes, come into the circuit – as they turned, their wings seemed to catch the sun in a series of winking flashes. A moment later, he realized his mistake, as the fighters came diving at him, the flashes of cannon and machine-gun fire now quite distinct. As the first two passed overhead and rocketed away, the Blenheim caught fire, and Tarr, followed down by clouds of smoked ducked into a shelter, the occupants of which immediately assumed that a gas attack was in progress.

When all six had passed over, Tarr emerged. Sparks from the blazing Blenheim were being blown all over the bay; the tanks of the other two aircraft had been holed and were pouring out petrol. An old fire engine came racing up, two men quickly ran out hoses from it while another man sat high up on the vitals of the apparatus, which was making steady grinding noises and producing a few apologetic drips from the hoses; then it made a supreme effort and the man disappeared in a splendid burst of foam. They put out the fire with hand extinguishers, but trying to service Blenheim night fighters under these conditions was a heart-breaking business. Curiously, it was the quiet and inoffensive types who usually remained to work until literally the last minute on the aircraft; the tougher characters, including those with distinguished AWOL records, tended to fade away at a very early stage of the proceedings.

According to British records, the Germans lost seventy-one aircraft while the British lost twenty-seven fighters[3] during the twenty-four hours of 18 August; certainly, the German daylight losses were high. High enough to compel a complete reappraisal of the situation. A conference was held on the 19th, a directive was issued on the 20th, and by the 24th it had been implemented. In the meantime, there were five days of cloudy weather which enabled the Germans to do little more than hammer Manston and send out reconnaissance aircraft which frequently did not come back. 'To carry out reconnaissance, compared to the previous campaigns, presented considerable difficulties,' wrote Major Bechtle in his Staff Study. 'The planes of the H-Reconnaissance Staffel could hardly manage to reach the British coast.'

On 20 August Squadron Leader Satchell, with a section of 302 Squadron, now operational, intercepted a reconnaissance Ju. 88 over Hull. He chased it in and out of cloud, trying to estimate the point at which it would reappear. It was the first enemy aircraft he had seen while in the air and it was most important that he, as the leader of the squadron, should score their first victory. He guessed right, got in a long full-deflection burst from above and behind – and then the Ju. 88 vanished into cloud, and they never saw it again.

As they taxied in at Leconfield, an exuberant crowd of Poles greeted the three Hurricanes; the Ju. 88 had crashed in flames. Later the Station Intelligence Officer interrogated in hospital two of the three surviving members of the crew. The rear-gunner had been killed by Satchell early on and his final attack they had not even seen – they had just felt themselves hit by the bullets and

[3] Actually 69 and 31, plus 37 other British aircraft, some destroyed on the ground.

then the machine had burst into flames. The pilot, who never regained consciousness and died a few days later, had no fewer than seventeen bullets in him. With extra-ordinary gallantry, the other two had dragged the uncon-scious man out of his seat, and had then jumped with him, one of them pulling the pilot's ripcord for him before he pulled his own.

Satchell, who had feared that he would get too excited when he first went into action and so fluff his chances, was relieved, and also a little disappointed, to find himself ice-cold, concentrating on his calculations to such an extent that he experienced no more emotion than in a camera gun exercise.

Next day, 21 August, the New Zealander, Flight Lieu-tenant Blake, found himself in much the same situation – his first action, plus the responsibility of leadership, against three Ju. 88s on 'armed reconnaissance'. He was now at St Eval in Cornwall, where he had taken over 238 Squadron, formerly at Middle Wallop. In a single day they had lost half a dozen pilots, including the CO and a flight commander, and had been withdrawn to rest and be brought up to strength. In the areas flanking 11 Group there were now many such decimated squadrons.

With two other pilots, one of whom had been badly shaken by his experiences, Blake flew due west, directly out to sea. The Ju. 88s were reported coming up the north coast of Cornwall, and he intended to turn south and come down on them from out of the sun; it worked exactly as expected, but Blake committed the normal mistake of the inexperienced pilot – opening fire too soon – and the Germans split and dived into a heaped cumulus cloud, each one pursued by a Hurricane.

Blake knew he had made a bad initial error; if any of the Germans got away, it was his fault. He therefore hung on grimly to the Junkers he had picked, into and through the cloud, keeping tight formation below the enemy bomber, which was weaving violently and preventing him from getting a shot at it. Then they both broke cloud, both of them diving, the German a little way ahead; Blake's Hurricane was shaking and shuddering with the speed. Still diving, the German began to turn – and Blake was straight across the circle at him. He could see the pinpricks of light from the rear of the cabin and knew he was being fired at; it didn't seem to matter, he was absorbed in his calculations and mentally cursing himself for his first mistake – he was not going to make another.

'We were talking, speaking, dreaming of this sort of thing,' he recalled, 'and if you practised enough, you did as you had imagined.'

There were flashes all along the cabin of the Ju. 88, where his bullets were striking; then he was pulling out, his legs shaking with sudden nervous reaction, his mind whirling with wild doubts. 'Were they German? Such sitting targets – my God, could they have been ours?' But they were not, and two were down; the shaken pilot had failed to score.

Manston, attacked again on the 19th and the 21st, was now a shambles of chalk-covered ruins and bomb craters. Even when some of the barrack blocks had still stood, attacks were so frequent that few people used them but preferred to sleep in the shelters. Here, as everywhere, people divided into two sharp classifications – the fatalists and the fearful. The latter underwent the harsher experience of being unreasonably afraid all of the time instead of being reasonably afraid part of the time. When the mass of men from the shelters filed in each morning to one barrack room where some half dozen fatalists had been sleeping in their beds, the youngest fatalist, a mere lad, sang out cheerily, 'The rats come out of their holes!' Sullenly, the fearful filed past.

Every night, 600 Squadron had to mount a guard on
their Blenheims; between them the Corporal and five or
six men had the total armament of the unit – two rifles
and a Very pistol. If a German landing occurred during
the night they were to make their way to the nearest army
unit; there was to be no attempt to hold the aerodrome.
But the only Germans to scale the cliffs were the crew of
a crashed bomber – as they reached the top they found a
row of bayonets pointed at them. One other German
turned up, with a Home Guard escort; he shook his fist at
them and announced that the Führer would rescue him.
By day, some of the enemy flew so low that they could
see the pilots' faces.

Casualties were not high, but the administrative
arrangements for feeding so many men scattered over so
large an area gradually collapsed. Often, there were no
hot meals and once, there was even a shortage of tea. The
men were hot, dusty and tired from terribly long hours of
work; additionally, the tea ran out when the first half of a
queue had been served, leaving the others to look on.
There was nearly a riot. Then came a high-pitched Cockney wail, 'Cor, whadyer fink we are – flippin' camels or
sumfing?' and the tension exploded in laughter.

600 Squadron were withdrawn to Hornchurch on the
22nd. Shortly before, a small group of men, led by
Corporal Hunter, were wandering in the wreckage of the
guardroom and barracks to see if anywhere anyone was
organizing any food, when two brand-new 'sprogs'
appeared. Perfectly turned out, and in full equipment, the
recruits made the airmen look even more dishevelled than
they were. Seeing a Corporal, they sprang smartly to
attention. 'We can't find anyone to report to. What should
we do?'

'Take the next train back,' growled Hunter.

'Can't do that, Corporal – our orders are to report to RAF Station Manston.'

Silently, the airmen surveyed the white and dusty waste. Then Hunter had an idea for a gag. 'What's your name and last three?'

'Brickbat' (or whatever it was), replied their spokesman. '18079643.'.

Hunter half-peeled off his jacket. 'Right. You stay here as 80566 Corporal Hunter. I'll go back and get some more training.'

They left the 'sprogs' there, wondering what to do. Next day, the Squadron was evacuated, and on 24 August Manston itself was evacuated. And the word went round that Winston Churchill had said, 'The treachery of Manston will not be repeated.'

PHASE III:

Approaches to London

9

Concentration Over Kent

24–27 August

Continuation of the campaign against the British air force with
the present object of weakening the British fighter force:
The enemy will be forced to engage with his fighter forces by
uninterrupted attacks.
Furthermore, single aircraft during the night, and during the
day when the weather will not permit operations to be carried
out by whole units, will attack plants of aircraft industry and the
air force ground organizations.'

(Oberkommando der Luftwaffe order, 20 August)

This directive, issued as a result of the conference of
19 August, implied no drastic change of policy; it merely
codified the ideas which dominated the minds of the
German commanders throughout the battle. The British
fighter force was to be drawn into action with the German
fighter force and destroyed in the air; the bombers would
give what help they could by bombing, but their main
function was to attract the British fighters. The Germans
believed they were winning the battle in the air, the battle
of fighter versus fighter. They were less sanguine as
regards the battle from the air, the destruction of fighters
on the ground by bombing. For them, the fighter arm was
more important; it would win or lose the battle.

The vital decision which was taken at the conference of
19 August was not a matter of policy, which remained the
same, but of method. A more realistic appraisal of the
British defences had now been made; and as a result,
there was a drastic regrouping of the fighter components
of the three air fleets. In the first stage of the main battle

– 12 to 19 August – the German fighter force was diluted. Resistance over southern England was expected to be overcome in four days. The Germans felt that they had sufficient forces to be strong everywhere. The larger part of the fighter arm was in Pas de Calais facing across the Straits to Kent, but there were also substantial numbers of fighters in the area of Le Havre/Dieppe which, together with smaller forces in the Cherbourg peninsula and the Channel Islands, faced the sector between Portsmouth and Plymouth. Additionally, there were long-range fighters in Norway under command of *Luftflotte* 5.

The first week of heavy action had shown a surprising resistance by the British, which the easy victories over the Channel had not led them to expect. The advantage which radar gave the defenders was not clear, there were always more British fighters met with in the air than they had believed their enemy to possess, and their pilots were fighting stubbornly and skilfully. As a result, the German fighters had not been able to gain air superiority over England and the bombers which they were too few to escort were virtually out of the battle and could not be employed. The Germans had therefore twin problems, both of which were caused directly by Fighter Command:

(a) How to gain air superiority over England;

(b) How to use the bombers for which no escort was available.

The solution adopted for the first problem was to concentrate all the single-engined fighters in one area – Pas de Calais – under the command of *Luftflotte* 2, in accordance with the maxim of concentration of effort at the decisive point; the decisive battle would therefore take place over Kent on the approaches to London. They were not yet ready to attack London, although at the back of their minds was the thought that the capital might prove to be the Achilles heel of the enemy. Therefore, in the days following 19 August, *Luftflotte* 3 was stripped of

ts 109s; by 24 August they had all been regrouped under
the JAFU 2. *Luftflotte* 3 retained the 110s, which had
proved a great disappointment, but which might be yet
useful if the bulk of the British fighter force could be
drawn off into the battle over Kent. *Luftflotte* 5's 110s
were withdrawn and brought to France. The main
responsibility for victory now lay with Kesselring, and
24 August marked a turning point in the battle. The
bombers coming in over Kent would now be escorted by
virtually every single-engined fighter the Luftwaffe
possessed.

The second problem, of how to use the surplus bombers
from which all possibility of effective escort had now been
stripped, was to be solved in two ways. They would
operate by day in cloudy weather and it would be seen,
by mass attacks in good weather on the Portsmouth–
Plymouth front, if the British fighters could still put up
effective resistance there; additionally, a large force
would turn to making mass attacks by night, although
they would be available once more for daylight operations
if the fighter arm succeeded in its task. To prepare a large
part of the bomber force for night attacks took a few days
longer, and major night raids did not begin until
28 August. This date, then, marked another turning point.

The battle which began on the 24th was to see Fighter
Command drawn in, held down, and finally annihilated in
the south-east by the overpowering necessity to defend
the approaches to London and the threat to the city itself.
This change of plan kept step with the change which had
occurred in the invasion plan. Originally, the German
beachhead was to run from Kent to the Isle of Wight; it
had now been reduced in extent, at the insistence of the
German Naval Staff, to Kent and part of Sussex. British
critics, judging solely on the basis of the switch from
target to target, assumed that the Germans had some
rigid timetable in mind to which they were adhering

regardless of results, or alternatively that they did not
share the same splendid conceptions of the correct use of
air power which was the natural birthright of the critics
themselves. The truth was more simple: the Germans had
found the task set them more difficult than they had at
first thought.

The solution adopted was probably the best, but it
brought the Germans up against another difficulty – the
short range of the 109. As long as coastal targets were
attacked, all was well. But when the range was extended
to the London area, from Pas de Calais, the fighters were
operating at the extreme limit of their fuel. This meant
that there was no possibility of carrying out elaborate
deception measures, with frequent changes of course by
the bombers; that there was no possibility even of evading
opposition; that there was no margin of safety to allow
for faulty navigation by the bombers when above cloud;
and that the escort could not get involved in any battle
lasting much longer than ten minutes without using up, in
high-speed, full-power manoeuvres, too much of their
precious fuel. If they were involved in too much fighting,
then the pilots had the straight choice: leave the bombers
and go home at once – or go on with the bombers and go
down in the sea on the return flight. It was, in reverse,
the difficulty the RAF had experienced over Dunkirk.
Because they were always so short on fuel, the pilots of
the 109s grew to loathe the Channel – the 'Shite Kanal' as
they called it, for that was where so many of them ended
up. Oberst Carl Viek, chief of staff to the JAFU 2,
recalled a single case in which, out of 250 fighters sent to
the London area, only 80 landed back at their airfields:
the remainder force-landed short of them in fields, in the
dunes, or in the sea. And, of course, the targets of the
bombers were limited to the area which could be flown
over by the 109s. These were the German difficulties.

But to the British the potentially great strength of the Luftwaffe, based only just across the Channel – instead of across the Rhine – posed a number of problems equally insoluble. The initiative was solidly in the hands of the Germans; they had the bombers to threaten the targets which must be defended, and they could attack them, the English summer permitting, when they liked and in what strength they liked. Theoretically, they could marshal 300 bombers and send 700 fighters to escort them; with so short a warning, and so many scattered targets to cover, the British could never manage to bring together all their 600 fighters, in time, at the threatened point (if they had, the control system could never have handled them all). They could fling in only a few squadrons, one by one or at the most two by two, as they became available and as the direction of the threat became clearer. If they waited to amass a more substantial force of fighters, the Germans would have struck and gone back over the French coast while the British were still assembling. And if the threat proved to be merely a diversion in advance of the real attack, then the British fighters could be caught in the air and short of fuel or even on the ground, refuelling. For ground forces, the situation would have been impossible, but for an air force, with a capacity for high-speed hit-and-run, the situation might just possibly be tolerable – provided that the fighter commander was wary and that his pilots were bold.

But from this sort of fighting no immediately decisive results could be expected, except perhaps that the enemy might be gradually worn down. The obvious answer to the German concentration of fighters in Pas de Calais was, if not an equal concentration, then at least a substantial addition to the number of fighters in 11 Group, which was now going to bear almost the whole weight of German

attack. With greater forces available, two or three squad
rons could be sent instead of one and reserves would be
available to cushion the effect of diversionary attacks. Air
Vice-Marshal Park did in fact ask for reinforcement by
extra squadrons, the numerical factor, and also for the
experienced pilots from other squadrons outside 11 Group
to be sent to his squadrons as replacements for casualties
instead of partly-trained pilots, which was the qualitative
factor. Given this, he believed that the battle could have
been shortened by several weeks. On the German side
this view has been put very much more strongly; if the
whole of the British fighter force had been brought to the
threatened area, they believe that the battle would have
been over in three days (this is a retrospective view, based
on the fact that the British had twice as many fighters as
they believed them to have at the time). This was not in
fact possible, at least not at this stage, because the
capacity of the control system was extremely limited.

Park was the field commander actually fighting the
enemy and naturally he wanted every squadron he had
the facilities to handle, as well as the pick of the pilots.
Dowding, who bore the overall responsibility for the
defence of the whole of the United Kingdom and not
merely the small area immediately threatened, had
necessarily to consider the military and political repercussions of leaving the greater part of the country open to
attack at any time that it suited the Germans to make
another switch of their forces, or even merely to repeat
this time against no opposition, the raids on the north.
Militarily, it was desirable to reinforce Park, politically it
could be disastrous. Apart from this, there had to be
taken into account another aspect of the quality factor. A
battle-weary squadron was, as Al Deere has written,
merely 'a token force in the air'. They were unable to

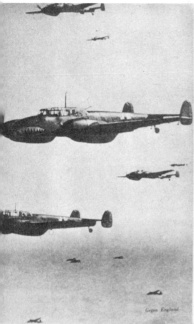

Left: Me.110s 'Gegen England'.
Photo: McKee collection

Gegen England

Right: From a German magazine. Stukas going down on an oil refinery at Thameshaven. 'Day and night the German Air Force is hammering vital targets in England.'
Photo: McKee collection

Above: Pilot and observer in a Heinkel He.111 of the *Löwengeschwad*
Photo: Willibald Klein collection

Below: Heinkel 111 of the staff flight of KG 55, shot down at South-wick, north of Portsmouth, while on a lone mission on 12 July, 1940
Photo: Portsmouth News

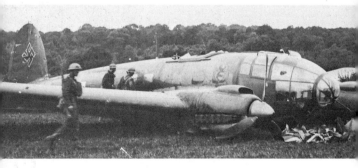

Right: Mechanic working on a Ju.87. The tiny propeller by the undercarriage leg produced the intimidating 'scream' when the Stuka dived.
Photo: Oberstleutnant Dilley's collection

Below: Briefing German fighter pilots at a Pas de Calais airfield.
Photo: McKee collection

Left: Waiting. F/Lt Gordon Olive DFC, an Australian of 65 Squadron, at readiness waiting for the 'Scramble'. *Photo : S/Ldr E.D. Glaser*

Below: For lack of sufficient escort fighters the Luftwaffe had to turn many of its machines to night bombing. Here the Heinkels of KG 55 have been painted black and daubed with soot to dull reflection. *Photo: Major Wronsky's collection*

shoot down many enemy aircraft and they were themselves liable to suffer unduly high losses. Rather than clutter up the strained control system with squadrons which were no longer of top-line efficiency, he preferred to take them out to rest in the less obviously threatened areas, bringing them south again a few weeks later, by which time they were fit to fight again. This, in Dowding's view, was the most efficient and economical way to use his force. His pilots agree with him.

The Germans had no such system, indeed the policy adopted by Göring was precisely the opposite. Not only had their airmen to fly on operations, without rest and regardless of losses, but the whole of the training organization in Germany was stripped of experienced men in order to place every single article in the shop window. Such a policy was effective over a short period of time, by bringing maximum strength to bear and also by impressing opponents; but in a campaign longer than a few weeks it was likely to prove a mistake of major proportions, particularly when the enemy was formidable. There were pilots on the German side who had baled out or crash-landed ten times in a matter of months, but they were ruthlessly driven to continue by that relentless tempo-tempo-tempo which the regime had made its own. If a unit was shot to pieces, the survivors continued to fly; the slogan was, 'The last man shall go again.' The German pilots disagreed with this system, some of the staff officers, such as Viek, tried to short-circuit it, and later it was altered – each geschwader had its own training geschwader to which the battle-experienced men went in rotation.

When the battle was renewed on 24 August Park was unable to concentrate on the bombers as he had planned, for they were now escorted by sufficient numbers of

fighters to provide a close escort, a top cover, and one or
more 'free-hunting' groups. He was forced to revert to
the earlier idea of trying to separate the bombers from at
least part of their escort by engaging it as early as possible
with the modern Spitfires; while the 109s dived and turned
in the dog-fight, the bombers would be going on steadily
at 180 mph, getting further and further away. The Hurricanes, less fitted to take on the 109s, would be held inland
ready to engage the bombers, against which they were
undoubtedly effective. Even if not a single 109 was shot
down, the Spitfires would have done their job if they
could separate the two components of the attacking force.
This idea arose from the actual division of the British
fighter force into two distinct types of aircraft with different values, but it also reflected a certain difference in
outlook. While the Germans considered the fighter battle
to be of paramount importance, the British not unnatu-
rally tended to regard the bombers as the main threat.
That is to put the matter perhaps altogether too tidily, but
there was such a difference of emphasis.

The Germans made no attempt to attack the radar
chain – that objective had been abandoned; but they
tended to drive back Fighter Command from its forward
aerodromes and secure air superiority over an increasingly
large area of south-east England. With sufficient aircraft
to make elaborate deceptions possible over the Straits,
they struck Manston twice, once in the morning and once
in the afternoon, and that was the end of 'Charlie 3'.
They struck also at two aerodromes of the inner ring
guarding London on the east – Hornchurch and North
Weald. Again, they were able to confuse the defenders.

Two Hurricane squadrons were paired at North Weald
– No. 56 and No. 151. 56 Squadron were airborne seven
times, Constable Maxwell logging five minutes short of
six hours' flying time; six times they chased vainly after

diversions, and the seventh time they were on the ground at Rochford when the bombers were passing overhead unmolested.

At about 3.45 P.M., after they had been on the ground twenty minutes, they heard the Southend sirens begin to wail, which caused laughter. 'There is a distant sound of engines,' wrote Maxwell. 'A squadron – no, many squadrons – our laugh becomes hollow. North Weald is rung up. No orders yet from Group. The noise of many engines gets closer. We get to our planes at very high speed. There are still no take-off orders. About 120 enemy aircraft pass almost overhead. "Take-off!"' The Hurricanes went racing across the grass and as they climbed up, so the 109s came roaring down on them. "Look out!" called Sergeant Smythe, "they're blitzing us!"

Meanwhile, 151 Squadron were taking off from North Weald. 'Large enemy force approaching base,' was the message. They climbed hard away to the west, to gain height, and then, still only at 3,000 feet, began to turn east towards the oncoming enemy. Above them, at 13,000 feet, they could see the massive German formation. There were seven Hurricanes in all, one being a private aircraft flown by the Station Commander, Victor Beamish, who ought to have been behind his desk. Still climbing, still turning, still below the bombers, they defiantly tried to put in their attack. 'It was an example of a thoroughly unsatisfactory engagement,' said R. M. Milne, who was flying one of the seven Hurricanes. 'We were at a disadvantage from the word go.' Now retired, as Wing Commander, Milne works for an aircraft company in London.

The 109s came down with a rush and not a single Hurricane was able to fire at a bomber. Looking down on North Weald, Milne could see large areas of the airfield covered in drifting smoke and dust – the bombs had fallen on the south side, where the hangars and other buildings were, and it looked as if the place had ceased to exist. Watch for craters and delayed-action bombs when landing, came an R/T message from below. But when Milne returned he saw that the aerodrome was not nearly so badly damaged as he had at first thought. Great heroism had been shown by an officer who had managed to save all the cars from a blazing garage, but he got no credit when it was realized that his own car had been at the far end. An incident of the other sort had occurred when some civilian workmen had run into Epping Forest to escape the bombing, followed by a number of RAF men. In the view of the Station Commander, this was desertion in face of the enemy.

Wing Commander Victor Beamish was an Irishman who had almost been thrown out of the RAF on medical grounds, but had gone to Canada to work as a lumberjack and was now extremely fit and active, although too old to be a fighter pilot. 'A rugged, square-jawed hero sort of type,' recalled Barry Sutton, 'very much like Al Deere in features. He was a kindly man, very arbitrary, very brave, with a tremendous affection for everybody who worked for him. Although he was the Station Commander, he didn't seem to get around to getting a proper flying suit – he wore a boiler suit, as a fitter might do, and he used to charge around the airfield in his big Humber station wagon, stop when he saw that some of the Works & Bricks chaps weren't getting on with the job of digging the drains or something, leap out of the car and upbraid them in his wonderful Irish accent. These poor fellows never quite knew who was addressing them.'

He now addressed the runaways to some purpose. Milne heard that it was with revolver in hand, and that they were actually paraded in front of him. The squadron ground crews were not affected, because they had not deserted the aerodrome. Constable Maxwell wrote that night in his diary: 'Beamish announces over the blower that he will shoot anyone leaving his post and means it! The flight mechanics in both squadrons are superb. It is only some of the others who can't take it.'

'He was not a tremendously good fighter pilot,' recalled Sutton, 'or so we thought, for we had the rather condescending point of view of young officers towards anyone over twenty-five – he seemed to us to be very old and I suppose he must have been about thirty-three. He used to leave his office when he heard of a raid coming up, leap into the air, and from the point of view of the orthodox, used to make a bloody nuisance of himself, just getting in to have a go at somebody, and more often than not he got in the way of somebody else. That didn't matter, because this demonstration was a tremendous fillip to the morale of the whole Station.'

The bombing of North Weald cost the Germans five bombers and four fighters; it cost the British eight fighters, but only three pilots killed or badly wounded.

At Hornchurch the AA guns interfered with bombing and little damage was done; at Portsmouth more than fifty bombers of *Luftflotte* 3 broke through the fighters without much trouble but appeared severely shaken by the gunfire and their pattern bombing went wild, bombs raining down all over the city instead of being concentrated on the dockyard, where as it was the stern was blown off a destroyer and there was a number of casualties. In the city, about a hundred civilians died in about sixty seconds. A friend of mine saw the bombers come in from the Nab, stepped up to the right in echelons of nine. He began to count them, as they slipped through the shell bursts. What seemed to be the leader got a direct hit just as bombing began; it flew up, wings and engines falling off it. The witness had now counted nearly fifty bombers, and there were more coming in; he decided it was time to take cover. Brigadier Stevens, a retired soldier, was standing outside a shelter in the Guildhall Square; he saw an aeroplane wing tumbling down alone.

Over the north of the city the bombers began to turn to port and went out over the back of the harbour where I and my uncle were watching. 'The sky was already speckled with the white puffs of shell bursts, but there was a lot of haze and glare and all I could see were a few tiny silver specks streaking through the bursts. The Portsdown battery was firing over the top of us but I wasn't really conscious of the noise. The animals and birds were, though. Horses and cows huddled together, as if for protection, under a hedge, and the birds were in a ferment. As the Germans turned south it was possible to see that there were a lot of them and then, directly over Gosport and under tremendous AA fire, there happened something I had never seen before. The German formation broke. They appeared to leap out in all directions, like goldfish after a stone had been cast into the pond. My uncle, with glasses trained on them, saw one bomber catch fire at the wingtip and lose height; then the fire went out and the German climbed up again.'

Mr Vince, then a soldier in the Royal Signals on leave from his unit in Kent, was sheltering a few hundred yards from a cinema in Lake Road, Portsmouth, in which a children's performance was going on at the time. It sustained a direct hit and some sailors who were sitting in the balcony were killed. A minute or so later Mr Vince saw a child running past, sobbing bitterly. He tried to calm the boy, who was plainly terrified, and at length extracted his story. He had been in the cinema when the bomb struck and in the confusion had lost the sixpence change from the entrance money; he was sure to be beaten when he got home. Mr Vince gave him a shilling, and the boy went off cheerfully to look for another cinema.

I investigated reactions at once, and concluded, 'The further from the bombs, the more fear. For instance, in a café remote from the nearest "incident", I was told, people had screamed, shrieked, panicked, dived under tables, and generally made spectacles of themselves. But a woman who'd had her windows blown out, had stuck her head through one of them and sent up a stream of filthy language in the general direction of the man who'd done it. Very near to the bombs, people were temporarily stunned, but unafraid. The wounded were best of all. A lady doctor we knew had crawled into the wreck of a surface shelter to give morphia to an old woman trapped under the debris; the hypodermic was refused, all the old woman wanted was to know if they'd hit the dockyard.'

Two destroyers had been damaged, one badly. One of the casualties was the captain of the destroyer *Bulldog*, Lieutenant-Commander P. Wisden. His wife and mother, living in Sussex, were notified that night; they drove through the darkness, made dangerous by Home Guard roadblocks, the sentries on which were liable to open fire if the driver did not stop promptly. When they reached Haslar hospital, Wisden was in the cellar, close to the operating theatre, with the badly wounded. Only the lightly wounded were kept in the wards above ground, because there were continual air raid warnings, day and night, which meant that they had to be moved every time. His relatives were allowed to stay with the wounded officer until, on the 29th, he died.

The Germans had now got into their stride and were making up to 1,600 sorties a day; rarely was it less than a thousand. And they were beginning to come over increasingly at night; on the night of the 24th they sent 170 bombers, some of which by accident dropped their load on London, still a forbidden target. On 25 August Warm-well aerodrome was raided by *Luftflotte* 3. Over ruined Manston there was a large-scale fighter engagement in which Colin Gray, after firing a full-deflection burst at a 109, saw it blow up, the pilot falling out of the wreckage with his blazing parachute streaming behind him and the fuselage, minus the engine, spinning down to join the other pieces of the aircraft smoking on the ground.

While the daylight battles still raged, Squadron Leader Oxley was at Bircham Newton, topping up with fuel for a long flight. Eighty-one bombers were to make the 600-mile flight to the German capital on the night of 25/26 August, as payment in kind for the bombs dropped on London the previous night. Like the sailing of the Channel convoys and the long retention of Manston, its object was partly political. The weather was good and Oxley was able to check off his pin-points all the way to the great city, but low stratus clouds prevented him from identifying his own particular target, the Siemens-Halske Electric Works. Even from 3,500 feet there was no sign of it. Had he gone down to 700 feet under the stratus, possibly it might have been visible. 'I was keen,' said Oxley, 'but not that keen. I should have brought my bombs back, of course, but I didn't, I left them in Berlin.'

Over the target there was little opposition, although a number of the bombers came down in the sea, possibly because they did try to bring their bombs back. Coming in over the English coast, one of the Hampden's two engines stopped; knowing that the aircraft was light, Oxley thought that there was a chance of going on to base. Then the second engine stopped and made his decision for him. He was then above Leconfield, the base of Satchell's squadron, and the controller was a Pole. When Oxley landed, the Pole exploded with rage because he had not taxied the aircraft in. 'Taxi it yourself,' said Oxley, 'because I can't.'

London was the imponderable city. Attacked at the right time, it might prove to be the key to victory, thought the Germans, remembering Rotterdam. The citizens might be panicked, or if not the public, then the Government. A city cannot surrender to an air force, but at the very least the disruption of life in the capital must greatly facilitate an invasion. The British thought so, too; they believed that the bombing of the capital would immediately precede an invasion attempt, and all their pre-war ARP measures had been based on the premise that the inhabitants would panic. And London would fulfil better than anything else the Luftwaffe's main requirement for a target – that it should be of sufficient importance to compel the enemy to engage with the bulk of his fighter forces.

There were, therefore, good reasons for turning the weight of German attack on to London. And now their enemy had presented them with the bombing of the German capital, the excuse they needed to justify as a reprisal the great attack on the British capital. But it seems that, as Churchill had been the prime mover in the raid on Berlin (which had not suited the Air Staff), so Hitler was the prime mover of the assault on London. 'I never saw a face with so little love in it,' had declared a relative of Johannes Fink's, after being presented to the Führer. Nevertheless, to his own people and to the world, Hitler needed to justify his acts. 'MAD DOG!' had screamed the newspaper headlines after the Portsmouth bombing of the 24th. 'Yesterday' (they screamed on the 25th) 'the Beast threw off his mask.'

The Beast also could speak that language, and in a broadcast to the German people on 4 September, he did so, raising the fury of his listeners at the indiscriminate attacks of the British air force on helpless civilians, and concluded with: 'Now you will understand that we shall have to give them our reply night after night and in ever-increasing strength; if the English declare that they will make mass attacks on our cities, we shall erase theirs.' And the cheers thundered back.

The bombing of Berlin on the 25th and on several subsequent nights therefore touched off events which culminated two weeks later in the mass attacks on London; meanwhile, the daylight battle continued and there was increasing activity by night.

On 26 August *Luftflotte* 3 again raided Portsmouth in force; it was to be their last large-scale operation in daylight for some time. There was a layer of stratus cloud above the city, with only a few gaps, and very little of the air battle could be seen. The sirens wailed, the red flag went up on the control tower in the dockyard, and the balloons were hoisted. Gunners and Air Raid Wardens put on their steel helmets, traffic across the harbour stopped, thousands of eyes peered skywards from the suddenly silent streets. The deep, harsh, uneven throbbing of German motors began to come in from seaward – a big formation up there. Bang-thump – the guns were firing. The rustling noise of the shells going upwards and the lighter crack of the air bursts. The whistle of descending bombs falling on the city through the clouds and the long-drawn-out ringing roar of the explosions, the earth vibrating slightly. Black smoke rising and drifting on the wind. The sound of other aero engines, fast approaching, then diving with a roaring hollow scream rising to unbearable pitch, punctuated by sudden drum-roll rattles, as if someone had drawn a bundle of sticks very rapidly across a piece of corrugated iron. A Heinkel came down through the clouds, steadily losing height on a northerly course and landing beyond Portsdown Hill.[1] The initial dive of the Spitfire squadron faded into the sound of individual diving, climbing and firing; then the clouds rolled back, nine silver, gleaming fighters flew south across the sudden blue gap; and the raid was over. The fighters had broken it up even more than the guns had done on the 24th, and little military damage was done.

Raids on Hornchurch and North Weald were similarly unproductive; only at Debden, a Sector Station northeast of London, was serious damage caused. But the gap between the losses of both sides had narrowed sharply: 41 German aircraft down, of which 22 were fighters, for 31 British fighters shot down. Sixteen of the British pilots were lost.

On the night of the 27th a considerable number of bombers crossed the coast, mainly in the Portsmouth area. For some weeks previously 'nuisance raids' had been taking place on a small scale over much of England; certain important targets were to be bombed and some, such as the Bristol aircraft factory at Filton, were damaged, but the primary purpose was to disrupt war production by keeping the night shift in the shelters. The aircraft flew singly and each had a particular 'beat' to patrol.

The line Portsmouth–Reading–Oxford was usually allotted to a Heinkel 111 of *Kampfgeschwader* 55 in which Feldwebel H. M. Wronsky was the observer. He retired as a Major and is now employed by the Henschel company in Kassel, but before the war had worked for Lufthansa in Berlin, Paris, New York and London, where he had been for a time at Croydon airport. His age was well above aircrew average, but the Luftwaffe accepted him

---

[1] I learned much later that the Heinkel was from 4/KG 55 'Grief', flown by Leutnant Klaus Walter. His observer was killed, the rest taken prisoner.

because of his flying experience and general aviation background. Two weeks before the French Armistice he was posted to III *Gruppe* of KG 55 at Villacoublay, just outside Paris. He had feared that he might be too late to see action, for it was the general belief that the English would either give in, be invaded, or be bombed into submission. It was the Heinkels of KG 55 which usually made the high-level attacks against Portsmouth, and it was one of their bombers which Paul Charrier had seen down in the field behind Portsdown Hill. By now, they were feeling their losses and were quite happy to change over to night attacks.

Although he knew Croydon well, Wronsky never visited it in wartime because it was outside the area allotted to *Luftflotte* 3; he usually entered England over Portsmouth or Gosport at dusk or just after, in a bomber which had been hurriedly prepared for night flying. The original paint-scheme of grey-green camouflage on top and blue below had now been smeared over with a black, non-reflecting mixture of oil, soot and dirt; and for each mission flown, a small flash was painted on the aircraft. Almost every night he flew either directly over my house or within a mile or so of it. 'It was very beautiful to watch,' I noted on one such night, 'with the searchlights illuminating the clouds, the shell bursts sparkling like jewels in the darkness, the occasional whistle of a bomb and the dull pink glow suffusing the sky as it exploded, and over all the distinctive irregular "beat" of the German engines.'

When Wronsky flew on inland he often saw red lights switched on down below and suspected that they were intended to mark out the course of the bomber to the waiting night fighters. He had all the time the feeling of someone creeping up behind him and looking over his shoulder. Yet most of the time there was no one there.

What few night fighters were sent up were wandering blindly across the wide sky, with nothing to guide them but the searchlights or the AA fire. The Germans saw the night fighters more often than the night fighters saw them. Once, somewhere near Reading, the red beacons were switched on below. 'Oh, that's bad, they got us,' thought Wronsky. Almost at once, the rear-gunner reported, 'Two night fighters!' The British aircraft appeared to be using yellow searchlights and to be closing in on the bomber, but the gunners were forbidden to fire because that would have given away their position. The pilot then turned the Heinkel and flew straight at the night fighters, flashing past in one direction at 180 mph while they were going the opposite way at a much greater speed. The bomber would be miles away before the night fighters could turn. For a night fighter at that time to shoot down a bomber was very nearly unheard of and the AA defences, as long as the Germans stayed high up, were almost as inefficient. The complicated technique necessary for success was still under development at nearby Tangmere, where the Fighter Interception Unit was stationed.

The night bombers could wander at will but as their technique also was fairly primitive, results were still meagre. Wronsky calculated that every time he came over, he kept a million people in their shelters, and this aspect of it could have been serious. To counter it, factories began to employ 'roof spotters' and the workers took shelter only when he reported the actual approach of enemy aircraft; the sirens were ignored. But on the evening of 27 August there were signs of a change.

'At 9.15 P.M. the sirens wailed over Portsmouth harbour, for the hundredth time since May,' I wrote. 'Cones of searchlights made pretty, glowing patterns on the ceiling of the sky. Gunfire was not intense, just a bang here and there, and the bombs showered down without rhyme or reason, east and west, north and south. Mostly they whistled but one which was particularly large, judging by the flash, made a rushing, vibrating noise and a few "screaming bombs" came down with an unearthly roar of whooooo-whooooo! Twice, splinters went shrieking overhead, one apparently red hot, for it looked like a spark of fire. Occasionally, the rising bomb whistles cut off abruptly without any explosion – either delayed action or dud. In a city most of this would have been blanketed by tall buildings, but here you got the full effect. Even so, I had to get down only once – and then it was a dud and two full fields away. We could not make out what the target was. Then an intense white light broke out quarter of a mile away and there was an irregular crackling that sounded like small arms fire. We looked at each other. Invasion? One sword and two African spears was our armament and we never were able to see ourselves putting up much of a resistance. Actually, it was a casket of incendiaries, something new to us, which had scored a direct hit on a pigsty. A number of pigs were burned to death. The railway line was cut, shortly after midnight, and was as good as new again by noon next day, by which time there was nothing to show for the raid except a few craters and the marks left by parachute flares where they had burned out on the ground.'

This was a typical night raid of the sort that was to be mounted in increasing strength for the next few months; even when the target was a city, the methods and results were much the same. A part of *Luftflotte* 3 was also employed in carrying out cloudy weather attacks in daylight. For the bomber crews, recalled Wronsky, there was a good deal of irksome discipline. Paris was out-of-bounds and they complained they could not leave camp, except to go to England. And when the weather clamped right down, drill periods under army instructors were provided, so that they should not be idle. The aircrews indulged themselves in those grotesque affectations which, in one form or another, are common to most flying men; in the case of III *Gruppe* of KG 55, the affectation took the form of pets, mostly dogs, in all shapes and sizes. When paraded for drill one morning, they formed up in tight ranks behind which were the dogs. When the unsuspecting army officer began to bellow orders and the men began to march and counter-march, the dogs trotted happily forward after their masters, halting and turning when they did, and the parade broke up in a riot of laughter.

On one occasion an inspecting officer flew in one of the bombers which had to return unexpectedly early from a night raid and he was curious to know the meaning of a code message (not in the book) which the radio operator promptly transmitted. The man stumbled slightly over his explanation but managed to produce some sort of indifferent answer; the message, when decoded, actually meant: 'Tell Jeanette I'll be along tonight.'

10

Day and Night

28–31 August

By day the attacks on aerodromes continued without a break and from the night of 28/29 August on were accompanied during the hours of darkness by major raids directed at cities and carried out by a bomber force numerically nearly equal to that involved in the daylight battles. Additionally, 28 August saw the end of the Defiant as a day fighter and its relegation to night-fighting and, eventually, target-towing.

Not only was it an unfortunate design but it was unlucky in its opponents. 141 Squadron, in their first and last patrol of the Battle of Britain, had met Major Trautloft's 'Green Hearts' *Gruppe* of *Jagdgeschwader* 51. It was a crack unit and Trautloft was one of the 'aces'; he is now a Brigade-General in the new Luftwaffe. 264 Squadron lasted a little longer until, shortly after 10 A.M. on 28 August, they met III *Gruppe* of *Jagdgeschwader* 26, led by Galland. Galland was then racing Mölders for the title of top-scorer of the German fighter pilots and his unit was one of the very best. But it was only by a matter of seconds that he prevented 264 Squadron from carrying out the peculiar type of attack for which the Defiant had been designed.

On this day Galland was escorting a gruppe of Heinkels from *Kampfgeschwader* 1 bound for Eastchurch aerodrome; like most of the bomber units now, they were not up to strength and there were only two dozen of them. They crossed the coast near Folkestone and for a few minutes single Spitfires dived through the formation, trying to get at the bombers, without much effect. Then, when they were passing Canterbury, Galland saw something quite extraordinary. He was with his staff flight flying fairly close under the bombers when, looking up, he saw yet another formation of aircraft, very close and orderly, just below the Heinkels. Puzzled, he wondered, 'What's that!' For a moment, it flashed through his mind that they might be stukas – certainly they were not fighters, because their formation was too tight. Then he saw guns sticking out of the top of these strange aircraft – the guns were pointed up at the bombers and they were just about to fire. Twelve sets of four machine-guns were ready to rake the bellies of the Heinkel formation.

Slamming the throttle forward and pulling back the stick, pressed against the back of the cockpit by 'g', he went straight up at the Defiants, and his staff flight followed him. In a moment they had broken that tight formation to pieces and scattered the unfortunate two-seaters to the four winds; there were Defiants going down in all directions. Galland fired at a number in succession. The first he could not finish off because it passed underneath other aircraft – indeed, he was actually flying alongside another when it burst into flames under the guns of Oberleutnant Horten. He dived on a third which was headed down but overshot completely, because it was going very slowly, with its engine stopped, then dived on a fourth, which was also pressing away down. Galland dived at once, opened fire at 100 yards, closing to 20 yards and using machine-guns only for his cannon ammunition was expended. The Defiant began to disintegrate. Pieces fell off the fuselage, then off the wings; white flames came out of both wing tanks and then both the wings and the fuselage were burning brightly. The 109 broke away with four bullet holes in it as a souvenir from the gunner. According to British records, this brief fight cost the squadron two Defiants lost and four damaged, after which they were withdrawn.

Now, climbing to meet Galland's 109s, were the Hurricanes of 79 Squadron which only that morning had moved into Biggin Hill from a period of rest at Acklington. Flying with them was a South African, E. J. ('Teddy') Morris, who had been away with meningitis when the squadron had suffered heavy losses during a previous tour at Biggin Hill, so that this was his first action. Morris, who is now a Group Captain with the OBE, DSO and DFC, had an elder brother, 'Zulu' Morris, also serving in the RAF.

79 Squadron attacked and were split up almost at once. Morris fired a burst at a yellow-nosed 109, saw it half-roll and dive away in the standard evasion manoeuvre which neither Spitfire nor Hurricane could follow, and then found himself apparently alone in the sky. Looking around, he caught sight of the bombers, pressing on for Eastchurch, and a single Heinkel turning away out of the formation and heading back for the coast, presumably a 'lame duck'. He chased it back over the Channel and came down on it at high speed. 'My closing speed was very high, through inexperience, and my first attack was pretty wild,' he said. 'As far as I can remember I attacked it a second time and got no return fire. I left it, losing height and smoking – whether from my attentions or from over-throttling, I am unable to say; if I had been more experienced I would have finished it off.' He now climbed back after the main force, which had just bombed Eastchurch, but before he could get near it, was met by three 109s which drove him down to ground-level. Altogether, according to British records, four squadrons had tried to halt the bombers on their way in, and failed; in all, the RAF lost eight aircraft and six pilots, the Germans only five aircraft.

An hour or so later Morris was airborne again over the Channel with two other Hurricanes, chasing a Heinkel 59 seaplane painted with the Red Cross. Flying Officer Bryant-Fenn attacked first, setting one engine on fire, and Morris followed him in. The seaplane came down at once, apparently in a sinking condition. 'I think at the time we were all rather in two minds about opening fire on this aircraft at all,' said Morris. 'But we were reassured when we landed that it was fair game.' The Red Cross plane was shot down, ironically enough, under the eyes of the man who had originally given the order. Winston Churchill had been standing on the ramparts of Dover Castle, watching the affair through binoculars.

At 12.30 Michael Constable Maxwell was at North Weald, talking on the telephone to his brother, Andrew, also a fighter pilot. Indeed, they were virtually a family of fighter pilots, Gerald Constable Maxwell having flown SE 5s. But Michael had to slam down the receiver with a 'Must go – flap!' A few minutes later 56 Squadron were climbing out of North Weald and heading for the coast. 'Rochford 15,000' was the order. Nearing Rochford, they were told to alter course to the south. And there they were. 'Twenty-seven bombers are going NW from Manston, a huge black pack of them; they look extraordinarily sinister. A big formation such as this can only be German and it is attacking England.' Maxwell was in the rear section as the twelve Hurricanes bore on for the enemy. 'Line astern, line astern – go!' The two leading sections changed from their vics into the attack formation and began to slant down towards the bombers, while the six aircraft of 'B' Flight climbed steadily towards a pack of thirty or forty 109s which were hanging over the bombers.

Then they saw below them a pair of 109s weaving slowly, apparently well throttled back, trying to stay with the bombers as close escort. Two of the Hurricanes promptly dived and shot them down, while the others engaged the top layer as they woke up to the presence of the British. Maxwell found himself under a single 109 which was weaving slowly and climbing. Looking behind him, and suspecting it to be a decoy, he followed and, surprisingly, found that he was gaining. That made him more suspicious, because the 109 was some 50 mph faster than the Hurricane, but this Messerschmitt must also have been trying to stay with the bombers. Glancing repeatedly over his shoulder, and momentarily expecting to hear the crash of cannon shells striking his machine, as they had twice before, Maxwell closed. 250 yards – the German was well inside his sights. 200 yards – Maxwell took another quick glance over his shoulder. Nothing there. He concentrated on the sights and fired a two-second burst.

Part of the engine cowling fell away from the 109, which began to bank steeply. A three-second burst. Flashes at the rear of its fuselage, to show where the de Wilde was striking. The Messerschmitt turned quite slowly on to its back and went vertically downward in the standard evasion manoeuvre, but with glycol pouring from the nose.

Maxwell took another quick rearward glance. Still nothing there. When he looked again for the 109, his windscreen was covered with oil. Thinking it was from the damaged Messerschmitt, and seeing a lone Dornier below, he began to dive on it but found that the oil on the windscreen was increasing and that he could not see forward to fire. He promptly dived out of it and found himself 2,000 feet up over the middle of the Thames Estuary. 'Oil pressure now zero and temperature off the dial, engine uneven, losing height although using a lot of throttle.' He tightened his straps and lowered the seat.

The Hurricane lost height slowly over Herne Bay until at 1,000 feet the engine raced violently and stopped. The beach was a mass of anti-invasion blocks and scaffolding. It was possible to jump, but in that case the Hurricane would go into the houses beyond. Maxwell glided straight ahead over the town and had nearly cleared the houses when clouds of white smoke poured back from the engine, usually the signal that it would burst into flames within a quarter of a minute. Maxwell saw a field, put his flaps down, turned into wind, and through the smoke and fumes could make out ahead a road lined with telegraph poles. At 95 mph the controls were already limp from lack of speed; the right wing dropping on the verge of a stall, Maxwell converted a gentle turn into wind to a terrific sideslip and, with just enough speed to keep the nose up, put his right wing into the ground. The Hurricane thundered on to the grass and spun round violently, disintegrating. Maxwell shoved the remains of the cockpit off himself and rapidly got clear; but there had been no hurry – the engine was burning, but it was twenty-five yards from the fuselage.

People began to arrive at the scene – a man who asked him if he was badly hurt and an army officer who took him to the mess of the 8th Royal Fusiliers. Hardly a word was spoken to him. The officers appeared uninterested. More probably it was the reaction of fighting troops, unable to do any fighting, confronted with a man who had come straight from battle, and moreover a battle whose principles they did not understand. A lady offered to drive him back to North Weald in her car, saying, 'I hate seeing you boys risk your lives and then be just sent off in a train.'

But Maxwell, who had now been shot down three times, was introspectively studying his reactions and preferred not to have to talk. He was glad to note that he was not depressed, possibly because of hitting that 109 – he now rather wanted to have a go at another, the affair had given him confidence. He reached London – by train – at 6.30 P.M., unshaven, hatless, dirty, with no collar, wearing scarf and flying boots, and with a porter proudly carrying his parachute. The porters at both Victoria and Liverpool Street stations refused to accept tips, as did the taxi man. 'You have risked your life for me, I would not dream of taking your money.'

By 9.30 P.M. he was back at North Weald, where his 109 was awarded as a 'probable'. 'We had a wonderful fight,' the CO told him. 'We shot down seven – a grand show; oh, and your brother Andrew got shot down, too!'

At that moment the first of 160 bombers of *Luftflotte* 3 were beginning to stream in over the coast to make the first of the Luftwaffe's major night attacks; their target, on this night and the three nights following, was Liverpool. They came in a long, straggly line, with two-minute intervals between each bomber, so as to keep as large an area as possible under attack for as long as possible; the defences were too weak to enforce a concentration in time and space on the attackers who, for their part, did not realize that concentration also had positive merits – it was the attacked who, as the night raids continued, learned that lesson. The weather, not the defences, was likely to be the major factor in what losses there were; during the four raids, 629 bombers crossed the coast and seven did not return, one only being shot down by a night fighter.

Even that one successful interception was a near-miracle; the total number of night fighter victories then stood at only three or four, two of which had been gained by 'Sailor' Malan in one night. This solitary success was scored over Bristol at 10.45 P.M. on 28 August as the bombers were streaming in over the west country on their way to Liverpool; the pilot was Alan Wright, flying a

Spitfire of 92 Squadron. Still serving, as a Wing Commander, he now flies Javelin all-weather jet fighters. As a Pilot Officer he had flown over Dunkirk with Bob Holland, killed after the war, and Bob Stanford Tuck, who retired as a Wing Commander and now grows mushrooms in Kent.

Wright was at 20,000 feet over Bristol in his Spitfire, not the most suitable aircraft for night flying, when he saw a Heinkel held in the searchlight beams. He turned in behind it and fired – and at that moment a well-aimed group of shells burst around the two aircraft and the fighter lurched violently; for a moment, Wright thought he had been caught by return fire from the bomber. But it was still flying steadily on, brilliantly illuminated by the beams, like a great silvery moth. He closed in, fired another burst – and immediately the searchlights went out, leaving nothing but the blackness of the night sky.

Then, straining his eyes, Wright saw among the stars two red-tinted glows which might be the exhausts of a bomber and not stars at all. Flying very carefully indeed and using the distance apart of the two glowpoints as a guide to show him if he was closing in or dropping behind, he crept up slowly behind the bomber. If he once lost sight of them, by overtaking too fast or turning too sharply, he would probably never be able to pick them up again. When he fired, it was with very short bursts, so that he would not be dazzled by the muzzle flashes of his own guns.

Repeatedly, the flashes of hits from explosive ammunition sparkled on the fuselage of the bomber, but it flew serenely on, apparently untroubled, unaware even that it was being attacked. It became increasingly difficult for Wright to remain in position behind his intended victim, because the Heinkel was flying more and more slowly. He fired a last burst, expending all his ammunition, and one of the red glowpoints, which marked an engine exhaust, went out. Speed down now to 120 mph, Wright hung on behind. Then, when he saw a lick of flame appear on the Heinkel and grow larger, he turned away for home.

He did not know where he was exactly, as navigation was by visual sighting or dead reckoning, and the Spitfire's endurance was limited; so he was anxious to go home as quickly as possible, and it was some days before he learned the fate of the Heinkel. It had glided towards the coast as far as possible but had come down at Fordingbridge near Southampton; until they were shown the bullet holes in their aircraft, the crew believed that they had been hit by AA fire.

Most of the bombs intended for Liverpool during the four nights were in fact scattered over a wide area around it; nevertheless, a race in technique between attack and defence at night had now begun, a race in which the Prime Minister took a great interest. He was Chairman of the Night Interception Committee which sat weekly to consider the results achieved by the experimental Fighter Interception Unit at Tangmere and to suggest new methods for trial, most of which were put up to him by his scientific advisers, among whom Professor Lindemann (later Lord Cherwell) was prominent.

FIU was commanded by 'Joe' Chamberlain, now an Air Vice-Marshal, and one of the pilots who joined him at the end of August was J. W. White, now a Group Captain, MBE. So urgent was the work that when the two of them were flying the results to London (White had the documents tied to his wrist), and the Blenheim burst a tyre on take-off, crashed and caught fire, Chamberlain tried to get into the wreck to extract White (who had already got out), and then, much relieved, was taking off in another aircraft within minutes.

'This night fighter business was toil and trouble, with

very little joy,' recalled White. 'We were continually experimenting, and it was hurry, hurry all the time.' The pilots who actually had to carry out the ideas of Lindemann and others were perhaps less enthusiastic about the scientific brains of the nation than was the Prime Minister; some of the suggestions they were required to try out were so downright childish that an actual experiment was hardly necessary and others were a good deal more dangerous for them than they were ever likely to be to the enemy.[1]

'In one experiment,' said White, 'I was to fly at 11,000 feet over Portsmouth, beneath a bomber stream going to the Midlands. The navy would fire a five-inch starshell over Portsmouth, which would explode below me, and so light up the bombers for me, as well as dazzling their gunners. When we tried it, it actually exploded above and dazzled me, not the Germans. It also lit up all Portsmouth harbour with brilliant clarity; I could see every ship in the harbour.'

The real answer was a complicated three-stage interception. First, a very accurate ground control to place the fighter behind the bomber with approximately the same height and course; second, a small radar set in the night fighter to bring it gradually up behind the bomber on the same course, at the same height and at only slightly greater speed, so that there would be no danger of an overshoot; and third, a visual kill by the pilot when the radar had brought him sufficiently close to see his victim. Anything else was nonsense. But the actual gadgetry involved was still far from perfect and progress was too slow for Churchill's mercurial temperament. The first success with airborne radar was eventually scored by

[1] For some diverting illustrations, see *The Defence of the United Kingdom*, by Basil Collier (HMSO).

Squadron Leader Ashfield, flying a prototype Beau-fighter, a vast improvement on the Blenheim as a night fighter. This was the first occurrence of its kind anywhere in the world – the Germans had only bulky radar sets which could not be installed in an aeroplane, and the Americans, who were to invent the word, had never heard of radar at all. But in September, 1940, they learned everything, at Churchill's express command.

Until then, RDF, as it was called at the time, had been the most closely guarded British secret of the war. In early September, however, a party of Americans, led by a very senior General, arrived at Shoreham which was now the base of FIU. They had been bombed out of Tangmere. The visitors were taken up in an aircraft fitted with an AI set, as airborne RDF was called; then they had dinner in a Shoreham hotel which had been taken over as an officers' mess.

A technical discussion began, in which the Americans kindly expressed amazement at the progress made; they confessed that they had nothing like it, not even ground RDF, let alone airborne sets. Meanwhile, the soup was being served by a blonde Cockney waitress – each time she entered it was with three brimming platefuls of soup balanced simultaneously – and at that moment an incoming German bomber released a stick of bombs which whistled down towards the hotel, the noise rising to a shriek as they passed over the roof and straddling the building in a series of thunderous detonations. As the echoes were dying away, the heads of Americans began to appear from under the table – and they beheld the blonde waitress still balancing the three plates of soup from which not a drop had been spilled. They conceded that these stories of the way the British reacted under bombing must surely have some basis of truth.

* * *

On Friday, 30 August, began the 'Bad Weekend' at Biggin Hill. For three days the already damaged aerodrome was repeatedly attacked, sometimes several times a day. On the Friday morning, Teddy Morris was leading six Hurricanes of 79 Squadron overhead on aerodrome defence when he saw eighteen Heinkels escorted by some twenty fighters. Bill Igoe tells the story that when Morris had first arrived at Biggin, three days before, he had asked, 'How do you actually attack these beggars?' and someone had replied, 'Oh, you just go straight at them.' Morris denies it and says that he simply misjudged, owing to the very high closing speed. He had sent one section to keep the fighters busy while he led the other two Hurricanes down almost vertically through the bomber formation, with the intention of splitting it up.

He saw too late that the second vic were flying very close behind the three leading Heinkels and that the gap through which he had to dive at 400 mph or so was much narrower than he had supposed; and at the last moment he saw that the second vic were not in line with the first but stepped up above them. He went straight into a Heinkel in the second vic.

'All I saw was a grey blur, and felt an awful thump on my right wing. I immediately went into a violent spin. I tried to get out of the cockpit and succeeded after what seemed an age but in reality was only a few seconds. There was no hesitancy to jump, things happened so quickly that I didn't have time to take stock of my emotions. It was great fun floating down – luckily we were at 16,000 feet.' Away to one side, he could see the Heinkel plunging to earth, both engines on fire and the best part of both wings gone; it went in with an almighty explosion – hanging above it were the parachutes of three of the crew who had managed to get out.

The attack had split the bomber formation, not surprisingly, and Morris was to become famous as the pilot who put in a claim for 'one Heinkel confirmed destroyed, by collision'. He landed in a grassy lane with trees on either side, somewhere near Dorking, and had hardly picked himself up when two men – probably farm labourers – burst through the hedge, shouting, 'There the bastard is!' One had a pitchfork, the other a shotgun. 'I remember letting go a volley of Elizabethan epithets to indicate I was friendly,' said Morris. The men took him to a farmhouse where he got a warm welcome from some middle-aged women, one of whom insisted on kissing him. They rang up the nearest army unit, which was Canadian, and shortly Morris was at their headquarters, surrounded by Canadians patting him on the shoulder and saying, 'Hard luck, Mac.' A man from the Heinkel was there, guarded by two huge Canucks armed with rifle and bayonet. 'He looked like a gunner, a small scared little man with bad teeth, no advertisement for the Master Race.' His hosts gave Morris lunch and then drove him back to Biggin Hill just in time for the second attack of the day.

The morning raid had not done much damage; this one did. Each squadron had a number of reserve pilots and aircraft, so that although the front-line strength was twelve, the full strength might be eighteen or more. Group Captain Grice ordered all pilots at stand-down to get airborne in any machine that was airworthy. A WAAF driver, already briefed for this duty, drove to the mess in a big Humber belonging to the Engineer Officer, R. J. B. Jackson, now Wing Commander, OBE. She took the spare pilots out to the aircraft – but there were one or two pilots for whom no machine was available, and one of these was Morris. As they were returning to the mess the Germans arrived; the Humber skidded to a halt, they dived into the nearest shelter, and ten seconds later a bomb arrived twenty-five feet away. The German force was small, only a staffel, but the bombing was accurate and the damage devastating. When they came up from the shelter, they found an altered landscape; worst of all, for the WAAF, was that her Humber was gone. She went to Jackson, nearly in tears, to report that someone had stolen it.

The Humber was found next morning, in a hangar, its point of entry being the roof, as was indicated by the hole; it had been blown sixty feet through the air. Elsewhere, direct hits had been scored on hangars and workshops and a shelter in which most of some forty fatal casualties had occurred. One man only was alive down in the darkness under the wreckage, trapped in an upright position and surrounded by the corpses of his friends. When the dust and smoke began to clear, he groped round in the gloom, touching the faces of the dead, to see if any flicker of life remained. And there he stayed, for eight hours, quite unperturbed, even when the men digging their way down to him started to cut the legs off a corpse which was lying on top of him and pinning him down.

Shortly before the afternoon raid on Biggin, and synchronized with it, there had been two other equally successful attacks – one on the aerodrome at Detling and one on the Vauxhall factory at Luton, north-west of London. Shortly before this the newly formed 303 (Polish) Squadron, not yet operational, took off on a training exercise led by Squadron Leader R. G. Kellett. They were to practise attacks on a Blenheim squadron north-west of London and were flying in that direction at 10,000 feet when Pilot Officer L. Pasczkiewicz saw 'many planes twisting around 1,000 feet below'. He reported this to

Kellett, but receiving no answer, dived out of the formation to attack.

'I saw before me the suburbs of a little town, where there were several fires, and a Hurricane going down burning. Then I saw a plane with two rudders, so I assumed it was German – I thought a Dornier. But the German noticed me and went down in a sharp dive underneath me. So I half-rolled on to him from behind. I started firing at 200 yards, aiming first at the fuselage and then at the port engine, which burst into flames. The German did a half loop, on which I attacked him again. He simply went straight down and crashed.' Pasczkiewicz was a serious, religious type of man, not at all reckless, and his example had its effect: two days later, 303 Squadron was declared ready for operations.

These raids, taking place all around London, caused the sirens to be sounded in the capital several times during the day. The morning alert at 11.55 brought female air raid wardens, clad in trousers (or 'siren suits') out on to the streets, where they dashed about energetically blowing whistles, in an endeavour to get people to take cover. The traffic moved stolidly on, the conductor of one bus remarking to a passenger, 'Nar, they'll never get to London.' In Piccadilly, the pavements were as crowded as usual and hundreds of people sat in the sun by the fountains in Trafalgar Square and on the steps of St Martin-in-the-Fields, enjoying their lunch hour and waiting for something to happen. At about 4 o'clock six bombers, probably on their way to Luton, passed over Roehampton Swimming Club on the outskirts of the capital; they were flying in a very tight formation of two vics at about 20,000 feet. The bathers looked up at them languidly and someone hazarded the opinion that they might be Dorniers; otherwise, no interest was shown. A little later there was the distant thud of bombing followed by the rising whine of a diving fighter and then the sound of his guns; then two fighters were seen turning overhead, obviously looking for something, and that was the end of the raid.

Next day a sober newspaper reported:

'Wave after wave of enemy planes were shattered and hurled back yesterday in fierce air fighting . . . it was the greatest effort the German air force has made at mass daylight raids on the Metropolis. More than 600 bombers and fighters were flung into a three-phase attack. It failed.'

It had not failed. All three objectives – Biggin Hill, Detling and Luton – had been hit and severely damaged by German forces which had broken through and in doing so caused heavy losses to the RAF. The crisis of Fighter Command was at hand.

11
The Crisis of Fighter Command
31 August–6 September

In the first week of September the German plan came near to fulfilment. The concentration of German fighters in Pas de Calais swept repeatedly across Kent, shooting to pieces the handful of squadrons sent up against them and carrying the bombers again and again to Sector Stations, laying them in ruins and putting out of action vital parts of the control system. In the air, the British lost more fighters than did the Germans, indeed their losses were higher than the total German losses of both fighters and bombers; and on the ground, they lost more fighters still, so that the reserve of machines became seriously depleted. If the process was continued, there could be only one end for Fighter Command.

The strain on the outnumbered British pilots was intense. 'It was no picnic,' said Colin Gray, 'despite what anyone might say later. I've seen Al Deere and others push away their breakfast when told to go up. Most of us were pretty scared all the bloody time; you only felt happy when the battle was over and you were on your way home, then you were safe for a bit, anyway.'

The strain on the Germans was equally terrible. Unlike the British, they were not being taken out of the line for rest. Every fighter pilot in the Luftwaffe, apart from those in a small unit held back to guard Wilhelmshaven against possible attacks by Bomber Command, was on the Channel coast and flying two or three sorties a day over England. For the Germans, time was running out. Invasion was timed for 21 September and, in any event, not later than 27 September; there had to be a preliminary warning given to the navy ten days in advance, so that British resistance in the air had to be broken by 11 September and, in any event, not later than 17 September, otherwise invasion for 1940 was out of the question.

The atmosphere on the German fighter airfields can best be gauged by the photographs taken at the time. The pilots are demonstrating with their hands how they shot down that Spitfire or Hurricane, but the faces are both tense with strain and at the same time drained of emotion and nervous strength. For the leaders, especially, there was the burden of responsibility. As soon as a gruppe commander landed, he had to worry about his losses. How many shot down – or missing? And who? How many aircraft serviceable? How long to repair the damaged aircraft? And then the order for the next take-off. And the crossing once more of what the German pilots with fury called the 'Shite Kanal', that 'sewer', that 'bit of dirty water'. 'I emphasize', said Galland, 'that this fear of coming down in the water did as much damage to our morale as the British fighters.' This sentiment, surprising as it is to an Englishman accustomed to regard salt water, and especially the Channel, as basically friendly, was echoed by all the German airmen who fought in the battle, whether in fighters or bombers, but more especially in the single-engined fighters. When the battle was on, they were too excited to feel fear of the enemy, but the nagging thought of that merciless sea waiting for the man whose engine failed either from enemy bullets or a mechanical fault, was continually with them.

On 31 August the Germans struck at three Sector Stations in 11 Group – Biggin Hill, Hornchurch and Debden – and one Sector Station in 12 Group – Duxford. The 12 Group squadrons, held back to guard the Midlands and to act as flank guard and reserve to 11 Group, were through no fault of their own seeing very little action;

consequently, they were fit and rested. The Duxford attack, the first of the day, failed.

At 7.30 A.M. the Spitfires of 19 Squadron scrambled from Fowlmere, a satellite field in the Duxford Sector. There were nine of them, led by Flight Lieutenant W. G. Clouston; the second section was led by J. B. Coward, now Group Captain, AFC, the third section by Flight Lieutenant F. N. Brinsden. Clouston is now retired, but Coward and Brinsden are still serving. Coward had seen action over Dunkirk, but he had been away having his tonsils removed, and had rejoined only two days before, so that this was his first action in the Battle of Britain. All nine Spitfires were fitted with two cannons instead of the normal armament of eight machine-guns.

With adequate warning of the raid they climbed away eastward and ten miles from Duxford sighted the enemy – about fifteen Dorniers escorted by perhaps sixty fighters. 25,000 feet below them, at Little Shelford, was Coward's home. The nine fighters pressed on in loose line astern, then Brinsden led his section of three up towards the escort while Clouston took the other six Spitfires into the bombers in a 'copybook' pre-war formation attack.

Coward chose the number two Dornier in the second kette, the other two pilots of his section aiming at its companions. Diving in from the beam, Coward aimed at the nose of the bomber and opened fire. 'The whole experience was an exhilarating one,' said Coward, 'for we were fighting over our own homes.' His cannons thundered briefly, 'boom-boom' – and then stopped. Almost instantly, there was a thud as something hit the Spitfire. Coward felt no pain, but saw his bare foot lying on the floor of the cockpit, almost severed from the leg. The Spitfire went out of control, the nose falling violently in the beginnings of an outside loop, which forces the pilot forward against his straps, out of the cockpit.

With the 'g' behind him, Coward got out quite easily, but his parachute became caught on the fuselage, his gloves were ripped off by the screaming slipstream and his nearly severed foot was banged repeatedly against the falling Spitfire. He had intended to do a delayed drop, but the pain in his foot caused him to pull the ripcord.

The opening parachute pulled him clear at 20,000 feet and, looking down, he saw the blood pumping out of his leg and dropping away far below. His bare hands, numbed by the cold, were unable to force aside the straps of the parachute harness so that he could get at the first aid kit and handkerchief in his pockets, but if he was to survive he had to improvise a tourniquet quickly. Frantically, feeling his strength ebbing away and aware that his life depended on it, he struggled with half-frozen fingers to undo the strap and buckle of his helmet, to which was attached a wireless lead.

Once the helmet was off, Coward wound the lead round his thigh, just above the knee, pulling it as tightly as he could to choke off the supply of blood, and at the same time holding his leg almost up to his chin. By these means, he managed to reduce the flow of blood to a trickle. In this position he drifted slowly across Duxford airfield, where the rest of the squadron were now landing. Then the wind changed and he sailed back over Duxford again and came down in a field near the roundabout on the Royston/Newmarket road. The impact was hard and painful and, worried about infection of the wound, Coward tried to keep his leg off the ground.

'A youth came running up with a pitchfork at the charge, obviously thinking I was a German (I was wearing a black flying overall). He stood looking at me, speechless with horror at the sight of the blood. This maddened me because I was hoping for some help. My language was a bit coarse and he departed without saying anything at all.'

Years later, when Coward was instructing at a Fighter Operational Training Unit, he met the boy again – now a Pilot Officer. He remembered their previous meeting in the field by the Newmarket road, and told Coward that he had actually run to find a doctor and that the first car he had stopped had contained one. Within half an hour an ambulance had driven him away to hospital in the charge of Squadron Leader Brown, an RAF doctor.

Brown had then driven on to Little Shelford to break the news gently to Coward's wife. As he was knocking at the front door, the baker was round the back, telling the kitchen staff that he had just passed the wreck of Coward's Spitfire; he thought the pilot had been killed. So when this story reached Mrs Coward she knew already that her husband had been operated on and that he had lost one leg below the knee. When he recovered, Coward was posted to Chequers to take charge of the Prime Minister's roof spotters.

The bombers had jettisoned their load before reaching the airfield and 19 Squadron claimed three victories. But they were certain that they would have got more if their cannons also had not packed up after firing only a few rounds. Cannon-armed Spitfires had been successful in combats against reconnaissance machines off the north-east coast, but in dog-fights there occurred these exasperating and inexplicable jams. They caused such fury among the baulked pilots that it was suggested to Lord Beaverbrook that the armament should revert to machine-guns. Instead, he ordered an immediate enquiry. Consequently, a few days later, when the attack had begun to switch to aircraft factories, Mr E. L. Cooper, of the Supermarine factory at Southampton, was to find himself solving the practical aspects of this problem under fire.

Shortly after the Duxford fight had ended, Teddy

Morris, leading six Hurricanes of 79 Squadron, was vectored down the Thames Estuary to intercept what was probably the raid on Hornchurch coming in – half a hundred Dorniers with a large escort. The Hurricanes were still climbing, too low to put in a fast attack, but Morris engaged. He passed under the bombers, firing as he went, and then turned to attack the rearmost bombers. He was knocking pieces off a Dornier when he saw a 109 nose up alongside him about twenty yards away. Just time enough to finish off the Dornier, he thought, wrongly. Cannon shells and machine-gun bullets ripped into the Hurricane; Morris, struck by several bullets, his legs sprayed with shell fragments, took violent evasive action and limped back to Biggin Hill where he crash-landed on the airfield. Lying doped in Station Sick Quarters, he was vaguely conscious of bomb explosions and of other casualties being brought in.

Before Morris had even reached Biggin Hill the raiders were over Hornchurch. Below them, the Spitfires of 54 Squadron were racing across the airfield in a belated attempt to get airborne. Colin Gray, who was flying with them, noted in his diary, 'Red Section blown to blazes but no one hurt. Miraculous.'

This is probably the most famous single incident of the Battle of Britain. The official *Fight at Odds* prints the Station diary, Richard Hillary, a Hornchurch pilot who saw the affair from the ground, described it in *The Last Enemy* (Macmillan), and Al Deere, the leader of the section 'blown to blazes', has given his own account in *Nine Lives*, as it was an occasion on which he lost one of them.

After several false alarms, the engines of the squadron's Spitfires had been started and stopped so many times that they were overheated and difficult to start again, when the agitated controller screamed, 'Take off! Take off!'

Colin Gray, one of the first eventually to get away, and climbing up under the raid, saw Hornchurch disappear in smoke and dust. Al Deere had swung into the wind, to find his take-off blocked by a Spitfire from his own section. 'Get to hell out of the way, Red Two!' he bellowed. Deere had got his tail up and was bumping over the grass when he saw the first bomb exploding, ahead and to the left, then the bumping stopped and he was airborne, his section close behind him. The bombs were still falling.

'Out of the corner of my eye,' wrote Richard Hillary, 'I saw the three Spitfires. One moment they were about twenty feet up in close formation; the next catapulted apart as though on elastic. The leader went over on his back and ploughed along the runway with a rending crash of tearing fabric; No. 2 put a wing in and spun round on his airscrew, while the plane on the left was blasted wingless into the next field. I remember thinking stupidly, "That's the shortest flight he's ever taken," and then my feet were nearly knocked from under me, my mouth was full of dirt, and Bubble, gesticulating like a madman from the shelter entrance, was yelling, "Run, you bloody fool, run!" I ran.'

When Gray landed after the action he saw Deere's KL-B over on its back, a sorry mess; he thought, 'Poor old Al's had it.' But no, he found Deere had lost only his helmet and a streak of skin and hair torn off the top of his head. His Spitfire had skated along the ground, upside down, at over 100 mph, dirt and stones battering at his face and the top of his head virtually in contact with the earth over which the fighter was careering, close enough anyway nearly to scalp him. When the wreck wrenched to a halt, he was trapped upside down in the tiny cockpit, with a sea of petrol soaking into the grass around the crash, and no possibility of getting out.

His number three, Pilot Officer Edsell, who had crashed right way up but had hurt his legs so badly that he could not walk, then began to crawl over the aerodrome, which was still being bombed, towards KL-B. While he wrenched from outside and Deere pushed from inside, they got the cockpit door open. Deere wriggled out and, as Edsell could not stand, helped his rescuer to Station Sick Quarters.

Of Sergeant Davies, Deere's number two, there was no sign, although his aircraft could be seen, minus its tail, lying just beyond the boundary fence. His fate was a mystery for some time. He turned up hours later, carrying his parachute – there was no gap in the boundary fence, and he had had to walk several miles round it to get on to the aerodrome again.

The airfield was a mass of craters, in which lay the three wrecked Spitfires of Red Section, and in the dispersal area four of their reserve aircraft had been destroyed, but not a great deal of damage had been done to hangars and workshops. Hornchurch was bombed again that day and next morning Deere, Edsell and Davies were in action again; Deere, in particular, had baled out or crash-landed many times before, a split-second escape being involved in each case. Later in the war the qualifications for the VC were amended, in the case of Group Captain Cheshire, to recognize the fact that unremitting performance and endurance may rank as highly as the single exceptional act of courage. Had this been so in 1940, there might have been more than merely a single VC awarded to Fighter Command.

In the evening Biggin Hill, bombed already three times in two days, was the target. Worrall, Frankland and Igoe were in the Operations Room as the raid came in. Frankland was controlling with Worrall helping him. The

WAAFs continued to plot the steadily approaching bombers as Frankland and Worrall passed the orders to the fighters. 'The WAAFs may have been scared to death,' said Frankland, 'but if so, they certainly didn't show it and their work wasn't affected.' With the bombers right on top, the WAAFs were ordered under the table. Corporal Henderson, however, remained at her post, the telephone connection with 11 Group, and Sergeant Turner had to be forcibly dragged from the switchboard. Frankland felt as a crunch rather than heard the bomb which came through the roof and struck the top of a safe fifteen feet away in the Signal Officer's office. The Operations Room was plunged into darkness as the lights failed, a substantial part of the roof fell in, and choking clouds of dust filled the air.

Desmond Sheen had moved in that morning from Acklington with 72 Squadron, which was relieving 612 Squadron at Biggin Hill; he had hardly settled in before he was airborne again on the interception being controlled by Frankland at the time of the bombing. When he landed, most of the remaining hangars and workshops had either been destroyed or were so full of holes that they could not be blacked out for use at night. A WAAF Armament Sergeant was having the time of her life going round the bomb craters and marking with red flags the small significant holes which indicated delayed-action bombs. The WAAF who drove Sheen across the wrecked airfield with a nonchalant disregard of the DA bombs had lost her husband and many of her friends in a previous raid; it was the attitude of this girl and some of the others which impressed Sheen most of all. That night, the mess having been badly damaged, he remembered eating his supper by candlelight while seated on the steps, and the Station Commander, Group Captain Grice, walking around heavily bandaged.

As a landing ground, Biggin Hill was still usable, in spite of the craters; but as a Sector Station it had ceased to exist until an emergency Operations Room could be set up in a shop in the village, and as an aerodrome for handling fighters it was crippled to the extent of being able to operate for a week afterwards only one squadron instead of three. At Debden also serious damage had been done.

Meanwhile, the severe fighting had caused significant attrition among many squadrons. 56 Squadron, for instance, had virtually ceased to exist as an effective fighting unit; in the space of only a few days it had lost most of its leaders and a number of other pilots – dead, burned, wounded or just badly shaken. The gallant 'Jumbo' Gracie – 'a fat chap, full of fun, full of life, a most positive cavalier character', Sutton called him – had been shot down and crash-landed on the 30th. He flew again on the 31st, joking about the stiff neck he had got in the crash, then bounced into Epping Hospital for a quick X-ray, cheerfully exaggerating (he thought), with 'I've got a broken neck!' He returned after X-ray, rather white – 'It really is broken.' Three pilots were in hospital with severe burns, one of them Barry Sutton.

He was shot down, he always thought, by a Spitfire. At any rate, when returning alone from an attack on a bomber formation, he was 'bounced' and the aircraft that circled his parachute was a Spitfire, presumably exulting over the demise of a 109. Just previously, he had been with the squadron, had sighted the German formation, which looked like a 'great swarming mass of flies', had reported them, but presumably had not been heard, for when he streaked off in their direction he found himself alone, with no sign of the rest of the squadron. His first instinct was to run, but suspecting that the Germans had not seen him and that a quick dive into the middle of them could hardly fail to get one, he went straight through them, spraying bullets. 'Looking back on it afterwards with the experience of years, I am quite certain I shot well up out of range and I doubt whether I did much damage.'

Grateful still to be alive, Sutton flew back over the Thames Estuary towards Hornchurch, gradually losing height. It was a beautiful evening, so he slid back the hood, raised the seat for a better view – and began to sing.

'Absolutely reprehensible', he commented afterwards. 'One should never do this . . . but I thought I was well away from the battle area. Then the instrument panel suddenly began to break up and there was a great explosion, rather like a bang from an oven door.' The hood was already open, and Sutton got out so fast that all he remembered of it was the tail plane going past his face, very close. He pulled the ripcord, but could not hold on to the shroud lines because the flames which had blown back into the cockpit had raised large blisters on his hands.

'So I just swung about helplessly and listened to the birds, and saw the Spitfire coming round, and finally I began to see the trees and telegraph wires coming up very closely, and a road, and then people running. The people running turned out to be women and I actually landed in the middle of the street in a village near Canterbury, and these old dames came running out, I am not absolutely certain, but I think with rolling pins in their hands – they were very hostile-looking and quite certain I was a German. Then there arrived an ambulance and a Wolseley 14 car with a soldier in it, and I was not going to get into the ambulance and insisted on the car. I was very rude to the ambulance driver, but he must have won; he put me back in the ambulance – this shows the power of one's will in conditions of shock, which is what I had.

Next morning, the Sister produced a "T" piece from my badly burned tunic, as she thought it might be of value. She didn't know what it was, and I couldn't identify it for a moment, until I realized it was the door-piece of the ambulance, which I had pocketed out of spite because they had insisted that I went in this bumpy old thing instead of the nice Wolseley.'

After these losses, 56 Squadron were taken out of the line and sent to Boscombe Down where the few surviving experienced pilots would train the reinforcements. A few days later, 54 Squadron were also to be taken out of the line, but on the 31st Colin Gray got a 109 near Maidstone, which gradually slowed down, spewing glycol, and landed in a field. Circling the crash, Gray saw the pilot get out of the wreckage and three men advancing on him. Each time the Spitfire whistled over the three men, they went down flat on their faces, so that it took some minutes to reach the German; he, meanwhile, took off his parachute and jumped on it. Gray assumed he was an 'ace' whose vanity was hurt.

A few hours later, at dusk on 31 August, the first of 145 bombers approached the south coast, bound for the fourth night in succession for Liverpool. Twenty-five other bombers also crossed the coast to carry out nuisance raids. The whole of *Kampfgeschwader* 55 took part, including Wronsky's machine; he came in over Portsmouth at 16,500 feet, intent on picking up his pin-points. Inland, England was simply a black, featureless carpet, but the indented coastline at Portsmouth, with the Isle of Wight lying in front and a maze of harbours behind, was picked out precisely by the quite different shimmer of the water; day or night, water is the best landmark from the air, making a village pond more conspicuous than a fair-sized town.

Everything was quiet and Wronsky was checking the exact point of their landfall, when there was a muffled bang and the bomber rocked. Looking out to starboard, Wronsky saw that the engine was on fire. The pilot, beside him, put on gentle bank and rudder and turned slowly out to sea, while they tried to smother the engine in foam from the extinguishers. At that moment, Wronsky felt sure that they were all going to burn.

It was not the custom in KG 55, any more than it had been in the *Löwengeschwader*, to wear parachutes – these were simply stacked against the bulkhead, so that an immediate bale-out was impossible. But the extinguishers worked and the fire died down and flickered out. The Heinkel, still turning clumsily, because only the port engine was pulling, straightened up on a course for home.

Wronsky's belief was that they had been hit first shot by AA guns from a warship lying off Portsmouth; that, at any rate, seemed the most probable explanation. But it could have been a night fighter.

As the crippled bomber approached Calais, one of the invasion ports, they saw that a British air raid was in progress. They had intended to put down at the aerodrome behind Calais, but any bomber approaching from seaward would undoubtedly be assumed by the defenders to be British, and in their damaged condition they would be unable to evade the flak. So they carried on, hoping to limp in to their base at Villacoublay, outside Paris. Below them now were the white chalk roads of Pas de Calais, standing out against the black shadows of the fields, but the port engine was over-heating and running roughly. It was time to abandon the attempt to get home and to bale out.

When putting on their parachutes, they were startled to find that there were no ripcords. In the hurry and excitement in the dark, they had put them on upside down, so that the ripcords were there, but not in the place they had expected them to be. Before they could rectify the mistake, the Heinkel had lost so much height that they were too low to jump.

The ground seemed suddenly to rise up at them – they were actually flying into a hill – and the bomber just failed to clear the top of it, ploughing through bushes and small trees on the summit and breaking its back. They were thrown about violently by the impact. Wronsky had an arm, a foot and his nose broken, one man was seriously injured about the head, and another was hurled through the perspex in the nose and landed clear of the bomber. The other hurt men lay helpless inside the wreck, waiting for it to catch fire, thinking in fact that it had already done so because they could hear a hissing noise which they assumed to be from a burning engine.

In fact the port engine was lying clear of the crash, eighty yards away; the hissing came from the fractured oxygen bottles inside the aircraft. The serious aspect of their plight was that they had crashed in open country, miles from anywhere, and that no one knew even that they had come down. In spite of his injuries, the man who had been thrown clear got to his feet and went to look for help. He came to a railway line and, with no torch to signal to the driver, stood in the middle of the track to wait for the next train. When at length one came rumbling out of the night at him, the driver saw him in time and applied the brakes. After coming out of hospital a month or so later, Wronsky was commissioned and, with one arm strapped in plaster, was soon flying on raids to London and Coventry.

Sunday, 1 September, was the last day of Biggin Hill's 'Bad Weekend'. Colin Gray attacked a Heinkel formation while they were actually bombing it and was hit by just one bullet from some German gunner – which severed both elevator control wires. He could turn and bank but not dive or climb, so he turned on to the bearing for Hornchurch, intending to use his trimming tabs to get the nose down. This he did, and brought off a successful landing in the middle of a new rash of bomb craters.

During the day Desmond Sheen took off from Biggin with 72 Squadron and engaged an escorted Dornier formation coming in south of the Thames; he was brushed off a bomber by the 109s, had to mix it with six of them, collected a cannon shell in his engine – and finally got away. Then he climbed up after the bombers once more. And his engine promptly burst into flames. He slid back the hood, turned the Spitfire on to its back, pulled the harness-release pin – and shoved the stick hard forward, so that the fighter tried to do an outside loop. Out he went, 'clean as a whistle', and fell free, somersaulting, until he had counted ten and pulled the ripcord.

'The parachute opened smoothly and there was a reassuring jolt as it took effect,' he recalled. 'I found myself swaying gently some twelve to fifteen thousand feet above the ground. The descent took some time and was very pleasant, moreover it gave me a perhaps unusual opportunity to survey the battle. It was a clear cloudless day, in fact a beautiful Sunday morning.

'But on my right I could see bombs bursting in the Dover area with the answering fire of the AA defences. The AA were also very active in the London area on my left, and in between a series of running fights was taking place. Above all could be heard the crump of bombs and AA shells, the roar of bomber engines and the distinctive whine of climbing, diving fighters. There was a smell of cordite in the air. Quite close to me a 109 went down vertically in flames. I think it was the pilot of this one who baled out but had a faulty harness – he parted company with his parachute. Another 109 turned towards me, but a Spitfire turned on to his tail and both quickly disappeared.

'I landed in the middle of a field with nothing but a slight jar. I got out of my harness and began to roll up the parachute. A young girl came up and eyed me shyly and a few minutes later a young army Lieutenant appeared, doubtfully waving his revolver in my general direction. I was wearing my old Australian Air Force uniform, which was then a generally unfamiliar sight, and there was no doubt that he wondered whether I was a German. However, I ignored the revolver, continued to pick up my parachute, and started as normal a conversation as possible under the circumstances.'

Since Friday morning some seventy people had been killed or wounded at Biggin Hill and every hangar had been destroyed, although the shell of one was still standing. 'It was grim that week,' recalled Pamela Beecroft. 'My most vivid recollections are of the hits on the equipment trench and the WAAF trench, of the general noise during bombings, and the smell – of dust and from broken gas mains. There were DA bombs everywhere and it was difficult to get around. We felt very cut off – at one time, only one telephone line was working. Our two regular squadrons, old friends, had gone just before the blitz started, and we felt completely lost. It was like sitting on top of a volcano. We lived packed up in suitcases, expecting the Germans to invade, feeling that this must be the climax . . . I had the keys of two cars and was to see that they got away.'

An emergency Operations Room had already been fitted up in Biggin village and the transfer was quickly made; but capacity to operate aircraft was cut sharply by the destruction of the hangars, equipment and stores and the impossibility of night work. To keep a fighter fit to fly under normal conditions required a team of about five men, who had to carry out daily more than 150 inspections on the aircraft, its airframe, engine, instruments, electrics, radio and armament. Many of the aircraft were now coming back shot to pieces and if the squadrons were to keep flying at full strength most of the repairs would have to be done on the spot. The sheer pressure of work on the ground crews was tremendous; they slaved to keep the fighters airworthy and suffered casualties while they did it. 'Pilots who were on the ground when there was a raid couldn't get into the air quick enough,' said Jackson, the Engineer Officer. 'When you can hit back it's a build to morale. But to sit on the ground, without a gun, unable to hit back, and just get blasted, is a terrifying experience.'

Biggin Hill was the worst hit of the Sector Stations, but what happened there during this climax of the battle against Fighter Command was different only in degree from what happened to most of the other Sector Stations. All except Northolt suffered a similar experience, and the cumulative effect of the attacks was becoming serious.

The destruction of so many buildings at Biggin meant finding billets in the village for a number of WAAFs. Section Officer Beecroft, who called at the houses to arrange this, met a reception which varied from the friendly to the frankly hostile. One woman told her that she wouldn't take anybody, because it was the RAF which had caused all the 'trouble'. Some bombs had fallen in the village and her attitude appeared to be based on a fear that the Germans would find out that she was billeting WAAFs and single out her house for attention.

Reactions differed greatly from district to district and from time to time. On 30 August I had been in London during the Sector Station attacks – no one had taken much notice. 'They didn't yet know,' I wrote, 'what the word "aeroplane" could really mean.' On 31 August I was in Portsmouth, alongside the dockyard, the favourite target, when the sirens had begun to wail. 'The streets were evacuated with speed and decision, pedestrians running to shelter and vehicles either speeding up to get clear altogether or pulling up to allow their occupants to shelter.' On 1 September I went to Bristol by way of Salisbury. 'On entering a square in Salisbury I found it so packed with gaping people that it was hard to make out what the attraction was; then I saw they were looking at a pub which had been partly and recently destroyed by fire – some bomber had unloaded a few incendiaries over the town in the first air raid they had ever had; this was the sum total of the damage.

'It was dark by the time I passed through Bath and a "nuisance" raid had just begun. In Bristol, I went out from my hotel for a stroll, and got a severe shock from a sentry. He jumped out of the darkness from beside some barrier, holding a bayonetted rifle, and said, "Halt, who goes there?" In a quavering voice, I assured the lad that I was his friend.

'The searchlights, wavering at first, converged and exposed a tiny silver moth, beautiful but deadly, moving steadily across the sky. The thunder of the guns, in the tall canyons of the streets, produced a really solid sound; battery by battery, the searchlights passed him on. Later, while drifting off to sleep, I heard the whistle of falling bombs pass across the hotel roof, followed by three explosions which made it rock. Next morning, at breakfast, I expected to hear excited discussion of the events of the night – those three bombs had landed 150 yards away, started a fire, and killed people, some of whom were still in the wreckage. Instead there was an uncanny pre-war calm; the clientele sat stolidly entrenched behind its newspapers and no word not strictly necessary was spoken. "The butter, if you don't mind." Grunt. Butter passed. Grunt. Acknowledged.'

The attack on the Sector Stations continued without intermission; Hornchurch was raided on 2 September, North Weald on 3 September. The Germans were getting their thrusts home with distressing frequency, partly because of the enormous concentration of fighters in Pas de Calais, partly because they were becoming more expert in protecting their bombers. But the 109s, flying to the limit of their fuel, were vulnerable on the return; they could not fight, but only dive for home. On the 2nd, J. Feric of 303 Squadron pursued a 109 with such enthusiasm that he was still firing at it over France. Park mildly rebuked the Poles, saying that although he appreciated their fine offensive spirit, 'this practice is not economical or sound now that there is such good shooting within sight of London'. On the 3rd Colin Gray met a 109 returning from the big raid on North Weald and chased it all the way to the French coast; it was streaming glycol but very determined to get home. As it was steadily slowing down and he was low on ammunition, he waited to fire until he had crept up to 150 yards. It promptly turned over, pretending to be dead, flipped right way up again, and carried gamely on, the propeller slowly ticking over. There, Gray had to leave it, 'because its chums were coming out'. The Germans were forced to include yet one more refinement in their escort technique – 'Fighter Recognition' – groups of 109s waiting over the Channel to greet the bomber formations, possibly broken up and certainly with 'lame ducks' lagging behind, and possibly separated now from the escort which would be low on fuel and unable to fight.

4 September marked the introduction of a new type of target for the German bombers on the western flank,

those largely under command of *Luftflotte* 3. Whereas in the last week of August they had been employed against targets which had direct connection with the invasion – the bombing of naval bases, particularly Portsmouth – they now began a systematic series of raids on aircraft factories, but without discriminating between those making bombers and those engaged in fighter production. What might have happened if they had concentrated on the fighter factories and done so earlier, in mid-August, is an interesting speculation; possibly, it might have been fatal.

At mid-day on the 4th Mr C. F. Andrews, who is now Public Relations Officer of Vickers-Armstrong at Weybridge, was arguing with a colleague in a bank at Woking, where he was then employed, as to the possibilities of recognizing enemy aircraft by the sound of their engines. He maintained that it was not only possible, but easy; his colleague scoffed. 'Well now, it's a most extraordinary thing,' replied Andrews, 'but there's a formation of aircraft coming straight up over the railway line now. And I'll take a small bet that this is a hostile formation, probably Ju. 88s.' Before they could even reach the door, the guns were firing. When they looked out, the bombers were scattering and they counted at least six parachutes. The man in command of the battery which had brought down two bombers with its first salvo was a Sergeant – the officers were away at lunch. He had seen about fourteen aircraft flying low and fast up the main railway line from Portsmouth to London, taken one look at them, roared, 'Bloody Ju. 88s! Take post! Fire!' (or words to that effect), and the first shell had burst between two of them, bringing both down.

This was most extraordinary. Everything in this case had depended on quick and accurate recognition of the aircraft as German, and most AA gunners (the navy were particularly notorious) had no grasp whatever of this subject. The army gunners relied on the warnings passed to them by Fighter Command, with which they were integrated. This situation and the poor quality of the recognition material had caused a group of aviation enthusiasts, mainly full-time or part-time members of the Observer Corps in nearby Guildford, to form the Hearkers Club. A purely private organization – it met in a café – it received help from the Technical Editor of *The Aeroplane*, Peter Masefield, and Leonard Taylor of the Air League, and set such a standard that it was eventually taken over officially. Andrews was a member and so was the Sergeant who had put his knowledge to such good use.

But he had not stopped the bombers; the remainder, rather scattered, pressed on to their target. This was the Vickers-Armstrong factory, producing Wellington bombers, at Brooklands aerodrome near Weybridge. It was 1.25 P.M., so that large crowds of men and women were leaving the canteen and washrooms or were clocking in; there were not many actually on the factory floor among the machinery, which afforded good protection from blast. Mr C. Pipe, who had been delayed, had not even reached the building. He had got as far as number three gate, where an old man was standing, leaning on the gate and looking up at a segment of sky across which came four bombers, roaring in low and fast. 'Now I don't think I've seen any of those before,' observed the old man. There were women and girls passing through, but the sight of the black crosses on the wings of the bombers temporarily distracted Mr Pipe. 'Don't stand there – get down, for flip's sake!' he bellowed, and set the example. One of the four planes banked steeply and a bomb fell away from it, plunging through the roof of the factory.

Watching from the door of the machine shop at that

moment was an assistant foreman, Mr J. Hilyard. His segment of sky contained two planes, from which bombs fell at the exact moment someone exclaimed, 'Look at those Spitfires!'

Mr F. W. Hackney, a storekeeper, had had lunch in the canteen and was just leaving the adjoining washrooms; both were on the upper floor with a 'well' in the centre. On the floor below was the clocking-in area. Canteen, washrooms, the stairs leading down, and the clocking-in area were crowded with men and girls. The roof above was of glass. One heavy bomb detonated here with maximum effect. It went down through the 'well' – passing Mr Hackney on the way – and exploded actually underneath him, on the top of a large rubber die-forming press. He heard no explosion. The place just started crumbling away, falling to pieces around him, dissolving and filling the air with dust. He ran down the stairs, saw the body of a girl and after a moment's hesitation took her to the First Aid Post. Because of the dust, smoke and ruin, every man's view was, for the moment, localized.

Mr A. G. Bugden, an assistant foreman, had stopped for perhaps one minute later than he usually did, to buy a bar of chocolate in the canteen; so he was coming down the stairs when he heard aeroplanes and was abruptly blown some distance by the bomb. He recovered consciousness, saw a man who was blood-stained, wiped the blood off him – and discovered that he himself was similarly streaming blood. He went into the machine shop through dense clouds of dust and saw that the glass from the roof was hanging down in slices, held up by the wire underneath. Two men were lying under the wreckage of the stores, but part of the roof girders had come down on top of it all, and there was nothing that could be done for them. He went to his own desk and found it crushed by a roof support – buying the bar of chocolate had saved his life. Many of the men went home, to tell their wives that they were all right, then came back to help.

It was fairly quiet, except for a low, persistent moaning which seemed to come from everywhere. One girl was sitting on her stool, quite lifelike, and quite dead. Of another girl, only the legs were left – with not a crease or crinkle in the stockings. Many other bodies had been wholly or partially stripped of their clothing by the blast, but there was little blood, often none at all, except among the people cut down by the flying slivers of glass. The blast had killed apparently without a wound. ARP precautions had familiarized everyone with gas but not with the effects of large amounts of high explosive inside a thin covering of steel. They were freakish, streams of blast streaking out as unpredictably as water from a running tap when a thumb is placed under it, and striking anything in its path with a force equal to collision with a fast motor car. The delicate internal organs – lungs, liver, spleen – were crushed or ruptured by the blow; the wounded were shocked and bleeding internally. Ordinary First Aid was useless; morphia, not bandages, was required.

Mr Hackney, anxious to see if his brother was all right, searched for him without result, and then began to help in the work of carrying out the dead. When the supply of stretchers ran out, they piled the bodies on the completed wings of Wellington bombers, and carried them out that way. He saw a man's foot sticking out from under wreckage, but decided to leave him. The general feeling about this was, 'They're gone. Leave it.' Over one body he had an argument with another man as to how to move it; they decided to turn the corpse over and Mr Hackney got hold of an arm – but it came right out of the body, which had been broken by blast.

Mr Pipe saw a removal van drive up to where he also was engaged on this task. The driver asked casually, 'Can

I help?' So they unloaded its cargo of shiny new bicycles, and put in the wounded and the dead as they were brought out from the factory. After three or four trips to the hospital, there seemed to be an end to the job, so the driver calmly took a broom, swept out the thickly-caked blood from the floor of the van, reloaded his shiny bicycles, and drove off without even giving his name.

First casualty lists were put up in Sub-Post Offices throughout the district at 6 P.M. One list alone contained 132 names, but the total was not known for several days – 88 killed and more than 600 wounded.

'It was eerie walking round the works that night,' said a Fire Officer. 'Bits of glass kept tinkling as they fell from the roof. Then there was the rubble covering the big press and you knew, as you went past, that there were people under there. Next day, I remember, there was a chap with a concrete breaker working to uncover the bodies; hat pushed back on his head, he was singing away quite cheerfully.'

That night, at eleven o'clock, Donald Connacher was 120 miles away to the north-east, in E-boat Alley. He was now second mate of the collier *Fulham V*. The Luftwaffe, concentrating on Fighter Command, had much less to spare for the convoys and sinkings by direct air attack were not so serious as they had been during the Battle of the Channel. This was just as well, for Park had nothing to spare with which to protect them and indeed on 1 September he had been formally relieved of responsibility for close convoy protection in the 11 Group area. But parallel with the Battle of Britain, and indeed as part of it, the Germans were carrying out blockade of the sea routes with mine-laying aircraft, surface mine-layers, and E-boats. It was the latter which attacked this convoy.

Connacher was below when the first bang came. 'I was

very bang-conscious then,' he said, 'and I made straight
for the bridge.' On the starboard bow the collier *New
Lampton* was burning fiercely. From somewhere out on
the dark sea there were voices calling. These were survivors from the 'flatiron' *Joseph Swan*, subsequently
machine-gunned on their raft, so Connacher was told later
by Captain Beattie, the only one of them who was not
killed. Connacher was halfway up the companionway
when the torpedo hit, port side and forward of the bridge.
He fell to the deck as the ship shuddered violently, half-
buried in the water thrown up by the explosion. He saw
that the port side had been blown out and part of the
cargo of coal had poured into the sea. Soaked, but still
feeling that he didn't want to get wet, he ran along the
hatches to one of the two lifeboats.

'It was a beautiful sinking, no bother at all. *Fulham V*
went down by the head, we heard the boilers crushed, she
gave a toot on her whistle, and just disappeared.' They
were picked up, landed at Southend and went to London
to report to the Fenchurch Street office of their company.
'We looked like a bunch of tramps, in rags and tatters and
lifejackets.' After accepting tea and cakes from the girl
telephone operator, Connacher walked across the street
to the office of the Shipping Federation, where he drew
his survivor's allowance in respect of the sinking of the
Henry Moon on 25 July and applied for another on behalf
of the *Fulham V*. 'You're making a bloody habit of it!'
said the clerk.

On 5 September, as 72 Squadron were climbing up over
Kent to get height over a raid reported coming in from
the east, Desmond Sheen was 'bounced' from the rear.
He heard a warning shout from one of the 'weavers', and
almost instantaneously the Spitfire shuddered from what
must have been an accurate and heavy burst from astern.

FIGHTER FORMATIONS

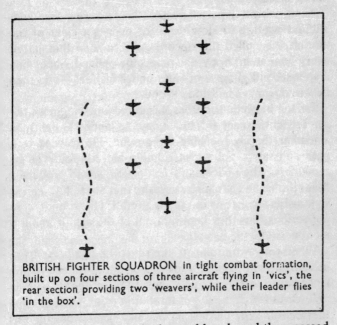

BRITISH FIGHTER SQUADRON in tight combat formation, built up on four sections of three aircraft flying in 'vics', the rear section providing two 'weavers', while their leader flies 'in the box'.

He felt sudden pain in the leg and hand, and then passed out. Possibly his oxygen bottle had been hit and exploded.

The Spitfire went whining down vertically with large pieces missing from the port wing; when Sheen recovered consciousness, he had no control over the aircraft, he could not even level out or roll over so that he could drop clear. And the fighter was going straight down at the deck, speed rapidly building up towards the 500 mph mark. The hood was already open, and when Sheen pulled the harness pin to release himself from his straps, he was sucked out of the cockpit; but his feet were trapped by the top of the windscreen. He lay straddled along the top of the fuselage, struggling to get free, with no idea how much height or time he still had. Not very much, he suspected.

Then, for no apparent reason, his feet were free and, without waiting to slow down or even get clear of the aircraft, he pulled the ripcord. With a snap that jarred every bone in his body, the parachute opened; Sheen had a split-second glimpse of trees under his feet – and then he was down in Maidstone Wood.

He fell between the trees, his parachute caught on the top branches to act as a brake, and he landed as lightly as a feather, barely touching the ground. He crawled to a path and saw a policeman riding a bicycle, followed by spectators. The policeman's first action was to produce a flask, the second to express surprise that Sheen had waited so long before getting out of his aircraft. His wounds were not serious, but they kept him out of the air for about a month.

When they were jumped, the squadron had been flying in the old tight formation of vics of three, instead of the loose pairs used by the Germans; to offset the difficulties of lookout which made this formation vulnerable, the two rear machines of the last section had been 'weaving' but this method was not satisfactory and the 'weavers' had seen the Germans too late to avoid the 'bounce'. Superior numbers and the holding of the initiative combined with the rigid and inflexible thinking of their opponents, enabled the Germans to inflict heavier losses than they themselves suffered; the Hurricanes particularly, with their comparatively low ceiling and poor performance above 18,000 feet, suffered from the 'bounce'. Malinowski was three times with formations which were jumped on from the top: the first time, he was shot down; the second time, the attackers consisted only of six 109s but they got two Hurricanes as they dived through; the third time, there was only one 109, but he also shot down two

Hurricanes. These were ambush tactics pure and simple, which, rather than dog-fighting, were the essence of fighter versus fighter combat.

On the morning of the 5th the staff of Vickers-Armstrong had reported for work as usual, but most were not allowed inside the factory because the structure was unsafe. What work there was consisted largely of moving out the machine tools and stacking them for dispersal; this took four days. Lord Beaverbrook's Ministry of Aircraft Production ruled that buildings in the neighbourhood should be requisitioned to house the machine tools as, in effect, small aircraft factories, and that the main factory should do only assembly work, so that never again should such a concentrated, vulnerable target be presented to the enemy. A bookbinding works, a cable works, a timber stores, many garages and one film studio – which proved ideal for building main wings – were taken over.

The company had been producing 134 Wellingtons a month, nearly two-thirds at Brooklands, the rest at Chester, out of range of day bombing. Production never actually stopped – the lowest weekly figure following the raid was four Wellingtons – but it was not until eight months later that production again reached peak. Coming three weeks after the raid on Shorts, Bomber Command had been struck a substantial blow. Two important factories in the area were intact, both producing fighters – Hawkers, on the opposite side of Brooklands aerodrome to Vickers-Armstrong, and Supermarine at Southampton. No sooner had Park been relieved of the responsibility for escorting convoys than he was directed by Dowding, as a result of the Weybridge raid, to give 'maximum fighter cover' to the remaining factories, thus imposing maximum strain on his already inadequate forces, whose bases were largely in ruins. Nevertheless, those factories were vital and had to be protected – and they were on the Luftwaffe target list.

On 6 September the debris was being cleared at Weybridge and unsafe parts of the structure brought down. Canadian troops, brought in to do this job, were walking the girders, high above the ground, or sitting on them and knocking out broken glass, singing to their hearts' content. When the whistles blew to signal another raid, and they were told to shelter, they shouted back, 'Aw, hell! We came here to work and no goddam Jerry's going to stop us.' At mid-day the raid came in, directed at Hawkers on the far side of the aerodrome. A bomb hit the banked racing car track which encircled the landing ground, bounced along the concrete like a football and ended up at the bottom, unexploded. The Engineering Division was hit and also the Home Guard armoury, from which rifles showered out; and cannon shells and bullets punched holes in the parked cars of the directors. But the effect was much less devastating than that caused at the Vickers factory.

The Home Guards – most factories provided their own battalions from members of the staff – worked the unexploded bomb by the banking on to a sheet of corrugated iron and then lifted it on to a truck driven by a Canadian. With one man sitting on the bomb to keep it steady, they drove across the airfield to the nearest bomb crater, lowered the bomb into it – and exploded it there.

While Weybridge was being bombed, the main effort was being made over the eastern outskirts of London; the vapour trails of the dog-fight could be clearly seen from the centre of the capital. The target, the oil storage tanks at Thameshaven, were set on fire and burned furiously. Below the battle, busy betting on the dogs at a greyhound racing stadium, were a dozen tired pilots from 66 Squadron who had been flying four and five sorties a day, and had been given the day off. 'There was a terrific dog-fight going on overhead,' recalled Oxspring, who was betting with Rupert Leigh. 'He appeared to take no notice, borrowed ten bob off me to put on a dog, then looked up and said, "You know, I can't help feeling this is a case of Nero fiddling while Rome is burning."'

Oberst Carl Viek, Chief of Staff to the JAFU 2, had in the beginning been able to do the same thing for his pilots, giving them the day off by squadrons to go down to the beach and have a swim, and also on his own responsibility grounding the leaders who appeared to be on the point of cracking under the strain. This now was no longer possible; he had been accused of 'softness' and nearly lost his job because of it. Nevertheless, in his opinion, greater than the physical strain was the psychological effect of their being told by the high command that, according to arithmetical calculations, there were no British fighters left. 'But when they went up they found lots of them – and that caused doubts about the Government.'

However, on this day the British defences were torn apart by the improved escort methods of the Germans. The radar system helped the British to offset their disparity in numbers – but only up to a point. Park was trying to engage with as many squadrons as possible – but usually there was insufficient time to assemble more than two squadrons together. The Poles of 303 Squadron, successful the previous day, failed on this day with heavy losses. Squadron Leader R. G. Kellett, who was leading them, saw that the rearguard of 109s was already being engaged by a Spitfire squadron and took his Hurricanes down on the bombers. He alone reached them, setting the engine of a Dornier on fire, before being hit and slightly wounded by cannon fire from a 109. Two of the Polish pilots were wounded and the Polish CO, Major Z. Krasnodebski, was so badly burned that he was in hospital for a year. Four Hurricanes were lost and two damaged. The new

Polish CO was Flying Officer W. Urbanowicz, who was to take over the squadron when Kellett left. Later, he became a Wing Commander and Polish Air Attaché in the USA, during which appointment he managed somehow to visit the Japanese battlefront and to shoot down two 'Zero' fighters. His combat report of 6 September contained much pertinent comment.

'Only two of our squadrons in the area – and a hundred Germans,' he wrote. 'The Germans had now developed a new principle of covering the whole length of the approach to London – a sort of blanket of fighters – under which the bombers had free passage. That made it very difficult to get at them, because invariably we had to engage the fighters first and in view of their superiority in numbers there was no chance to deal with them in time to catch the bombers. So – heavy fighting, considerable losses, where pilots had to engage one Messerschmitt after another and only Kellett was lucky enough to get to the bombers. The English are a bit too cautious in restricting interception to one or two squadrons, which cannot be effective, instead of, on such occasions, putting everything in the air and sweeping it clean.' He added, as an afterthought, 'I was lucky enough to shoot down a 109. Gave it a very short burst; to my surprise it went straight down in flames; the pilot did not jump.'

In the week beginning on 31 August and ending on 6 September, Fighter Command lost 161 fighters in air battles alone, against a German loss of 154 bombers and fighters. The battle in the air – of fighter versus fighter – was being decisively won by the Luftwaffe. If this continued, there really would be no British fighters left, or at any rate not enough to put up an effective defence. Then the whole of the German bomber force could sweep over southern England, destroy the aircraft factories to make their victory complete, and turn finally to the essential

'VALHALLA' WITH FULL ESCORT

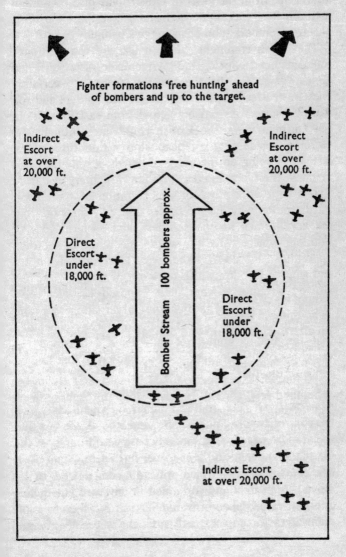

Fighter formations 'free hunting' ahead
of bombers and up to the target.

Indirect
Escort
at over
20,000 ft.

Indirect
Escort
at over
20,000 ft.

Direct
Escort
under
18,000 ft.

Bomber Stream 100 bombers approx.

Direct
Escort
under
18,000 ft.

Indirect Escort
at over 20,000 ft.

bombing of targets connected with the invasion. And that afternoon, from the cliffs of Dover, part of the German invasion fleet was sighted, steaming west past Cap Gris Nez to its embarkation ports in the Channel.

The Polish comment, 'the English are too cautious', found its echo later on the German side. The RAF had almost as many fighters as the Germans, certainly enough to sweep that carpet of German fighters and roll it up by squadrons passing across from east to west. In the German view, the British could have brought the German onslaught to a dead stop within three days, instead of being on the verge of defeat, if only they had matched the German concentration of fighters in Pas de Calais with an equivalent concentration of their own. Furthermore, why did the British doggedly carry on from the aerodromes on the southern and eastern sides of London, which were just within the range of German operations, instead of withdrawing to aerodromes north and west of London which were out of range? They had already withdrawn from their exposed forward aerodromes, why not withdraw the target altogether and leave the Germans to beat at the air? They concluded that the British could not fully have understood the weakness of the German position caused by the limited range of the 109.

Unknown to them were the weaknesses of the British position. First, the limited number of squadrons which the control system could handle, and second, the fact that the aerodromes were not merely base aerodromes, as the Germans understood them to be, but Sector Stations of the control system which was too complicated to be moved in a hurry and for which in any case emergency alternatives had been provided. The British therefore felt themselves forced to stand and fight where they were, instead of withdrawing. But certainly they could have engaged with greater numbers, if Dowding had taken the risk of stripping other parts of the country of fighter protection in favour of concentration on the main battle. It was not even necessary to control them, merely to get them airborne in time so that they could indulge in a British 'free hunt' across the German fighter 'carpet'. In the last analysis, it was not even necessary to retain fighters at the Sector Stations, for the control aspect consisted of an Operations Room and its annexes, together with landlines to a transmitter and telephone lines to Group; it was convenient and efficient for the control staff and the fighter pilots to be in personal contact with each other but it was not strictly necessary. On the other hand, a withdrawal could produce a momentarily critical situation if the Germans landed suddenly on the south-east coast; the British fighters were just as short-ranged as the 109s and from bases behind London they could not intervene effectively against bombers supporting the troops on the beaches.

The British reaction to the new German tactics was not altogether satisfactory. Instead of bringing the fresh 12 Group squadrons into the battle area, under Park's control, he was merely given to understand that they would relieve him of responsibility – at some time while attacks were in progress – for guarding his bases north-east of London. In practice, they either did not take part in the battle at all or came in too late. As these squadrons were fully efficient and indeed exceedingly impatient for action, the failure to use them fully partly justifies the criticism of undue caution. But it should be remembered that Dowding held the major responsibility in a battle to which he could see no certain end, at a time when the facts could not be fully known, and when a false move could lose the war. What might have happened if the German attacks on the Sector Stations had continued further to disrupt the effectiveness of his Command is guesswork; for on 7 September the Germans chose another target for their bombers.

PHASE IV:
London

12

The U-Bend of the Thames

7–14 September

On Saturday, 7 September, Reichsmarschall Göring in person took over nominal command of the attack; he stood on the cliffs of Pas de Calais and watched the bombers and fighters of Kesselring's *Luftflotte* 2 set out – for London. Shortly afterwards, from their bases around Paris, a powerful force from Sperrle's *Luftflotte* 3 was due to take off – also for London. Partly this was reprisal for the RAF raids on Berlin, partly it was a continuation of the policy of bombing vital targets and so forcing the British to fight in the air, but also it was an attempt to see if the British or their Government could be panicked and poleaxed into surrender by mass attacks such as had been delivered at the appropriate time and with maximum effect on Warsaw, Rotterdam[1] and Paris. The targets were the great commercial docks in London – on what the Germans called the *U-bend* of the Thames – important blockade objectives, but having no connection with the defeat of Fighter Command or the gaining of an invasion beachhead. This abrupt switch of targets took the British off balance, and the attacks were completely successful at small cost. The defences were almost totally disorganized, and the Government was stampeded into ordering an 'invasion imminent' warning that night. And with the night came a fresh series of attacks on London, delivered by bombers unable to venture over the capital in daylight because of the lack of escorts.

[1] Rotterdam was a tactical air strike to defend a paratroop bridge-head, but the morale of the Dutch Government was shaky already.

That Göring was a simple, not to say childish personality, was an opinion held in the Luftwaffe by many who knew him. He was also a forceful one; it was his ruthless drive and energy which had built up the Luftwaffe from little more than a collection of gliding clubs to the point where, not only had it overtaken and then far outstripped the Royal Air Force in striking power, but was now to deliver its blows at the heart of the enemy capital.

Göring was perfectly receptive to criticism in private, although not in public, where it would damage his authority; and he had no real political convictions in the doctrinaire sense. He was even heard to say that he was not a National Socialist at all but a believer in Monarchy – at which the Luftwaffe Generals nudged each other and hinted that the system of government he was referring to would turn out to be Monarchy by Popular Vote, with Göring as the Monarch. On another occasion, Göring made a derogatory remark about Christianity and General Fink at once got up and left, actually to answer a telephone call. Göring suddenly remembered Fink's views, and remarked, 'Oh dear, I wouldn't have said that, if I'd known Fink was here.' Göring was not really convinced of what he was saying; he had in him a strong element of the swashbuckling adventurer and had seen, quite rightly, that the best place for his talents was the Nazi Party. It was this man who now stood watching the bombers go out and, intoxicated by the power of the force he had created, made a bombastic speech into a waiting microphone.

But it was Fink, the professional soldier and a deeply religious man, who led the bombers of *Kampfgeschwader* 2 over the White Cliffs and into England. Geschwader after geschwader thundered across the Straits. 'Right from the French coast, on the way in, we could see the vast columns of smoke from the burning oil tanks, bombed the previous day,' recalled Paul Weitkus, who led II *Gruppe*. Each gruppe had been allotted a different target in the docks and had been provided with a sketch map of it.

Over Sevenoaks, their close escort turned back, already low on fuel; and Fink led the bombers on alone. British fighters, in ones and twos, came diving from directly above, straight through the formation, going vertically down; Fink had the impression that they were not keen to expose themselves to the mass fire of the bombers. All the same, it was a terrifying experience as the Spitfires and Hurricanes fell like plummets towards them at over 400 mph, each having apparently picked out a particular bomber for its target. A Dornier close in on Fink's left fell away out of the formation and crashed; but the bombers hung together and the fighters could not break them. There is something incongruous in the spectacle of the old Christian gentleman, for Fink was 45 – old even for a bomber pilot – pressing on doggedly, without a fighter escort, into the heart of the most powerful air defences in the world. To his crews he said, before each operation, 'You must make your wills.' Only then, he thought, was it possible to stand up to the strain and immerse yourself in your job. There was more to it than that; there was his duty to his country, notwithstanding that it was governed by men he considered a menace to Christian civilization, and there were his own Christian beliefs, which made of life on this earth a temporary thing, unimportant compared to the way in which one conducted oneself while on it. Many outwardly tough characters tend to fade away in battle because they cannot face the final thought of dying; often the gentle man goes on. Fink went on, to Victoria Docks, and his formation bombed it heavily and accurately.

Paul Weitkus, leading II *Gruppe* of the Geschwader,

came in over India Docks; their bombs, too, were well-placed and he could see the fires starting as he turned away. Leaning downwards, he pointed the telephoto lens of his Leica at the scene below and took several pictures. He thought them better pictures than those taken by the professional war correspondents; a precise, soldierly man, his objection to the press men's photographs was that their huge cameras tended to exaggerate the scene of destruction.

They turned away, gruppe by gruppe, not much bothered by the AA fire. When, occasionally, a stray shell splinter thumped against the belly of a bomber, the crew yelled, 'Come in!' Weitkus could make out the gun positions around London – the battery positions, that is, not the individual guns. Then, with bombs gone and streaking for home, they met the first furious attacks by full fighter squadrons – the defenders had reacted at last.

'When over London, on this day or on any other,' said Weitkus, 'you couldn't tell a 109 from a Spitfire in the chaos of diving machines and bursting flak. Whoever saw who first, was the victor.' Roaring back, with fighters tearing into the formation, Fink saw in a machine ahead of him a rear-gunner firing wildly into his own tailplane; in his own Dornier, every man of the crew, except himself, was wounded, and a map he was holding in his hand was knocked away by a bullet. When they landed, a crowd formed round this other machine, the rear-gunner excitedly pointing to the tailplane and asking everyone to count the hits he had sustained. Fink walked up and, making allowances for the strain of the flight, quietly told him who had done the shooting.

111 Squadron intercepted a *Valhalla* over Redhill on its way to the docks and fought it all the way to London. They had too little warning, had taken off too late to gain a height advantage, and were forced to make their initial

attack head on and at the same level. But these bombers, with hundreds of fighters swarming round them like bees around a hive, refused to accept the deadly head-on attack; they evaded it by turning away, and the Hurricanes had to come in from the port quarter. Squadron Leader Thompson remembered shooting a Heinkel in the tail and had a brief glimpse of bombs bursting on the docks; that was all he had time for – '109s were popping up from behind like corn on a summer's day.'

303 (Polish) Squadron were climbing up over London when they saw AA bursts away to starboard and heard some British pilot calling on his R/T: 'Tally-Ho!' Then 3,000 feet below them they saw a Dornier formation, flying tightly together, so many they could not be counted. The Hurricanes came in from above and astern.

Corporal Wojtowicz, in the last section, saw several bombers trailing smoke already from the attacks of the leading sections; he closed on a Dornier which had broken formation, shot it down, and immediately after another one flew straight into his sights – all he had to do was press the button. But this bomber was tough and did not start to burn until he had given it six bursts. As it fell in flames, he saw a burning Hurricane go whining down on his port side.

At full throttle the Poles chased the bombers back to the coast. Pilot Officer Jan Daszewski, an enormously tall, strong man, chased a staffel as far as Dover and had set one of the bombers smoking when a 'Fighter Reception' team got him. A bullet struck his upper arm, a cannon shell struck his thigh, tearing an enormous bloody wound; glycol and smoke filled the cockpit, and the fighter began to spin. The controls were out of action, so Daszewski tried to get out; with no power in an arm and a leg, it was desperately hard. He hung half in and half out of the cockpit, unable to do anything more, while the

Hurricane, its nose pointed at the earth, rotated violently in the spin.

The slipstream suddenly sucked him clear, but it seemed an age before he was able to grasp the ripcord and pull, and then the jar of the harness biting into his mangled thigh was terrible beyond description. The descent seemed to take too long, the earth appeared miles away, and he was losing blood so fast from the hole which the cannon shell had blown from one side of his thigh to the other; he fell like a sack into a ploughed field and was dragged across it by his parachute. He was out of action for nearly a year and the wound never closed up.

Corporal Wojtowicz, a simple, uneducated man, entirely without polish, wrote in his combat report the epitaph of the day. 'I turned back from this chase but I was returning with a heavy heart, in spite of my victories, for the whole eastern suburb of London seemed to be burning. It was a very sorrowful sight, reminding me of a flight a year ago over Poland, near Lublin; it was the same spectacle.'

'Nobby' Clarke was sitting in a Gosport cinema later that afternoon, when a message for him was flashed on the screen: Return to the aerodrome at once. He was there within ten minutes and his Skua had been wheeled out and was waiting for him, bombed up. The bombs were incendiaries, intended to 'set the sea on fire'. At various points on the south coast, from Beachy Head to Weymouth, fuel tanks had been installed; from them a mass of oil and petrol was to be piped out to sea off the best landing beaches, just before the first wave of the German invasion armada grounded. Clarke, in his Skua, was to dive-bomb the inflammable mixture with incendiaries as the invasion craft entered the area. He was supposed to escape in the smoke and, on the way back, had permission to let his rear-gunner engage any surviving invaders at low level. His solo efforts would be supported by Tiger Moths and other unarmed light aircraft, carrying in newly-fitted racks an inconsiderable load of anti-personnel bombs.

'This is it!' he was told. 'The Jerries are on the way! Get cracking and. light all the points, working from east to west.'

Clarke climbed into the cockpit, the engine fired at once and while it warmed up, he pulled on his helmet and strapped himself in. He took straight off the tarmac into a westerly wind and the setting sun. A climbing turn to the left, undercart retracted, coarse pitch – and as the revs changed he could look down on the waters of the Solent and as far east as Selsey Bill. There was no sign of shipping.

He passed over Selsey, with its flat fields and little villages, its tide-scoured coast. To the west was the place where he had carried out his one practice ignition, scream-ing down vertically, letting go the bomb at 1,500 feet and pulling out. 'The sea erupted with an unheard woomph! which made the aircraft quiver. Almost instantaneously visibility was cut to zero by a black cloud of oily smoke which stunk like hell. Anyone afloat in that inferno would certainly have recognized the similarity . . .'

Ready now to carry out the operation in earnest, he flew eastward to Littlehampton, and was then recalled. He strained his eyes staring out across the Channel for a sight of the invasion fleet; but there was nothing – only the sea, grey after sunset, and the white surf stark in the fading light.

The bombing of London had convinced the Govern-ment that invasion was imminent and units in the threat-ened areas were warned to that effect; in some places the church bells were rung. At Southampton, the Home

Guard at the Supermarine factory were told that the enemy was landing in the Portsmouth area and that they were to defend the works at all costs. Mr E. C. Cooper went out through the darkened streets to call at the homes of some of the men who had not turned up. He was knocking hard at one door, when it gave way completely and fell in – to reveal nothing but bomb ruins, the front wall of the house being the only part of it standing. But most people were not aware that an invasion was supposed to be taking place. The events of that night, however, were later to be a rich source of myth and legend. There were tales that the sea *had* been set on fire (which could not be true, because Clarke was the pilot who would have done it, and he confirms that he did so once only, as a practice), and that charred corpses had drifted ashore. I was not even woken up that night, but I heard two different stories and noted them in my diary at the time. 'Two persons vouched for Story A – Invasion attempted, transports sunk right and left, 20,000 Germans drowned. (I see that I did not believe this, on the grounds that if fifteen Germans had been drowned in the Channel, the Ministry of Information would have added two or three noughts and announced it, but they had said nothing.) According to Story B, however, it had all been a silly scare – a destroyer had passed close to a buoy at Spithead and set it ringing, this had been heard on shore at Gosport, and some idiot had promptly rung the church bells.'

In a sense, some idiot had.

Across the Channel, the German preparations for an invasion had exactly that air of unreality and amateurishness as the British preparations to resist them; naturally enough, as both were hurriedly improvised affairs. Paul Weitkus had been given invasion tasks for his gruppe. The first, which was practised as a battalion-strength exercise, was to lay smoke screens round invasion barges. The troops had no Mae Wests, and thought they might need them, so they collected empty tins and tied those on to themselves; additionally, said Weitkus, 'they were so seasick that they could have been killed off with fly-swatters'.

Weitkus had not been told what the overall plan was, nor could he assess the effectiveness of the Rhine barges in which the soldiers were going to cross; but he knew the British navy was intact – he had seen it at Dunkirk operating on the Luftwaffe's doorstep – and that boded ill for an invasion attempt. His second task, timed for when the troops would be well established ashore and beginning to advance on London, was to cut the electricity grid carried on pylons between Bristol and London; they had tried this out, trailing cables behind the aircraft, and it worked well in practice, although they never did it in fact.

As darkness had fallen on 7 September, the first of 247 bombers had crossed the coast, heading for the enormous beacon of burning dockland. All night the bombs rained down on London, adding to the fires kindled by the day bombers. Liverpool had been hard to identify and much of the bomb-load had been wasted; but London, because of its sheer size and its river, could hardly be missed. Now, moreover, the actual target – the docks – was brilliantly illuminated. For the people who lived in dockland this was the first night of many nights of terror; but the rest of London was as yet hardly affected.

On 8 September the Sunday newspapers, printed in London, arrived late in the provinces ÷ but they arrived. The BBC was putting out news bulletins saying that 400 people had been killed and 1,400 wounded. Londoners were dazed by the extent of the calamity, all the more so since they had not been led to expect it; momentarily, the world seemed to have come to an end. That feeling came over quite clearly in the announcer's tones, but later in the day the same bulletin was being read differently, in the normal passionless manner.

From now on, until the end of the month, the main weight of the daylight battle would be directed across Kent and Sussex to London, with smaller forces in the west endeavouring to reduce the remaining aircraft factories to rubble. The switch to new targets had given Fighter Command a much-needed breathing space to rebuild its battered bases and strained control system.

At Biggin Hill, 92 Squadron came in to replace No. 79, sent away to rest. Alan Wright was still with them; they rarely had a Squadron Leader, having them shot down one after the other, and were usually led in action by Flight Lieutenant Brian Kingcome. Kingcome was not interested in the 'ace' conception fostered by the press; anyone who wasted time trying to confirm a 'kill' or hung on unnecessarily to a damaged bomber was quite simply not doing his job. Split them up with a quick head-on attack from a high position, was his method; 'continuous and unremitting performance' his record, according to Bill Igoe. 11 Group were now trying to use Wings of two squadrons – the 'train'; when Kingcome was 'driving the train' or simply leading 92 Squadron, he inclined to ignore the controller's instructions to go south and meet the enemy direct. That might mean an attack at the same level or, worse, an attack from the rear, with the bombers' guns in front and the 109s coming down behind. Instead, he turned north and flew away from the enemy, then turned and came back, gaining height all the time, so that he was poised high up ready to take the squadron down in a vertical dive on the bombers from head on. That would split up at least a portion of them before the fighters could interfere.

'As soon as they saw you coming, you could see the wings of some aircraft wobbling, occasionally a collision,' he said. 'I don't blame them, I've been in a bomber when a mock attack has been made by a fighter. Usually, we'd get in one good attack on the bombers, probably demoralizing them, and then, in two cases out of three, there would be fighter trouble. As the battle went on, they became more and more reluctant to come down and engage – but some exceptions were keen.'

92 Squadron were a relaxed, rather scruffy crowd of pilots, with a brilliant record in the air (in contrast to another squadron to surface appearances perfect, with the polish and discipline of the Brigade of Guards and a mediocre record in action). Sartorially, they affected cravats, predominantly red, and it may have been the 92 Squadron pilots whom the crews of *Kampfgeschwader* 2 referred to as the 'Red Pullovers', who seemed to be wearing something red at the neck and specialized in the high-speed head-on from-above attack.

They went into their first action of the Battle of Britain on 9 September, the previous day having been quiet, and had a sharp lesson in survival. Six of their Spitfires were between Canterbury and Margate on a course to intercept bombers, coming in for London, when they were bounced by a staffel of the 109s which were now flying in small groups ahead of the bombers, behind the bombers, and on both flanks. Two pilots baled out, wounded, and Alan Wright collected a burst which smashed the reflector sight a few inches from his head. Some people made up their minds that the orthodox, inflexible way of doing things was no good.

On 11 September the big formations came to London again. 92 Squadron put in their attack, and then every pilot was on his own. Wright found himself quite alone, looking down on a *Valhalla*, possibly 200 bombers and fighters in all, advancing steadily against the capital. Quite apart from the fighters, the intensity of the fire power which the bombers could concentrate on a single attacking fighter was enormous. Wright hesitated. He had been in action already and had fired his guns; if he ignored so many enemies, no one would ever know about it, let alone blame him. But he still had ammunition left and he ought to attack. How then? Get in and get out quickly, seemed the answer, and pick a bomber with plenty of room behind it, so that when he broke away downwards there would be no risk of collision with the next astern. Wright turned the Spitfire over on its back and dived 5,000 feet into the German formation.

His target was a Dornier, which he hit and may possibly have brought down; then he pulled up with all the speed of the dive behind him, and found a lame Heinkel being attacked by other fighters over East Grinstead. He joined them in finishing it off.

'I have often thought about this incident since,' he said. 'A fighter pilot is very independent and for most of the battle he fights on his own. He must know what is expected of him and the standard must be the highest attainable. If this is so, and I think it was in those days, then even the imaginative and maybe the nervous individual will do well. It struck me later on, how many fighters were always finishing off the lame duck, the bomber that had to fall back from the main force. It was wrong, really. True, no crippled bomber should be allowed to get home, but there were often more fighters after it than necessary. The real reason was not lack of sportsmanship, nor was it sadism; it was just having to attack, and naturally taking the easy meat. No one had thought to instruct us to use more discretion in choosing our target; if they had, I have no doubt the advice would have been followed, with more bombers destroyed.'

When the bombers were returning over Kent, 303 Squadron, paired as a Wing with 229 Squadron, intercepted, the latter going for the Dorniers and Heinkels, the Poles climbing towards the 109s which had already started to come down. After the dog-fight had scattered them, Pilot Officer Lokuciewski tore for the coast where he circled round waiting for a target; it came, in the shape of a Dornier which he put into the sea. He was last heard of driving a taxi in Warsaw, after five years in a Communist prison and four years in a German POW camp, with an interlude as CO of 303 Squadron. Corporal Wojtowicz, who had been saddened at the sight of burning London four days before, was shot down and killed in defence of the capital that afternoon, falling very close to a 109 which he had shot down near Westerham. It must have been an epic battle against odds, for the local Fire Brigade took the trouble to write to the squadron, describing the manner of his death as 'magnificent'.

Synchronized with the main assault on London – the blow to the jaw – was an attack on aircraft factories at Southampton, the close-range jab to the kidneys. At the factory itself there was no advance warning. A small force of bombers, probably only a staffel, entered England to the east of Portsmouth and then turned 90 degrees and flew west to Southampton along the back of Portsdown Hill. When I saw them there they were unusually low and already in line-astern formation, that is, each machine was to bomb individually; and they were only a few minutes' flying time from the target. I heard the pop-pop-pop of cannons, mingled with machine-gun fire, and a big twin-tailed monoplane at the rear of the formation, probably a 110, banked away to engage something.

At Eastleigh airport, just north of Southampton, a foreman of the Supermarine factory, Mr Nigel Johnson, heard the sirens, ran outside – and saw a crowd of German aircraft 100 feet up over the top of the brand new, four-bay aircraft factory being erected for Cunliffe Owen and due to be officially opened in a few days' time by Lord Beaverbrook. A single Bofors crackled from a corner of the airport and a company of the Hampshire Regiment blazed away enthusiastically with rifles and Lewis guns, while workers from Supermarine and Cunliffe Owen tried to take shelter in the few seconds available, or like Mr Johnson, simply watched, fascinated. Before the men could get clear, the bombs had detonated with maximum effect on the new factory, making Lord Beaverbrook's journey unnecessary. Three of the four bays collapsed and the other was damaged. The tragedy was that men had been working in them at the time.

I visited Eastleigh a few days later, and found that echoes of the tragedy still lingered. 'The bays of the factory looked like the broken-backed carcases of burned-out airships, a tangle of silver girders lying on the grass. There was a kind of raw tension there. Fifty-four names on the official list of killed and real total nearer 70, grumbled an old man I talked to. A terrible thing, he said, that the men had to keep working during raids. And no interference with the bombers either, they just did what they liked. Some people were missing still, and of others only an arm or a leg had been found. As I walked on I overheard two women discussing bitterly how the men had died in agony there. They were blaming the lack of warning and the government. It was the first time that I had come upon bitterness against the government, after a raid.'

A few hours later, the Prime Minister was on the air, warning of invasion. 'Several hundreds of self-propelled barges are moving down the coasts of Europe . . . convoys of merchant ships in tens and dozens are being moved through the Straits of Dover into the Channel . . . There are now considerable gatherings of shipping . . . all the way from Hamburg to Brest . . . If this invasion is to be tried at all, it does not seem it can be long delayed . . . Therefore we must regard the next week or so as a very important period in our history. It ranks with the days when the Spanish Armada was approaching the Channel . . . or when Nelson stood between us and Napoleon's Grand Army at Boulogne . . .'

The preliminary condition, of German air superiority over the threatened area, was well on the way to being established. The losses in the air fighting on 11 September were 29 British fighters and only 25 German bombers and fighters. If the invasion was to take place on 21 September, then the decision to sail on that date had to be made on this day, the 11th, to allow the German Navy ten days in which to sweep the British minefields barring the way across and to lay their own mine barrages on both flanks of the projected beachhead, which they could not do until the superior British naval forces had been driven out of the Channel. On the 11th the decision was taken to wait until the 17th – ten days before the last possible date for invasion – and to see if in that short space of time the Luftwaffe could both gain air superiority and then exploit it to a sufficient extent as to deny the Channel to British warships. This is to simplify, to a certain extent, for not everyone on the German side realized what would happen if the minesweeping and mine-laying programme was not fully carried out and if the Royal Navy could still operate in the Channel; but the German Admirals knew. The Luftwaffe had six days left in which to succeed in both tasks; if they succeeded after that, the victory won could not be put to practical use in 1940.

Until 6 September the invasion ports had been empty, but after that date they began to fill with shipping, mainly barges, which offered a close-range target to Bomber

Command. On the night of the 14th, Squadron Leader
Oxley took off from Lindholme in Yorkshire. After an
hour and a half he saw ahead the signs of battle over
Ostend, a cone of searchlights over the port, with a fixed
barrage firing up the beams at British bombers held in the
glow. But beneath the cone was a wall of darkness where
no flak was bursting, so he decided to go through that,
making two runs – the first to identify the target, the
second to bomb it. Letting down to 2,000 feet, he found
the pin-points easy to pick up in the reflected glow from
the searchlights and dropped a flare over the harbour area
where the barges were supposed to be concentrated.
Down it went, burning for ten long seconds.

'It was burning right in the middle of them,' he recalled.
'There were enormous numbers of barges, all tied up to
one another; the area was black with them.'

Round he went and out to sea again to the point where
he would begin the bombing run. They came in steadily
at 2,000 feet, the Hampden heaved as the bombs fell
away, then Oxley was turning and diving out of it for
home. Up in the nose, he could not see the results of the
bombing, but the rear-gunner had a perfect view – the
bomb-load had exploded in the middle of the barge
concentration. Almost every night after that, Oxley was
out to Ostend, to Calais, to Flushing and to Antwerp,
hammering away at the 'Sealion' fleet. 'We felt that there
was not enough night to do as many trips as we wanted –
that was the sense of urgency we had.'

13

Decision Over London

15 September

On 15 September London was twice attacked by mass formations – in the late morning and in the late afternoon. Diversionary targets were shipping in the Thames Estuary, Portland harbour and the main Supermarine factory at Southampton. The Germans flew 328 bomber sorties and 769 fighter sorties; as many of the aircraft flew twice to England that day, the number of aircraft actually used was smaller. The average strength of the bomber gruppen was now down to about twenty aircraft instead of twenty-seven. The strain of continued operations had sharply reduced the number of serviceable aircraft available – for every bomber destroyed a larger number were damaged and temporarily out of action. Fighter serviceability was normally rather higher. On the British side, aircraft reserves were diminishing and more than a quarter of the fighter pilots had been killed or seriously wounded. The struggle on 15 September differed from that of 15 August in that it was waged by air forces both of which had been seriously weakened by four weeks' heavy fighting. After a lull on the 12th and 13th, there had been a resumption of the day attacks on the 14th, which had cost both sides fourteen aircraft. The trend of the battle continued to favour the Germans as far as the exchange rate for fighters was concerned.

The extent of Park's problem can be judged by the nature of the picture developing on the radar screens and being collated at his headquarters on the morning of 15 September. One track is fairly easy to read – the normal morning down-Channel reconnaissance flight to check on shipping, probably one bomber with fighter escort. There is a large build-up above the German bases in Pas de Calais – obviously the bomber formations are circling slowly and being joined by the fighters, but they have not begun to move off yet and although the obvious threat is to London their allotted targets could just as easily be the Sector Stations; until they have crossed the coast and are being tracked and reported by the Observer Corps, this will not become clear – and they could even be a bluff – a mass of Ju. 87s or 110s, or even 109s. In fact, it is the main raid and its target is London. But there is also a force out over the North Sea, composition unknown – it could turn in and attack the Thames Estuary or the aerodromes to the north, or it could be a shipping strike which, in fact, it is. Then, in the south and in the south-west, other forces begin to appear out in the Channel at the limit of radar range – one or both could be a stuka diversion, but just as easily one or both could be a threat to the surviving aircraft factories, some of which lie uncomfortably near the coast. Until they arrive at the coast, nothing can be known for certain. It is imperative to decide early which are the real threats, because at least twenty minutes must be allowed in order to get the fighters into the air and up to a reasonable height; if caught under the Germans, while still climbing, they will risk heavy losses at the hands of the escort and will in any case be ineffective against the bombers. And Park's force is too small to enable him to be strong everywhere. With a wealth of scientific 'magic' at his disposal, he is still in the position of a Marlborough or Wellington – forced to guess at what lies 'on the other side of the hill'.

Neither his superiors, nor his pilots, not even the watchers on the ground, could easily judge whether he did well or ill; only his opponents were in a position to know exactly how much their plans were frustrated. The testimony of the Germans is overwhelming, although they tend to give the credit to the radar (which was primitive) rather than to the commander who interpreted what it said. Their view was summed up by Generalmajor Kurt Bertram von Döring who, for a part of the time, was virtually Park's opposite number:

'The German fighters were superior in numbers, but English radar evened up this disparity. Sometimes we were forced to get a Jagdgeschwader airborne sixty minutes before the bombers attacked – the fighters taking over from each other in relays – either to provide continuous protection to the bombers when they were penetrating deeply inland, or simply to distract the RAF fighters from an attack coming shortly elsewhere. But somehow the RAF were always there.'

Of course, often enough the Germans were in sufficient force to sweep aside the opposition, but nevertheless the radar did enable one British fighter to do the work of two or three German fighters by being in the right place at the right time. But because the radar was inaccurate as to height and numbers and because it told him nothing about the composition of the enemy force, he now instituted the technique of 'spotting'. On 15 September Alan Wright twice performed this duty. He was to take off early, in advance of the raid, and watch it come in, noting all these points and some others also – if escorted, how it was escorted, and whether it was splitting in order to attack two targets instead of one. Both attempts were failures.

In the morning, he was scrambled too late and saw, not the start of the raid but its end, some bombers and fighters straggling back from London to the coast. In the afternoon, he took off from Hawkinge to carry out this lonely task once more, was vectored incorrectly and met two 109s. His orders were to avoid combat but there was no avoiding these, they were climbing up after him; so Wright dived into them from 28,000 feet and when they broke away followed one down. The 109 was extremely fast in the dive but Wright's Spitfire had already picked up speed; he tied on to it, firing, over Dungeness and when he eased back on the stick promptly blacked himself out; he recovered consciousness, upside down, over Maidstone – thirty miles away. The Spitfire, which becomes tail-heavy in a dive, had pulled out of its own accord; the Messerschmitt had the opposite characteristic, and Wright doubted whether his opponent ever did pull out.

Later, a flight from 92 Squadron were based at Hawkinge purely for 'spotting' purposes and eventually 91 Squadron took over the task. Meanwhile, 12 Group had been experimenting with tactics. As their function was to act as reserve to 11 Group, and in particular to guard the Sector Stations north of the Thames when all Park's squadrons had been committed, they had more time available in which to mass a number of squadrons into a formidable Wing, never in lesser strength than a jagdgruppe of three dozen fighters. Even so, however, the time taken to assemble the 'Duxford Wing' or 'Balbo' (as it was sometimes called, after the Italian leader of mass formations), led frequently to late interceptions, as it had on 7 September, when it was first in action at three-squadron strength. It now consisted of no fewer than five squadrons, two equipped with Spitfires and three with the slower Hurricanes. The Hurricanes were those of 224 Squadron, led by Douglas Bader who also led the 'Balbo', the Czechs of 310 Squadron, and, since 11 September, the Poles of 302 Squadron, led by Satchell. They were based at Duxford and two satellite fields. Air Vice-Marshal Leigh-Mallory, who commanded 12 Group, inclined to the policy of giving his fighting leaders their head, as they were more closely in touch with the battle, and the whole conception owed a great deal to Douglas Bader, already famous as the world's only legless fighter pilot. Satchell recalled Bader, on one occasion, stumbling to his tin feet and replying to Leigh-Mallory with, 'You appointed me to lead the Wing, sir. I'll lead it my own way, or not at all.'

Bader's basic idea was simple – the German fighters were flying in big formations, we ought to fly in big formations, too. Leigh-Mallory, who cared more for winning the air battle than guarding ground targets, agreed – and the disadvantage of the Wing, the time taken to form up, was accepted. According to Satchell, it took about ten minutes to get from the 'scramble' to 2,000 feet over Duxford and climbing hard. If there had been no need to rendezvous over Duxford some of the squadrons, particularly the Spitfires, could have got into action earlier, intercepting the bombers before they reached the target. On the other hand, the fighter exchange rate would have been favourable to the Germans, whereas the actual losses of the Duxford Wing were very light. Park was not in principle opposed to big Wings, he had used them himself during the Dunkirk operation – sometimes three squadrons, known as the 'Grice Fighter Force'; but he did not favour them in the utterly different circumstances of the Battle of Britain, in which he had to react to specific threats and the methods of the fighter 'sweep' were inappropriate.

He expressed himself forcibly after the war:

'On a few dozen occasions when I had sent every available squadron of No. 11 Group to engage the main enemy attack as far forward as possible, I called on No. 12 Group to send a couple of squadrons to defend a fighter airfield or other vital targets which were threatened by outflanking and smaller bomber raids. Instead of sending two squadrons quickly to protect the vital target, No. 12 Group delayed while they despatched a large Wing of four or five squadrons which wasted valuable time . . . consequently they invariably arrived too late to prevent the enemy bombing the target.

On scores of days I called on No. 10 Group on my right for a few squadrons to protect some vital target. Never on any occasion can I remember this group failing to send its squadrons promptly to the place requested, thus saving thousands of civilian lives and also the naval dockyards of Portsmouth, the port of Southampton and aircraft factories.'[2]

A lively, sometimes embittered, controversy developed, the 11 Group pilots criticizing the 'Balbo' on two additional grounds – that it was so large as to be unwieldy and also too conspicuous. Mutual recriminations soon passed the boundary of purely technical discussion. Often enough, during September, after a day of hard fighting in the 11 Group area, 12 Group would be rung up with the taunt, 'Where was the Duxford Wing today?' The factual answer usually was – going up and down the Barking Patrol Line and hearing on R/T the babble of voices from a stiff fight going on somewhere south and being unable to join in, even by disobeying orders, because they did not know where the fight was and controllers were forbidden to handle them south of the Thames.

Satchell's logbook contains eleven times the entry '*Wing Patrols – No Action*' and only three times the entry '*Wing Action*' for the period 11–25 September, when mass assault after mass assault was being made on London. Two of these memorable actions were concentrated into the space of a single day – 15 September. They took place in the forbidden area, south of the Thames, after the targets had been bombed. In an unpublished history of the squadron Satchell wrote, of the morning action: 'We were a bit late arriving over London . . .' and of the afternoon action: 'Again we arrived at the scene of battle

<hr />

[2] *New Zealand Herald*, 9 September, 1952.

late . . .' On the other hand, the effect of five squadrons of fighters hitting the Germans simultaneously was certainly impressive.

At 11.30 A.M. 11 Group had eleven squadrons airborne, mostly in pairs, on either side of the approaching German formations; to the north, the five squadrons of the Duxford Wing were coming south en masse, and one squadron from 10 Group was coming up from the west. The Germans had therefore to fly through what was virtually an ambuscade, with the Duxford Wing poised to give the coup de grâce.

92 Squadron, followed by No. 72, put in the first attack, over Canterbury, shaking the incoming formations by plunging into them head on; thereafter, there were running fights all the way up to London as the 11 Group Wings of two squadrons came successively into action. Steady toll was taken of the bombers, as the fighters whined through the *Valhallas*, crippled machines falling away below or lagging behind; in the bombers that still thundered on there were many gun positions unmanned and dead or wounded men in the cabins. Much of the bombing was ragged, and as the shaken formations turned away they flew straight into the five massed squadrons of the Duxford Wing.

The three Hurricane squadrons – Bader's, Satchell's and the Czechs' – were flying close together in normal 'sections line-astern' formation; the two Spitfire squadrons – No. 19 and No. 611 – were a little apart and up-sun. As they flew south they saw the German formation ahead of them and above; it promptly went into a turn, having apparently unloaded on the target, and reversed course to go home. As the Germans swept slowly round, the 'Balbo' was still gaining height, and by the time the enemy were head-on to them, they had climbed above. As the Duxford Wing wheeled in to the attack, Satchell saw 109s streaming down on the leading British squadron, which was Bader's, and heard Bader shout, 'Weigh-in, everyone for himself!' The whirling dog-fight which resulted left the Poles of 302 Squadron still in formation, still unengaged, with the way held open for them to go straight at the bombers, numbering, thought Satchell, about 130.

The Poles roared in from the beam and Satchell picked a Dornier; the rear-gunner stopped firing almost at once and then the port engine burst into flames. Satchell nosed in close to have a look – and saw that what he had taken to be some kind of red light in the cabin was actually an inferno of fire in the fuselage. He broke away, seeing four other German aircraft on the way down, and joined a gaggle of Hurricanes and Spitfires attacking a lagging group of five Dorniers. Opening fire, he set the starboard engine of a bomber smoking and caused the rear gun to point up in the air – then there was a terrific clang in the cockpit, a sharp, infuriating pain in his left leg, caused by splinters, and a 109 swept overhead.

Although the splinter wounds were not serious, he was out of ammunition, so Satchell returned to base. Four of his Hurricanes did not come back from the fight in the morning. One was at Hornchurch with a holed petrol tank, another had crash-landed, and from two others the pilots had baled out. One had hit the tailplane when he jumped and had broken two bones in his foot, the other had not pulled the ripcord at all – possibly he also had struck the tailplane, with more serious results.

The afternoon attack came in the same way as the first and was met in the same way as the first. The fighter versus fighter combats were particularly hard-fought and vicious. The tired German pilots were meeting squadrons which previously had hardly been engaged and were thoroughly fresh; it seemed to them as if the British had conjured new squadrons out of the ground. Sweeping far ahead of the bombers, leading the assault, were Galland's fighters; they were to arrive at the target first, clear the sky of British fighters and remain above the target while the bombers unloaded. 'Our mission was "free-hunt" on the target,' he recalled. 'I had a ten-minute fight, without success, against Hurricanes and Spitfires – and in air fighting ten minutes is a long time. Then I saw two Hurricanes 1,500 feet below; I got one of them in flames over the Thames.'

'Again we arrived at the scene of battle late,' wrote Satchell, 'but there were large numbers of bombers scattered about in all sorts of formations all over the sky and also a number of 109s with them. These 109s attacked us as soon as we arrived on the scene and we had to break up before we could get into position to attack the main mass of bombers as a Wing.' Engaged by the escort, the Duxford Wing split up, but were later able in little groups to attack the broken-up bomber formations and chase them out to sea. One of the Poles was savagely determined to score a 'confirmed' because a claim he had put in for the morning action had not been allowed, as he had not actually seen it crash. So when he attacked a Dornier in the afternoon he set both engines on fire and then began to blaze away at the fuselage from just astern. The crew began to bale out hurriedly and so close to the burning bomber was the Hurricane, that one man went straight into its propellor, smashing the blades to pieces and breaking the radiator. The Pole force-landed at North Weald in a Hurricane covered with the ghastly remains of the wretched German airman.

In addition to the five 12 Group squadrons there were ten squadrons from 11 Group engaged over London, and others elsewhere; and two reinforcing squadrons came in from 10 Group. One of these latter was 238 Squadron, led by Blake, now a Squadron Leader, and based at

Middle Wallop, where they had arrived on 10 September. They replaced 234 Squadron, which had lost nine pilots in a single sortie, and was withdrawn to rest. Two days after settling in at Middle Wallop Blake had added a reconnaissance Ju. 88 to his bag in a very brief encounter over Brooklands. 'I just went up behind him and pulled the trigger.' On the afternoon of the 15th he was again over Brooklands, this time leading the whole squadron at 22,000 feet.

Flying towards West Malling, he saw a formation of eighteen Heinkels, in vics of three, coming back from London. They were on the left and ahead and about to fly in front of him. Blake decided on a stern attack, turned to port to let the bombers go by, then turned in behind them and came down with a rush from dead astern in a perfectly timed manoeuvre. As the Hurricanes straightened up out of their turn they went through the Heinkels in formation, two sections firing almost simultaneously from very close range, sixty to seventy yards. Virtually at the same moment, the three Heinkels in the last vic blew up.

Blake, in the leading section, went straight through the Heinkels and found himself almost on top of another group of bombers, Dorniers this time, going in towards London. He flashed through this formation, finishing off his ammunition on one of the rearmost bombers, with tracer bullets from the whole formation streaking at him.

Oil began to come back from the nose of the Hurricane and when Blake opened the throttle smoke and fumes blew into his face; at 2,000 feet the engine seized up. But there was West Malling down below, so he did a circuit and came in, cutting it a bit fine, for he had to give a quick blast of throttle to ease the fighter over the hedge.

A banner of flame forty feet long streamed out instantly

from the damaged engine. Blake cut the throttle, flattened
out and touched down; with the Hurricane still rolling
and, he thought, about to go up in flames, he started to
get out, forgot to disconnect the wireless lead from his
helmet, slipped on the oil-covered wing, and very nearly
strangled himself. As the Hurricane bumped to a stop a
young man and a girl ran out towards it and pulled him
upright. Within sixty seconds, just after his own arrival in
a tremendous sheet of flame, they saw a Heinkel skim-
ming over the boundary, trailing smoke from its engines,
with three Spitfires, some distance behind, blazing away;
but it touched down and rolled to a stop.

The Heinkel was from the formation his squadron had
attacked, so when the Intelligence Officer had arrived,
Blake managed to have a word with the pilot. The
German seemed to be very confident that his country
would win. By the time Blake had reached London, the
nightly 'Blitz' had begun and he walked through the
streets underneath the bombers, carrying his parachute,
to a flat belonging to friends. Their conversation, he
recalled, did not ever mention the possibility of defeat;
the attempt to win the war by bombing London day and
night had been a failure from the start. When he reached
Middle Wallop the following morning, a new Hurricane
was waiting for him. Even at the height of the battle, the
efficiency of squadrons was not hampered by any shortage
of aircraft. Badly damaged fighters were streaming to the
factories and being repaired within an incredibly short
time; but most of the repairs were being carried out at the
aerodromes, RAF teams working under the supervision
of key men detached from the factories for this purpose.

One of the 11 Group squadrons engaged had been No.
66; they had tangled with one of the big formations but
although Flight Lieutenant Oxspring had fired at several
aircraft he could claim no definite result. He was returning
alone from this running fight when, over Rochester, he

saw a lone bomber – a Dornier 17. As Spitfires usually had to take on the 109s, a bomber, and particularly a lone one, was a gift from the gods. He put in two quick attacks, out went the crew, and down went the Dornier – on to a house on the outskirts of Rochester. 'There may have been exaggerations about what happened on 15 September,' he remarked, 'but there was no doubt about that one.' Worried that he might have killed the people in the house, he went to see for himself where it had landed; but the woman and her child who lived there had been in an Anderson shelter, from which they had crawled out unharmed.

Synchronized with the afternoon attack had been an unescorted diversion by *Kampfgeschwader* 55 against Portland, intended to draw the fighters from the main battle; and in the late afternoon, timed to come in shortly after the main battle had ended, *Erprobungsgruppe* 210, equipped with Messerschmitt 110s converted to light, fast bombers, streaked in to bomb the Supermarine factory unopposed.

At the time it occurred, Mr E. C. Cooper, chief draughtsman of Supermarine, was driving back from Northolt after a day spent supervising the work now going on to remedy the defects of the cannon-equipped Spitfires. While the Northolt squadrons had been taking off to give battle to the German bombers roaring up to London, Wing Commander 'Tiny' Vasse had been testing the new installation. The stoppages experienced by 19 Squadron had caused Lord Beaverbrook to set up a small Working Committee, consisting of Air Commodore Roderic Hill, Director of Technical Development, Professor Douglas of the Royal Aeronautical Establishment at Farnborough, Mr 'Bill' Adams, a gun expert from the Royal Armament Establishment at Enfield, and Mr Cooper of Supermarine. This was a typical Beaverbrook move, of the sort which created resentment in some quarters, but got results quickly. Locating the cause of the stoppages was fairly easy.

The Hispano cannon and feed had been designed to fire through the hollow propeller shaft of the Hispano engine, the cartridges being housed in a fifty-round drum mounted above the breech and fed into it by the pressure of a clock type of spring. The force exerted by the spring diminished after a few rounds had been fired; also it had to overcome the friction within the drum. All was well as long as the aircraft was not manoeuvring violently, but when the enormous 'g' pressures of a dog-fight were exerted on the spring, it gave up the struggle; the cannon simply went 'boom-boom' – and stopped. This explained why it had worked against lone reconnaissance machines but had failed in the dog-fights.

What they were working on now, as a complete answer to the problem, was a new type of feed, known as the Châtellerault, two or three prototype models of which had been saved from the collapse of France. It employed the continuous linked belt principle in place of the drum. Mr Cooper's task was to rehash the thin Spitfire wing to take the gun, now mounted upright instead of on its side and fitted with an ammunition tank for the bulky belt of 20-mm slugs. The two inner guns in each wing were removed, and a cannon installed in their place, the two outer guns being retained, giving a mixed armament of two cannons and four machine-guns. This was to prove extremely popular with pilots and its hitting power was only outclassed several years later when RP rockets were introduced. The battle which Mr Cooper and the others were fighting was still in the future, but the present battle was inescapable and often present in the background of their thoughts.

A great new factory at Castle Bromwich, near Birmingham, was being converted on Lord Beaverbrook's orders from the production of bombers to the building of Spitfires, but the bulk of Spitfire production was still concentrated at Southampton, in three factories, and the bulk of Spitfire repair was carried out by another factory at nearby Hamble. A continual stream of battered, bullet-riddled Spitfires passed along the south coast daily to Southampton, to be returned to the squadrons within a few days as good as new. This complex of factories lay almost on the coast, a tempting target for the Luftwaffe, and the homes of the people who worked there lay only a short distance away. That particular aspect did not unduly worry them at first. 'We had a too complimentary opinion of German bombing,' recalled Mr Cooper. 'We thought any place three hundred yards from the factory was safe!' The precision with which Cunliffe Owen had been destroyed five days earlier seemed to bear this out, but the first shock came on 15 September. On the outskirts of Southampton, Mr Cooper was held up by a police barrier. 'You can't go any further,' he was told. *Erprobungsgruppe* 210 had put on a brilliant display over the factory, but their bomb aiming had not matched their flying skill.

Returning from a visit to Eastleigh, I saw the attack from a hill just outside Southampton. 'A siren moaned half-heartedly for an instant. Then the drone of engines. I counted them aloud. Ten. They dived straight down on Southampton without any preliminaries, through a barrage of gunfire, one after the other. My uncle watched the first bomb fall away and then handed the field glasses to me. They had twin rudders, their dives were fast but shallow, and they pulled out at about 2,000 feet. Some soldiers began to pass half-inane, half-defiant remarks about "our ack-ack boys are having fun . . . nothing could live in that barrage", while very quickly and efficiently the

Germans re-formed and disappeared into a cloud. I never saw a better piece of flying – they got into formation like a well-drilled team, in the teeth of the guns. A second formation, which appeared to be of equal size to the first, appeared, slipped down to the attack through the ack-ack smoke, and also retired without loss. Two dense clouds of smoke rose high in the air behind the nearest hill; they were white, tinged with reddish brown – probably brick dust. Then, after it was all over, a solitary Spitfire flew low down towards Portsmouth. The proprietor of a teashop, outside which we were standing, was very outspoken about everything – when no one was listening. When the Germans bombed Eastleigh in daylight, he said, no guns fired, but they blazed away at night without a target; anyone who recognized the strength and ability of the enemy was supposed to want Hitler to win, whereas it was really those who said "Everything's all right, we're doing fine" who were helping him.'

Mr Cooper eventually got through the police cordon to find his own home – and the factory – intact; the bombs had fallen mainly around the railway station nearby.

And so the day ended, just another day of heavy fighting – but not so heavy as in August – with Park's tactics notably successful and the bombers having a much harder time of it; the RAF still fighting, and civilian morale unbroken. That it was also the decisive day no one on the British side could have guessed. The Germans had only two more days left in which to gain air superiority and on both bad weather prevented large-scale operations. On the 17th the final decision had to be made: to order the German Navy to begin the preliminary minesweeping and mine-laying operations which would culminate in invasion ten days later – on 27 September – or to postpone the invasion until the following year.

The decision was recorded in the War Diary of the German Naval Staff on the afternoon of 17 September:

'The enemy air force is still by no means defeated; on the contrary it shows increasing activity. The weather situation as a whole does not permit us to expect a period of calm. The Führer has therefore decided to postpone Operation SEALION indefinitely.'

On the other hand, the Luftwaffe was by no means defeated; it had failed to achieve its objective, but it was not destroyed. Its losses on 15 September were lighter than they had been on 15 August. But they were much heavier than they had been during the first two weeks of September, and it was this abrupt reversal of the trend of victory which made clear beyond doubt that the destruction of Fighter Command was somehow beyond their strength. The actual losses were 52 German bombers and fighters as against 27 British fighters.[3] The Germans believed that they had shot down 78 British aircraft and the British claimed 185 German aircraft, the Duxford Wing alone claiming 48 of them. But the figures, right or wrong, hardly mattered, it was the impression produced on the German pilots and aircrews by the day's fighting which counted. They had been told, and the figures seemed to prove it, that British resistance was weakening to the point of collapse; instead, it was stronger than ever. The fighter pilots, whose losses were not so heavy, nevertheless found the fighting very hard; the bombers, and particularly those formations which had been broken up, had been 'blasted out', as Otto Bechtle put it. One particular staffel which had set out, under strength

[3] The Luftwaffe Operations Map for 15 September shows 50 aircraft lost and two missing. British official histories give the number as 60 lost. They do not give their own bomber losses and therefore the picture is not quite complete.

already, with six aircraft, had come back with two. That night, the crews of *Kampfgeschwader* 2 held a drunken party, half-weeping, half-mocking, as they grieved for their friends who would not come back. Time and again, they had been told that their sacrifices were about to be crowned with victory, and always it receded into the distance. Mutinously and defiantly they sang, 'The steel wings are flashing, Tommy's given us another hiding . . .', a doggerel verse in mockery of the government.

In the bomber messes that night, the 'Red Flag' went up, to mark the RAF victory. This was a Luftwaffe custom, the flag was an actual one, a miniature; when it was hoisted, at the end of a spell of hard drinking, that was the signal for free criticism of Hitler, Göring, the Party, and their superiors generally, without restraint, a kind of psychological safety valve hardly to be understood outside a totalitarian state. As the party warmed up, they burst into a dismal song:

> 'This is the real Bommerlünder,
> Whether you drink it down or sick it up
> It tastes the same – bloody awful.
> It's a contribution from Oberleutnant Kruger,
> Who at the moment is a "retribution" flyer,
> Who usually overshoots the target,
> Which is why his schnapps sticks in our gullet . . .'

And when they finally staggered off to bed, the 'Red Flag' was hauled down, to signify that criticism was ended. Tomorrow, by no means defeated, they would continue the battle.

14

The Fight for the Factories

16–26 September

The German leadership was divided in its opinion about what to do next – call off the whole battle and then attack again with greatly increased forces in the spring of 1941, or go over to night attacks by the entire bomber force with the object of destroying industrial centres and strangling the ports. The decision taken was to continue with the day attacks as long as the autumn weather lasted, with London still the main point of effort both by day and by night – in the hope that there might be a collapse of morale – combined with blows in daylight at the aircraft factories in southern England which were within range of escorted bombers. Although invasion was no longer possible, there was some hope left of victory in 1940.

On the other hand, the selection of London as the main daylight target presented familiar difficulties and, with increasing bad weather, a number of new ones. First, instead of the bomber force being split into small groups attacking a large number of targets over a wide area, they had all to come in together, all too predictably, in a steamroller assault on the capital. Because of the short range of the 109 there was no possibility even of confusing the defence by flying zig-zag courses; they were compelled to go head on at London, the centre of the enemy defence. Second, the increasingly cloudy weather was liable to make the bombers late for their rendezvous with the fighters or to prevent the rendezvous altogether; in which case the fighters, having insufficient fuel to waste in circling over the French coast, would join the first bomber formation they saw, which would be doubly escorted. The proper formation would be unescorted and possibly have either to turn back or, at the most, bomb alternative targets. The bad weather also made it harder for the fighters to keep in touch with the bombers.

Additionally, the fuel margin of the 109 was insufficient to allow for unforeseen contingencies. If the bombers were forced by the defences to fly evasive courses, the situation for the fighters at once became serious. If, as was likely to happen in bad weather, the bombers made an error in navigation, or altered course and either did not or, through bad radio communication, were unable to tell the fighters what was happening, many of the escort would not get home. One formation, which took off from Pas de Calais to raid London at this time, afterwards found itself above the clouds, without sight of the ground, and presumably because of a change of wind direction, flew back to somewhere in the region of the Isle of Wight before getting a fix and turning for Pas de Calais. After two hours' flying and while still over the Channel, the fighters began to run out of fuel; those who had fought the most, and thus used up most fuel, went down first – seven into the sea and five on the French coast.

The next daylight assault on London took place on the afternoon of 18 September. For Leutnant Erich Bodendiek it was his second flight of the day. As Technical Officer of his gruppe, he was testing the first 109 to be equipped with a gear which automatically changed the pitch of the propeller. The morning flight had shown a drop in revs and above 18,000 feet it appeared not to work at all; it was also impossible to disconnect it in an emergency and change over to the mechanical gear. During his second flight, which was over Kent with a formation of eighteen 109s, they emerged from cloud at the same time as a much larger number of Spitfires which were above them and to one side – obviously a radar-directed interception. The 109s promptly turned in under the British fighters and vanished into the cloud, all except Bodendiek, whose aircraft lagged behind.

As there was no alternative except to climb hard for the cloud, he carried on, drawing very slowly away from his pursuers. But the Spitfires had the better rate of climb, so they began to climb above him, then used their height to gain speed in a dive, firing at him from the bottom of the dive. There were a number of them doing this, going up and down like roller coasters astern of him, but without scoring any hits. At last, one Spitfire dived past Bodendiek, carried on down, then pulled up underneath him and, standing on its tail, fired a shot-gun burst into the path of the Messerschmitt. The 109 flew right through it, and exploded.

Bodendiek went over the side, his face and hands burned by the flames, pulling the ripcord at well over 20,000 feet somewhere in the area of Tonbridge. He took some forty minutes to come down, drifting rapidly with a storm, but in the wrong direction; it took him back towards the coast and then along it, so that he was only some two miles out from Folkestone when he hit the sea. A coastguard vessel fished him out of the water and handed him over to a Royal Artillery unit, where he was treated as a spy.

In his pockets they found English money, obtained in Guernsey where he had been stationed a few weeks before. They refused to believe that he was, as he claimed to be, an officer in the Luftwaffe. Where was his uniform? He was dressed in a white pullover and a pair of trousers. The only single item of uniform he had worn at take-off had been his flying boots, lost when he baled out. They handed him over to the RAF, who were also deeply suspicious for an hour or two, although their pilots too were inclined to dress in just this casual fashion.

Meanwhile the bombers had ploughed through 11 Group to London and met the Duxford Wing once more. There were more aircraft visible that afternoon than I had ever seen in my life before,' wrote Satchell. 'Two enormous formations, each of at least 150 bombers and probably about 500 fighters – 109s and 110s stacked in layers above. It was a most impressive sight.[1] There were, of course, 60 fighters in our "Balbo" and I could see numerous other fighters about.'

Leaving the two Spitfire squadrons up-sun, to take care of the escort if they attempted to interfere, Bader led the three Hurricane squadrons up to the bombers from behind and above. When exactly above, Bader gave the word to go, and they dived simultaneously into the *Valhalla*, firing as they came. Three dozen Hurricanes hurtled through the mass of aircraft, some of them so close to a bomber that they had to put their noses down beyond the vertical and pass through partly inverted, and some skidding sideways with a violent kick of the rudder. The bomber Satchell fired at plunged like a shot duck out of the formation, falling bomber and diving fighter keeping company as they tore downwards; when he pulled out, the bomber was still going down vertically and above him the whole German formation was scattered all over the sky in ones and twos. Satchell flew with the Duxford Wing on five other occasions during the month, but no interceptions resulted.

All the German hopes of an immediate decision now rested on London. No great city had ever before been repeatedly bombed by day and by night; every night the

[1] The British history records that only about 70 bombers attacked London, in three waves, so that these estimates are too high. A big formation always looks at least twice as large as it really is.

bombs fell on London, and every day when the weather permitted the *Valhallas* surged up to the capital. The British press was calling it the 'Blitz' and proclaiming that 'London can take it.' But was this really so? The Germans had no means of knowing.

I stayed in London on the 20th and 21st, my first visit since the raids had begun two weeks before. 'I made pages of notes of what I saw and heard, but what it boiled down to was not a "Blitz" at all, with its echoes of rapid action; rather, what was taking place was the Siege of London. That was the atmosphere and that was the physical effect of the attacks.

'In the suburbs there was as yet no damage to speak of – about one bomb per quarter mile – in the central area about one bomb per street, and only in the dock area had there been concentrated attacks. Generally, the effect was of dislocation, not devastation. I tried to telephone – it was out of order. Streets were blocked, partially by bombs that had gone off, completely by those that hadn't. At the late rush hour there were hundred-yard-long queues at bus-stops – and police were halting private cars and forcing the drivers to take as many passengers as they could. The gas was cut off in some areas. Cinemas were open, but it was not advisable to go to one in the West End as, owing to disorganization of transport, one would have to walk all the way back. We decided to go to a cinema near my friends' flat, off Sloane Square. The performance began nightly at about 8 o'clock, with the first bomb five minutes later, I was told. And so it was.

'The warning was announced from the stage at 7.55 P.M. and at 8.00 P.M. exactly the first bomb shook the building. No one left the cinema because, of course, the routine was known, expected and discounted; but the cinema closed early, at 9.00 P.M. We went back to the flat and boiled tea on an emergency spirit lamp, which took ages, and there was no milk either. Curiously, although this was a "terror" attack, my friends did not see it as such – they believed that every bomb that fell in London was of military value, by the dislocation it caused to the life of the capital, and it was clear they thought it their duty to carry on unshaken. What they were facing was not one short, sharp attack, over and done with in a minute or so, but a steady, monotonous bombing stretching into the future as far as they could see. The Germans had not beaten us, but unless we beat them, what lay ahead was an endless night of endurance, with no foreseeable time limit set to their ordeal.

'They had their own particular German, they called him "Pumpernickel", who simply flew up and down, letting go a bomb at intervals; sometimes they referred to him as "No. 74", or whatever bus route it was he appeared to be taking. After a little while the clouds in the east began to glow a dull red from two fires, and then the kettle boiled. Two business girls lived in the flat and if one happened to be away, the other usually slept on the landing, so that, if injured, she stood a chance of crawling down the stairs for help. They were still a bit upset, because the previous night they had to listen to the screaming of injured people trapped under a wrecked house; but at the same time there was an indefinable light-heartedness, springing perhaps from the feeling, "Why take care for tomorrow, for tomorrow may never come?" It was a curiously happy atmosphere. "If a bomb blows this flat to pieces, our moral reputations will be blown to pieces with it!" they told me, as I was shooed off to a sofa.

'I think Londoners felt that London now really was the centre of the world, that it was good to be there, and still alive in the morning. The attitude was even more marked in East London. Next day, I toured the West End first.

There had been a recent hit on Buckingham Palace, for
the windows were out and there were two craters in front;
at Marble Arch a very big crater, smelling of drains, and
a smashed shelter, probably the tomb of the sixty people
I had heard about, and a bus had lost its top deck; a very
big row of stores in Oxford Street was still burning, shop
window dummies piled on the pavement, piles of glass,
hoses, and curiously quiet crowds moving slowly past.
Apparently the AFS, who used to be known as the
"Afraid of Foreign Servicemen", have become popular
heroes, now that the Auxiliary Fire Service are standing
up and dying under the Luftwaffe's bombs.

'I took a bus into the City and another along East India
Dock Road into the heart of East London, where the
bomb damage was conspicuous. A constant running fire
of commentary came from the bus passengers, as each bit
of fresh damage was passed. "That's yesterday's." "'E did
that larst night." "They 'it Lizzie's little place – just darn
there – got the front page of the *Chronicle*." No fear, no
hate, they talked about it as eagerly as the chances of
their favourite team. Often, the rubble was topped by
defiant Union Jacks, and there was one rather pathetic
sign on a fire-gutted mission hall for the poor – "Light
and Warmth Inside".

'I noticed one man walking with a mattress strapped to
his back, probably on the way to a tube shelter for the
night, and some others were carrying suitcases, apparently
bombed out; I saw only two vans making removals from
undamaged houses. A crowd was huddled under a railway
arch and others were hurrying to join them, although it
was several hours before the nightly performance was due
to start; few appeared to be British. The man on the seat
beside me, obviously bursting to inform an outsider,
began to talk about the bombing.

'The dockers should – must – carry on during air raid

warnings. Did soldiers knock off when there was shell-fire? he asked. Only one wharf left, for discharging wheat, it must be kept in action. The men – he was one of them – were willing to work through the raids, provided they got steel helmets and transport home, so they didn't have to walk three miles, after a hard day, under the shrapnel. There should be fire look-outs on duty all night. Incendiaries had done nine-tenths of the damage – 10,000 tons of sugar burnt, and only two sugar warehouses left standing. And he grumbled about the foreigners being able to leave the East End, while they had to stay and stick it out. Had I seen that lot under the railway bridge?'

The pre-war prophecies of panic – an article of faith with official planners – had gone very badly wrong, and got lost somewhere in the East End. The factor they had forgotten to take into account was a certain resilience in the population. Their imaginary public had fled, bursting aside police cordons. The real Londoners hung on, cleared away the rubble, swept aside the broken glass, repaired the railway lines, the gas mains, the telephones, and quietly fought back, but with a bitter tongue for any signs of lagging or irresolution on the part of the Government. This docker's suggestions must have represented the general feeling, for they were subsequently adopted throughout the country, as the provincial cities also began to receive the same treatment; nevertheless, it was some months before a system of 'fire-watchers' was brought into being.

On 24 September Mr E. C. Cooper was having lunch at the Woolston works of Supermarine with an American; very soberly dressed in a black morning coat, he was a Beaverbrook representative sent down to get production really moving. What both the British and German aircraft industries thought of then as mass production was in fact nothing of the kind, as they realized later, when they really got into their stride. They were lunching on a balcony high up on the office block, when the roof spotter came running in. 'Get out! Get out!' Then they heard the roar of diving aircraft.

I was watching from a distance through field glasses. 'We heard gunfire, the menacing rumble of aircraft coming in over Gosport . . . and there they were, a lot of little specks . . . one, two . . . three, four . . . five, six, eight . . . and more behind that. 109s, they're diving, one after the other. Then bomb after bomb. Bursts of AA fire stretching along the sky for about eight miles. Then the sirens sounded . . .'

There was no time to get out of the office block at Woolston, let alone reach shelter. One man flattened himself against the wall, maintaining afterwards that that was the safest thing to do. Another crawled under the table and Mr Cooper, leaping up, had to jump over him.

The workers in the factory alongside did not have to run down flights of stairs to get outside, and they managed to stream out on to the road and start to run for the shelters which were some distance away. 'The four-minute mile was then unknown, but plenty must have done it in three-and-a-half,' recalled Mr Leonard Gooch, now Production Manager.

No one from Woolston reached the shelters before the bombs struck. Those few who did came from the Itchen works of the factory, which was further down the road, directly opposite the shelters, and about a minute's walk away. The leaders actually reached the shelters, with behind them a great crowd pressing underneath a railway arch which separated the road and the factory from the large fields in which the half-buried shelters lay, looking like enormous graves. Seconds later, that was what they became in fact.

The bombs whistled over the top of the Woolston works and pitched further down the road, opposite the Itchen works, on to the shelters, on to the crowds running for shelter, and on to the railway arch – which collapsed on top of the men and women struggling through below. Mr Gooch was in a shelter which was not hit, but merely shuddering from the bomb detonations all around, and filling with dust. There were girls and men there, and also some girls from an ENSA concert party which had been visiting them. Someone started singing, and everyone took it up, amid the whistling of bombs and the roar of diving planes. Mr Cooper, looking out from the window of the Woolston works, had his last sight of the American – he was going away down the road and, in his morning coat, he resembled exactly a large, black beetle.

Water and gas were cut off, the First Aid Post had been hit, and the casualty list was very long; but no structural damage had been done to either of the factories. They began to pile the bodies inside the wrecked First Aid Post, using it as an improvised mortuary; there was annoyance at the lack of warning, anger about the complete absence of RAF fighters, and a sharp increase in general tension. This was the second time the Germans had tried for the factory. They obviously meant to get it.

After leaving Southampton the 109s, apparently converted to fighter bombers, made directly for Portsmouth over which they 'trailed their coat' for an insolent twenty minutes. 'They flew up and down over us in two loose gaggles of twelve,' I wrote, 'the guns blazing away at them and not a British fighter to be seen. Now and then one would shoot upwards again. Over the city, a black trail of smoke began zig-zagging downwards, not at all like a burning balloon, but as if from an aircraft in a spin. When the two formations again came roaring over us, one seemed to have only eleven aircraft. I heard later that a

Messerschmitt had indeed come down, after a shell had been seen to burst directly above him.'

On the following day, 25 September, in the late morning also, the sirens sounded at the Filton works of the Bristol Aircraft Company. This was an enormous series of aircraft and aero-engine factories at Filton aerodrome, also a Fighter Command base, just outside the city of Bristol. Among the aircraft being produced were the bomber and night fighter versions of the Blenheim and the new Beaufighter designed to combat the night bomber. Mr H. W. Pitt, now Fire Controller at Filton, was not then with the company; he was watching from a point three miles south of the city, as the bombers approached. He looked up in surprise, saw one or two fighters picking at them 'like gnats', and expended ammunition began to rain down into the road; he thought, amazed, 'This is real!' One or two fighters made no difference to that formation, and they roared on to Filton.

Mr E. W. King, a works fireman, stood watching from his post as the workers streamed out of the factory buildings and took shelter. A single German aircraft flew over, apparently dropping leaflets; he thought afterwards it was a target-marker. Looking towards Avonmouth, he saw a massed formation, some sixty or seventy planes, appear from out of a black cloud. Another fireman, Mr N. Harris, who was watching from the aero-engine works on the other side of the main road, saw them also – 'They looked like a lot of swallows.' Somebody near him said, 'They're all ours.'

'There was no AA fire,' he recalled, 'and I saw no fighters. I never heard the bombs coming down, but I felt the blast all right.' The Germans roared straight across Filton aerodrome from south-west to north-east, hundreds of bombs tumbling from their bellies, the majority falling on to the various factory buildings, gouts of smoke and dust shooting up above the roofs.

Mr Harris got into a shelter and went down on one knee, then something heavy struck him violently in the back – it was the body of a man who had been blown from one end of the shelter to the other. The walls were shuddering with the concussions, the air was filled with the dust and smoke, and for a moment Mr Harris thought his back had been broken. After five minutes, light began to penetrate again and they stumbled up into the car park, hazy with the smoke of blazing vehicles; the cars as yet untouched could not be moved, because the doors were locked, and the fires could not be dealt with immediately because the hydrant had been destroyed. On the aero-drome, a British fighter was burning, in a crackle of exploding ammunition, apparently caught taking off. Looking around, they saw that a bomb had landed almost on the parapet of their shelter, driving splinters through the two-inch-thick steel doors. Behind them, two of the five sheds engaged on aero-engine work had been hit. One had its roof smashed in, the other was on fire. There was damage to machine tools, not only from blast but from water spouting from the mains and the factory sprinklers and the hoses of the firemen.

Ernie King, who was at the aircraft works, recalled, 'Those two minutes were like a lifetime.' Then, with the bombers retiring (they were intercepted later), King dealt with a number of fire calls and afterwards went to help at the shelters. They were of the usual partly-underground type, proof against virtually everything except a direct hit. Some had received direct hits. In all, in these shelters and in various parts of the many factory buildings, there were lying 72 dead bodies and 166 wounded, 19 of whom were dying. Some of the shelters were just indentations in the ground, where their roofs had collapsed on the occupants;

others were burst wide open and their contents exposed to the sky. In one, the corpses were rammed up against one end of the shelter, as if a giant piston had pushed them there; in others there were many dismembered corpses. In many cases their clothing had been burned off on one side of the body, that exposed to the explosion, but was intact on the other side.

King was a man who would cheerfully and confidently volunteer for any job, no matter how grisly or unpleasant. He volunteered for this. 'Three of us had nothing else to do but pick up the remains with our hands,' he recalled. 'There was no other way. Many times a limb came away separately, and perhaps a head. I remember one head which had a large round hole right down through from the top, with nothing inside – it was uncanny. If I had stopped to dwell on it all I might have had to give up, but although I am not callous I was surprised to find that after a bit I carried on as just a job to be done.' The three men laid everything on the floor of two lorries, and King found a tarpaulin to cover the poor remains. Then they drove them to the church hall of Filton Church.

Meanwhile Mr Pitt, seeing that the target was Bristol, where his two children were at school, got into his car and drove after the bombers as fast as possible. 'I travelled about nine miles – all the way on a flat tyre – and didn't notice. I stopped at a garage, where they said, "It's up at Filton – they've ruined Filton." The bombs had in fact gone right across the works.'

Of fifty completed aircraft in various parts of the huge factory, eight were seriously damaged, including the third Beaufighter prototype with Rolls Royce engines, and twenty-four were slightly damaged. Dispersal began at once, into large houses, small factories, garages, and even farms. Next day, the workers at Filton watched with relief the Hurricanes of 118 Squadron landing; they were to stay as local protection to the factory.

On 26 September, the day after the bombing of Filton, 303 (Polish) Squadron were being inspected at Northolt by King George VI. They were on 'readiness' at the time and a scramble interrupted the inspection. His Majesty asked if they would telephone the results of the fight to him at Buckingham Palace. They roared due south, climbing, and then altered to the west for the Portsmouth area. Ahead of them, AA bursts began to appear in the sky.

The flags on the control tower of Portsmouth dockyard came running down. An officer at a Lewis gun post began to put on his steel helmet. Two little girls, playing on a swing by the harbour ferry, continued their game. In the distance the faint thudding of gunfire rumbled over the Channel. All along the coast from Portsmouth to Southampton, the sirens began to moan, their refrain being taken up inland. There were a few bursts of machine-gun fire very high up and out to sea. Nine Spitfires went racing seaward, in tight formation, over Stokes Bay, heading south for battle at 20,000 feet and 300 miles an hour. Southward, where massed and tumbled cloudbanks rose above the Isle of Wight, there was a distant droning, increasing to the harsh uneven roar of an immense bomber formation coming in. Across that sound the whine of diving fighters suddenly rang like a trumpet scream and burst after burst of machine-gun fire echoed in the heights. A grey streak of smoke, a blazing balloon, fell slowly down over Southampton, followed by a thunderous, long-drawn-out rumble, so many bomb detonations occurring simultaneously, that it was all one ringing blow. In those few seconds, seventy-six Heinkels and Ju. 88s unloaded bombs by the hundred on to an area of about one square mile, in the centre of which were the Woolston and Itchen works of the Supermarine factory. The factory buildings vanished in smoke, which billowed up thousands of feet into the air and began to drift down Southampton Water. When it blew away, the aspect of Woolston was quite different, hundreds of shattered houses and acres of rubble, and gaunt, shell-like structures, torn, smashed, empty, streaming dust and smoke – the Spitfire factory.

When the sirens had sounded, only a minute or two before, Mr Cooper was in his room on the top floor of the office block. He went racing down to the ground floor, which he reached as the first detonation rocked the works, and then dived into the test house and got under a concrete plinth. 'It was like being in a rubber box,' he recalled. 'That really surprised me.' The solid concrete of the structure flexed under the earthquake blows of repeated explosions from all directions, and battered at his back and sides. The whole structure was moving. When he came up again to ground-level, the atmosphere was a dark, yellow-green colour, the devastation appearing much worse than it was. Both factories were destroyed but the office block, although gouged and gutted, was still standing.

He went up to his own room, to find that the blast had first showered it with flying splinters of glass, guillotining a wad of printing paper in a locked drawer, and had then by suction stripped the room of everything except his desk. Looking down from his window on to the River Itchen, he saw barges lying on their sides and an enormous number of small holes in the mud – holes which were slowly collapsing inwards, so that within a few hours there would be no sign of them. These marked the arrival of bombs which, because of the soft nature of the ground, had not exploded; they are still there today, fused and ready. Out in a field an unexploded bomb was lying in the open, with a horse lazily scratching its back on the casing. Casualties had been very light, only two dozen killed, many fewer than in the previous raid, because most people had left the works and, avoiding the shelters, run towards Woolston station. One man was lying dead in the road there. Two other men running with him had escaped; he, an ex-infantryman from the first world war, had been killed. A surprised lorry driver was stumbling to his feet; he had got under his vehicle, and held both hands over his head. When the explosions ceased, he was still crouched there, but the lorry had vanished.

Just outside the factory, cut into the banking, was a deep shelter in which, for a few moments, there was pandemonium. It was reserved mainly for women and girls, but one man who had no right to be there had shouldered his way in, with 'My life is more to me than the girls'.' No one had guessed that this was the type he would turn out to be. Above the shelter was a store where Spitfire wings were stacked and painted; the store was hit, the ventilator which connected with the deep shelter blown open, and down it poured a rain of wing ribs, followed by a blazing tide of paint and dope, which flooded into the darkness of the shelter. 'My God, an aircraft's crashed on top of us, we'll all be burned to death,' was the instant reaction, but no one was seriously hurt down there and the pandemonium subsided.

At about the moment that happened, Flying Officer W. Urbanowicz, piloting one of the Hurricanes of 303 Squadron coming rapidly down from the north-east, sighted the bombers passing north of the factory, with 109s above them, and starting to turn in a wide sweep for home. As he ripped down on them, he passed two Heinkels on fire and losing height; to starboard a Hurricane and a Messerschmitt were both falling into the sea, and ahead some bombers were already trailing black smoke. He closed with a lagging Heinkel, set it on fire, and saw it go down into the Channel. Then he turned back, one of a number of fighters returning singly from the chase.

I was watching from Stokes Bay and heard two or three distinct formations returning over the Isle of Wight but hidden by cloud, and heard also the howl of the fighters diving on them. Then a rapidly growing cluster of white shell bursts appeared to the west, and I raised my field glasses. Over Southampton, across a patch of blue sky, streamed a massive formation of bombers, flying nose-up and majestically through the shellfire, an enormously impressive aerial parade, while below raged a vicious fighter dog-fight, the 109s beating off every attempt of the Spitfires and Hurricanes to get at the bombers. The sun shone on the wings of the fighters as they went whirling round, occasionally a momentary contrail appearing from the tightness of the turn. The bombers also began to stream contrails, as they rode through the white smoke of the bursting shells and eventually disappeared behind a cloud over the Isle of Wight. There were thirty in that formation, either Heinkels or Junkers, probably the latter. The Luftwaffe was certainly not going down tamely in defeat.

Within minutes a single bomber came from Southampton Water and flying at barely 4,000 feet passed directly across Stokes Bay; it was a big, fat Heinkel, as bulbous as a goldfish, the black crosses on the silver-grey wings menacingly clear in my field glasses. Behind it, low down and overtaking slowly, a single Spitfire was streaking up from astern. 'Now for it!' thought the little group of people who had gathered on the seafront to watch. 'My emotions, I must admit, were plain jealousy. An absolute sitter, he couldn't miss. But he did. Two quick beam attacks, and he broke away, doubtless out of ammunition. The Heinkel flew off insolently over Portsmouth.'

The British official history records that the enemy were engaged by four squadrons from 10 and 11 Groups, and that the Germans lost only three aircraft compared to the British loss of six aircraft and two pilots. Clearly, the bombers seen by the Poles to be on fire either got back or were simply trailing smoke from over-revving. Nevertheless, a number of pilots were believed to be down in the sea somewhere south of the Isle of Wight, and an hour or so later 'Nobby' Clarke was told to take off from Gosport and to 'search for survivors, 15 miles 200° from St Catherine's Point'. It was now sunset, there was not much time left, so when he was unable to find his air gunner, Sergeant Mercer, he took another Sergeant who was less familiar with the Fraser-Nash turret. For Clarke now had guns. Indeed, his Roc was the only armed, operational aircraft at Gosport, and he was very proud of it. He and Sergeant Mercer had harmonized the four guns in the turret to a hair's breadth, painted personal insignia on the fuselage, and always flew off on Air/Sea Rescue duty hoping for sight of something to shoot at.

It was late when they reached the area of search, the sun hidden by a black cloud low down on the horizon and a smoky haze on the grey, tumbling sea. While Hunt searched to starboard, keeping most of his attention on the sky, Clarke flew at nil feet and searched to port, looking at small sections of the sea at a time – it was only too easy to miss a man's head bobbing in the dark waves. Three miles away a Swordfish, presumably from nearby Lee-on-Solent, was also searching methodically in the deepening gloom. After half an hour, Clarke's search had taken him nearer to the Swordfish which he now saw was fitted with floats, a sensible idea for Air/Sea Rescue. A few minutes later he looked up, to rest his eyes for a moment from the strain of searching, and noticed the Swordfish again, now only about half a mile away. Somehow, it seemed larger than a Swordfish.

He began to check off his instrument readings, his mind still on the seaplane. What on earth were those things between its wings – long-range tanks? He corrected his course, trying to stay exactly ten feet off the water. Did Lee-on-Solent actually have any Swordfish with floats? Then the answer came to him – of course, those lumps between its wings were engines. It was a twin-engined seaplane, not a Swordfish at all.

Abandoning the search, Clarke climbed up and began to turn towards the stranger, trying to think of any British aircraft which it resembled. As he came in from above and behind, he could clearly see the markings on the seaplane – black crosses outlined with white. It was turning slowly to port. Then it straightened up, parallel with the Isle of Wight, and continued to look for survivors.

Clarke had no front guns, so that although he was 500 feet above and in perfect position for a fighter attack, he could not fire a shot; indeed, it was hard to see how he could fire at all, except from below, and the German was too low for that. Also, he would have to be careful, for the seaplane had both front and rear guns. Then the thought struck him – should he attack at all? 'I remembered now,' he wrote, 'that the Germans had been using floatplanes to pick up their pilots who had been forced to ditch in the Channel – and not only their pilots, but ours as well! Supposing this particular kite had already picked up the blokes I had been looking for? Furthermore, didn't these aircraft fly under the international Red Cross? They were "ambulance planes". If I shot it down, Lord knows what would happen to me. And wouldn't Goebbels enjoy making propaganda out of it?'

But really there was no doubt. Clarke had been a fighter pilot until a year or so before, and was continually bombarding his superiors with requests for transfer; this was the opportunity he had been longing for throughout the battle. 'I'm going to do a steep turn across the front of him!' he called to his gunner. 'Don't open fire unless he shoots at us. OK?'

'OK, sir.'

Looking over his shoulder, Clarke saw the turret begin to revolve, the four blue-black barrels coming slowly into view and dropping into the horizontal position like the mighty guns of a battleship – that was the awkward part of it, they would depress no further. Clarke dived and then turned right across the nose of the floatplane. Looking down at it from a hundred yards away, he saw the German's front turret slowly revolving to follow him. Brief muzzle flashes twinkled from the seaplane's twin guns and darts of red light came streaking at him; there was the thud of bullets striking, gashes ripped in the port wing, then the Roc was vibrating as its own four guns fired.

'I saw our tracer pouring into the enemy's fuselage and wing centre-section. I felt stark naked for one whole second as we hung in the air like a model on a string in an incredibly vulnerable position, while he shot at us and we shot at him. And then it seemed that movement restarted and I broke away to starboard, appalled by the pandemonium of my first action.'

Clarke began yelling to his rear-gunner; there was no reply. But he had not been hit, his earphone plug had come out, that was all. Impatient to get on with the strange battle, Clarke re-established communication and turned after the slower floatplane, which was now making away for home low down on the water. Then a shower of spray hit his windscreen, and he pulled up hastily to twenty feet. He had to get below the level of the enemy if his guns were to bear, but whereas the seaplane could fly low without danger, being warned by the touching of the floats on the water, Clarke could easily fly straight in.

He nosed up alongside his opponent, broadside on to it and 300 yards away, then dipped his starboard wing to let his gunner bring his guns on to the target. The Roc skidded dangerously towards the water, and as Clarke corrected, the answering fire came back – from three separate gun positions! The red tracer flashed past nerve-shatteringly close. Clarke ducked instinctively. He tried the manoeuvre several times, and one of the German guns eventually stopped firing. Then a smudge of coastline appeared ahead. France.

At that moment the seaplane fired again. The noise of bullets striking the Roc was no longer merely a sharp thump, but a frightening cacophony of shattering perspex, torn metal, and a suddenly faltering, choking engine. Fuel shortage at nil feet.

Clarke's left hand flashed round the cockpit, making adjustments and changing tanks, then he turned away and prepared to ditch. But the engine picked up and at less than 100 mph gallantly spluttered him back to Gosport. In the tank under his seat were two incendiary bullets which, if they had entered a few inches higher, into the fumes, would have fried him. The machine was a wreck; his personal insignia, an image of the 'Saint', had been, significantly, shot through the head. There was a painful interview with the AOC, who held that he should not have attacked the Heinkel 59 seaplane, and later congratulations from Sir Frederick Bowhill, head of Coastal Command, on having done so. Clarke himself is not sure, even to this day. But he got his transfer to fighters.

15

The Last Valhalla

27–30 September

On 27 September, the day after the bombing, I went to Woolston and looked down from a hill on to the maze of destruction. 'There was not an intact roof or window in sight. The ring of workmen's picks came from the railway line, which they were striving to repair; and also from the low ground where the shelters were and presumably bodies were still buried. Some small boys were excavating in a crater with pieces of broken slate, digging for bits of bomb casing as souvenirs and stuffing them into paper bags. My attention was attracted by what looked like a derelict and abandoned warehouse – no roof, no walls, girders and wires trailing down on to a concrete floor pock-marked with bomb craters. "What's that?" I enquired of another spectator, "a warehouse?" "Warehouse!" was the indignant reply. "That's the Spitfire works!"'

It was in fact the Itchen section of the factory. The Woolston section was worse, merely a flat jumble of tangled girders; it was never rebuilt but instead handed over to the Commandos as a training area for street fighting. No more Spitfires would be built or repaired at Southampton for a very long time to come. But the floor of the ruined building, bare as a tennis court, showed that the machine tools had already been removed and that dispersal was under way, exactly twenty-four hours after the blow had been struck.

Inside one part of the works was an unexploded bomb which had gone deep. A Bomb Disposal Team had arrived, those curiously brave people whose work elicited

not admiration, as did the fighter pilots and firemen, but
something more than that – awe. They cordoned off the
area, forbade anyone to approach, laid a wall of sandbags
round the hole . . . then sat down on them and ate their
sandwiches.

Another attack was expected and when a reconnaissance machine came over to photograph the damage, the
salvage lorries which were loading with debris got away
very fast. As one lorry came rocking round the corner a
man, an old labourer in heavy boots, fell off it; in a flash,
he was on his feet and running, and had caught up the
lorry before it had even got into the next gear.

Lord Beaverbrook, the Minister of Aircraft Production,
came down personally to discover the effect on production. Not all the bombs had been aimed at the factory –
one wave of attack had bombed the gasworks and the
wharves on the opposite side of the River Itchen – and of
those dropped on Woolston only eight had scored direct
hits. Many completed Spitfires had been damaged but
only three actually destroyed; some machine tools had
been damaged by falling debris or bomb splinters, none
had been destroyed. But the factory buildings were completely wrecked and unusable, and other production
centres would have to be found. It was this which was
serious, almost completely stopping production for several months. In August, 133 Spitfires had been built,
mostly at Southampton, as the new factory at Castle
Bromwich was only just coming into production; in
October only 59 Spitfires were produced, mostly at Castle
Bromwich. But by the end of November the Southampton
works had completed dispersal in thirty-five small sites
and had begun to produce again at something like the old
figure. It was in the measures needed to obtain these
premises that Lord Beaverbrook showed his hand.

England being a comparatively free country, even when

at war, surprising difficulties had been met with in the past. Supermarine had bought a row of houses nearby, for expansion, but one owner would not sell; he maintained that, so far from extending the factory, it ought not to be there at all, as it would draw enemy attention. The acrimonious litigation which ensued was brought to an end only by a German bomb, which abolished the owner in the retreat in Cardiff to which he had gone to escape the expected bombs on Southampton. Some dispersal measures had already been carried out and Mr D. Webb, while supervising a move, had met with opposition from their new neighbours, one woman remarking bitterly, 'Now I suppose *we'll* be bombed?' 'Share and share alike, madam!' replied Mr Webb cheerily.

Lord Beaverbrook forthwith nominated as his personal representatives, with practically unlimited powers of requisition, the well-known financier, Mr Whitehead, a Canadian, Mr 'Joe' Cowley, and an American, Mr Carlton Dyer. Mr Leonard Gooch, the present production manager, was to follow in their wake, installing jigs, tools and machinery and despatching chargehands and workmen in due course. At once, they came up against a most formidable opponent, the Lord Mayor of a town whose Corporation Bus Depot was ideally suited to aircraft manufacture. As this was a contest between one government department and another government department, they thought carefully – and fired the Canadian at him.

'Joe' Cowley noticed at once that the town was very Spitfire-conscious. The 'Spitfire Fund' had originated in an enquiry from Sir Harry Oakes, a Canadian mining millionaire (later murdered), to Lord Beaverbrook, asking to know what a Spitfire cost. The arbitrary figure of £5,000 was chosen (it actually cost much more), and Sir Harry duly sent a cheque for that amount. The idea, which had naturally no effect whatever on the actual production of Spitfires, had become amazingly popular, as a kind of token means of defying the Luftwaffe. So Cowley bowled in, looking very prosperous, and fired off with, 'Good morning, Mister Mayor, I hear you've got a Spitfire Fund?'

The Mayor beamed, visualizing a substantial cheque, and agreed that he had.

'Yeah,' said Cowley. 'What are you going to do with all that money? Build a statue to the Mayor who didn't think Spitfires were necessary?'

The Mayor got no cheque, but Cowley got the Corporation Bus Depot.

On 26 September, the raid on Woolston had been accompanied by another assault on London; on 27 September, while the debris was being cleared away at Woolston, there was another raid directed at Filton, accompanied by yet another assault on London. At Filton, when the sirens sounded, there was a rush for shelter. There, too, a sharp distinction between the fatalists and the fearful was obvious. 'Normally the men divided into two different types,' recalled Fred Hackwell. 'The first lot couldn't care less – if it does, it does, was their outlook. And they used to laugh at the others (dubbed the Filton "Yellow Bellies"), who used to scamper for shelter, getting on to cars and wagons, jumping up on tailboards to get away. There were so many alerts, you see, which meant nothing – nothing ever happened, it was a waste of time to go to shelter. We had a number of night raids at this time and one night the outside siren went. There was no reaction at all among the couldn't-care-less crowd, who were playing cards in the canteen. Then the works warning came over the loudspeakers, that was the playing of *Marching Through Georgia*, and it meant the raid was probably for the works. No reaction, they went on playing cards. Then a gun went off outside. BANG! The card tables went one way, the cards went another, and everyone got down on the floor, there were about six card packs all mixed, it was chaotic.' The factory was hit repeatedly at night, both before the big daylight raid and after it, but not substantially damaged.

The follow-up daylight attack on Filton entered England during the morning of 27 September; to get there, the bombers had to fly across some sixty miles of the west country, a deep penetration without effective escort. But the previous raid had cost them only five aircraft, one of which had fallen to the AA guns. The British defences were obviously weakened and strained after six weeks of heavy fighting, and five aircraft was not a high price to pay for extensively damaging so important a factory.

56 Squadron was now in 10 Group, resting and re-forming at Middle Wallop, and at the same time helping to guard the west country. They were scrambled at 11.05 A.M. to patrol base and then directed to Bournemouth against an incoming 50-plus raid which was actually the formation bound for Filton. As they climbed up, Constable Maxwell found that his oxygen had not been turned on, so he broke away and returned to Middle Wallop. He obtained permission to take off again, alone, and with the new, non-operational pilots watching him enviously, he taxied out; the groundcrew were wearing steel helmets. As the Hurricane rolled away over the grass, it was rather as if the retinue of a knight were watching him set off on his charger into battle, and hoping he wouldn't waste all their hard work by muffing things when it came to clouting the enemy.

That was precisely what was worrying Maxwell. He had not been very successful so far and now, how on earth, since he obviously could not catch up with the squadron, was he to tackle the 50-plus, supposing that he did find them? He could hear 'Bandy', the Middle Wallop controller, calling to 'Boffin Leader', the CO of 56 Squadron, that the enemy were approaching Shaftesbury from the south-east. Shortly after that, he reported 'Bandits approaching Bristol'. Maxwell turned on to a course that would take him south of Bristol in a position where he might be able to intercept something coming back from the raid.

Once again, Mr Pitt was outside Bristol, this time to the east; once again, he saw a massed German formation approaching. 'I felt a bit shivery – Blimey, here it is again!' Then, a moment later, he saw something new – another big formation approaching the first on an interception course. The two formations met, and a 'battle royal' began, from which three or four aircraft came whining down; then the Germans, harried by the British fighters, were turning away and going home, dropping their bombs at random and miles away from Filton. 'That's lovely,' thought Mr Pitt, 'why didn't they do it on Wednesday?'

Twenty miles south of Bristol Constable Maxwell, flying at 15,000 feet, saw a formation coming south and nearly 10,000 feet above him. Apparently Messerschmitt 110s, they were being attacked by Spitfires. Climbing hard towards them, he saw four miles to the north and 2,000 feet higher than he was, another black mass of aircraft approaching – the enemy bombers. Still climbing, he thought about a head-on attack – unwise, because the rear-gunners would rake him as he passed through. The mass of bombers passed him to starboard – about 25 to 30 Dorniers. He was now a little above them.

He banked in behind, chose the rearmost bomber, and fired very carefully from about 250 yards away. Spurts of tracer from the rear-gunner replied. A piece fell off the port side of the Dornier. The tracer was still whipping past the Hurricane. Maxwell nosed right in and fired a burst at the port engine. Part of the cowling fell off. Maxwell broke away hard left and then saw the Dornier going down with black smoke streaming from its port engine. He felt utterly surprised.

All his previous easy shots had seemed to produce no effect whatever on the enemy and he had half-expected the same thing now. Below him, another Hurricane appeared and had a quick nibble at the falling bomber. Indignantly, Maxwell went after his prey, feeling that this chap might at least have picked his own German, with so many of them about.

He went head on at the smoking bomber, which was still full of fight, and banked away; turning inside it, he fired a long burst from less than 100 yards. Its nose dropped, and trailing smoke it fell towards the ground some 6,000 feet below, with no sign of a parachute or even of anyone trying to get out. Maxwell felt almost sick at the sudden doom which had overtaken four men. Then he saw that the bomber was not seriously hurt, it was pulling out of its dive and turning. Instantly, his emotions changed. He roared down after it, eager to knock it into the ground, shoot its occupants to ribbons, kill without mercy. It was a menace to his country. Coming in for the final attack, he saw that the port engine had stopped. The Dornier was trying to land.

The fight was over; the enemy had given in, all he wanted was a safe place in which to get down. Again, Maxwell experienced a swift change of feeling.

'For five minutes I watch him from 500 feet above and out to his right. He tries to land in a field, but overshoots and opens up his one good engine. There are trees in front. I could not desire a friend to clear those trees more than I do that German. He gets over it and I am delighted. Suddenly he slows up. I nearly stall and lose him for a

second. There was a hill in front and he has not cleared
it. I turn and see a huge silver thing lying broken on a
grassy bank between two woods. The nose is askew, the
whole plane is steaming but is not on fire. No one gets
out . . .' This was the first time he had felt any strong
emotion in the air – and it was pity. He wrote, 'I felt they
were just airmen who were in a dangerous plight, such as
I had experienced myself. I was safe, they were in danger
of death. This last few minutes was the most unpleasant I
have experienced in this war.'

At a party the following evening, a civilian who had
been told of Maxwell's encounter with the Dornier,
turned to him and said, 'Oh, how absolutely splendid of
you, I do hope they were all killed.'

'The filthiest remark I have ever heard,' wrote Maxwell.
'I was staggered by its sadism. It is these old fools of fat
civilians who are unable to do anything and just become
venomous.'

At 9 P.M. on the 27th, two hours before the Bristol raid,
303 (Polish) Squadron had been in action against a
bomber stream coming up to the capital, with an escort of
109s sweeping in front of the bombers and another group
of them on the left flank stretching for five miles. It was
the last *Valhalla* – the final mass daylight attack on
London which penetrated to the target. Flying Officer
Henneberg, trying to close with the bombers, noted how
quickly the Polish squadron diminished in numbers as the
109s came roaring down to engage. As he came in to the
attack, and was almost through the fighter screen, he saw
Sergeant Andruszkow's Hurricane going down in flames;
in front now were only a pair of 109s, weaving. He
pressed the gun button and set one on fire. Before he
could even look round, he had been bounced, three bursts
had hit the aircraft and his cockpit was filling with white

smoke. The radiator had been hit and his aileron control wires cut, but Henneberg managed to get back.

In the afternoon they were scrambled again and ordered to form up with 229 Squadron and 1 (Canadian) Squadron. There were a large number of British squadrons airborne when Flight Lieutenant John Kent, leading the Poles, sighted the Germans coming in from the southeast through a heavy AA barrage. The Germans promptly turned and began to dive away for the coast from 15,000 feet. The Hurricanes had climbed only to 10,000 feet, so they turned also and waited for the diving Germans to come down to their level. Kent caught up with a Ju. 88 which was being unsuccessfully attacked by two other Hurricanes, closed in, knocked out the rear-gunner, hit both engines, and saw the bomber go into the sea a mile from shore. One man swam away from it.

92 Squadron, paired with another squadron, was also engaged with Ju. 88s flying towards Redhill; they attacked head on and then split up. There were about twenty of the bombers and many 109s – 'latter very shy', wrote Alan Wright in his logbook. 'Shot lumps off three, shared in another which crashed aflame.' Finding himself alone under the bombers he had tried a new method of attack, the 'snap-up' – possibly this was the first time it was ever used. He flew at high speed 2,000 feet below the bomber formation and out to one side, then pulled the stick hard back and lunged up almost vertically at their bellies, rolling over to fire, and then breaking away sharply downwards. It kept the fighter out of view of the front- and rear-gunners right up to the moment of the break away and it reduced the fighter's speed, at the moment of firing, to something like that of the bombers.

On 30 September, the German pattern of attack was almost precisely repeated. On London, a morning and an afternoon assault by *Luftflotte* 2; and in the west, an

attack on an aircraft factory by *Luftflotte* 3. The formations coming to London consisted of the usual groups of
about twenty bombers, escorted by perhaps one hundred
fighters; they were no longer trying to do real damage,
dropping their loads mostly on the outskirts, and the 109
pilots were obviously becoming increasingly weary of
fighting for air superiority. This was the very last day of
the mass attacks, and none of them got home on the
target.

Alan Wright arrived at mid-day at Biggin Hill after a
'day off' (which was from 12 noon to 12 noon), found 92
Squadron airborne and one serviceable Spitfire on the
ground. He took it, found a Spitfire fighting two 109s over
Reigate, and disposed in flames of one of its opponents.
In the afternoon he was airborne again with a two-
squadron wing. After attacking bombers and being
attacked by a 109, he found himself alone, so climbed up
to 25,000 feet. He sighted five 109s on their way out to
the coast, got in a hasty burst at one, holing its glycol
tank, and was then out of ammunition.

All he could claim was a 'damaged', so he determined
to follow the five enemy fighters, to see what happened,
reasoning that they would be too low on fuel to fight. The
damaged German fighter went down in a long dive for the
coast, crossing out to sea at about 5,000 feet, Wright
following on behind. Its flight lasted seven minutes, then
bursts of brown smoke came out of the engine, and it
cartwheeled into the sea. Satisfied, Wright turned back
for England, flying in a straight line 200 feet above the
water and looking round him. But he never saw his
enemy.

There was a bang, the cockpit filled with smoke, and
the Spitfire heeled over and plunged down to the waves.
The sea came up at him in a flash, appearing to fill the
windscreen, but with stick hard back he was pulling out

and then banking sharply to turn in to face his attackers –
two 109s. 'After a turn or two they were gone. But I had
great difficulty in maintaining an even keel – I needed
both hands on the stick in the forward left corner of the
cockpit. There was a roaring noise, which must have come
from a piece of the wing surface flapping, and air was
coming through a hole in the starboard side of the cockpit.
My right leg was numb and bloody, my map ripped by
bullets, and my temperature gauge smashed, so that I
could not tell if my glycol also had been punctured. I
headed north, but could not recognize my landfall. I came
across an airfield, but it was disused and covered with
derelict cars as an anti-glider measure. I pressed on along
the coast until I came to another airfield, which was
Shoreham.'

The damaged Spitfire limped round the small civil
airfield – most of the rudder had been shot away, half the
elevator, and the bottom of the fuselage had been ripped
open from the tail nearly to the mainplane. But Wright
managed to get his flaps down and make his approach;
the slowly turning propeller looked ragged from the bullet
holes and he could see from the position of the gashes in
the wing that one tyre was burst. He eased back on the
stick and touched down gently.

Meanwhile, a hundred miles to the west, Constable
Maxwell was coming down to a dead-stick landing on
Chesil Bank, by the Bill of Portland. 56 Squadron had
moved from Middle Wallop to the coastal aerodrome at
Warmwell, near Weymouth, where they were intended to
operate as a Wing with the Spitfires of 152 Squadron.
They were scrambled during the morning and were
brought into action without sufficient height. The first
enemy formation – two dozen 110s – went rocketing past
them very close and just above, 'a wonderful sight – at
about 600 mph closing speed', wrote Maxwell. 'They go

up and we go down – there being dozens of 109s spreading
up into the upper air. I hear and feel a rushing clattering
noise. I have never shifted quicker, and down I go on my
back. It was a single 109 which put two bullets in my port
mainplane from below. Marston and Sergeant Ray got
shot down – Ray breaks an arm and Ken is "shook up"
generally.'

In the afternoon engagement about forty escorted
bombers crossed the coast, the Westland aircraft factory
at Yeovil, on the borders of Somerset and Dorset, being
their target. When they arrived, it was obscured by cloud,
through which they dropped their bombs. None of them
hit Yeovil, the bombs actually landing at Sherborne some
miles away and putting the railway out of action. The
Germans had to fight their way in, against attacks by four
British squadrons, and fight their way out, under attack
by four more. 56 Squadron attacked them as they were
nearing the coast, both land and sea being hidden by a
sheet of cloud. Above them hovered an escort of 110s,
which were slow in coming down, as the Hurricanes
turned in from the quarter.

The bombers were Heinkels, which met them with
bursts of crossfire. Four Hurricanes fell to their fire, and
a 110 picked off a fifth. Two of the British pilots baled
out, two landed safely with glycol leaks, and Constable
Maxwell never fired a shot. At 400 yards from the
bombers, and still closing, there was a 'phut!' from a stray
bullet hit and at once oil began to cloud his windscreen.
'Herne Bay!' thought Maxwell.

His windscreen, compass and goggles were covered in
oil and the cloud sheet hid the land, so he turned away
blindly at first. Then he shut off the engine and the oil
ceased coming back at him. When at last he saw the land,
it was nearer than he had thought, within gliding distance.
It would be much safer to bale out, but the machine

would be lost. Ahead was a long stretch of shingle and behind it a lagoon – Chesil Bank. He decided to force-land there, but this time to keep a lot of speed in hand because the controls were ineffective when the propeller was no longer ticking over; it made a quite surprising amount of difference, as he well knew.

The Hurricane came whistling down on to the long stretch of shingle, the wind blowing directly across, so that Maxwell had to lower his wing into it. Wheels retracted, the fighter struck in a shower of stones, slewed round with a violent jerk, and stopped. It did not catch fire.

While Maxwell was trying unsuccessfully to find the bullet hole in the nose, the soldiers arrived, in this case Durham Light Infantry. He was taken to their mess for tea and it was just like Herne Bay again. 'They are quite nice, but are like Prussians with their men when ordering them about. An officer in a Highland Regiment or the RAF has a different type of man to lead; they will not be driven.' He was struck by the contrast with the relaxed discipline of his own squadron, where there was such keenness on the part of the men that hardly a word was spoken when there was a 'flap', everyone was too busy striving to strip seconds from the take-off time.

The Battle of Britain did not end – it died gradually away, through a fifth and final phase in which the bomb-load delivered in daylight was negligible but there were still a great many air battles, so that Hitler could maintain that the fight against England continued. The Germans had won a degree of air superiority over England, but not to the extent of making an invasion possible. They had calculated, at the beginning of August, that four days' fighting would break British resistance in the air over southern England; and six weeks after they had actually launched their great assault, the British were still fighting, still inflicting heavy losses, still preventing the mass of the German bomber force from sweeping over in daylight to bomb aside all opposition. Clearly, some fundamental decisions would soon have to be made.

In an article written in German and not intended for publication in England, Adolf Galland wrote:

'Indisputably, Germany had air superiority at this time, but the decimated English fighter units flew with stubborn courage. This was a factor which would certainly have to be taken into account in planning future operations. The battle put up by the British fighter pilots deserves the highest admiration. In numbers often inferior, untiring, fighting bravely, it was they who, in this most critical part of the war, undoubtedly became the saviours of their country.'

PHASE V:
Fighter-Bombers

16

Contrails Over the Coast

October–November

The autumn was crisp and cold, often with blue skies and high winds. This was the time of the contrails, rarely seen before, and known then as 'smoke' or 'vapour' trails. In October the novelty ceased. The fighting was going higher, up to 30,000 feet, where condensation more often occurred; the trails were a portent, showing that the battle was between fighter and fighter. The *Valhallas* were no longer thundering against England at 15,000 feet. It was a hard time for the pilots of the unheated Hurricanes, whose best performance was below 18,000 feet; frozen, dazed with cold, they hauled their soggy aircraft up under the high-flying Messerschmitts. Only the Spitfires could fight on even terms. But the duels at great heights were of a formal nature only, and could decide nothing.

The German bomber forces had been largely withdrawn from the daylight battle, for four main reasons: the weather was unsuitable for large-scale operations; the losses had made the attacks very costly; now that invasion was no longer possible, these losses were incurred without possibility of a decisive effect; and because it was necessary to preserve the Luftwaffe for a major campaign in the East. The serviceable strength of the fighter arm had been reduced by 25 per cent, and the pilots were extremely tired. Nearly 35 per cent of the bombers had been lost, but production and replacement had kept the bomber force more nearly up to strength. Nevertheless, the end of the daylight attacks came as a relief to the crews. 'All of us were happy about the stop, for the English fighters and anti-aircraft artillery took a heavy toll of our bomber squadrons,' said Wolfgang Berlin of KG 55. Paul Weitkus of KG 2 commented, 'Of one thing I'm sure, and that is – the British fighters won the Battle of Britain.'

That result had not been achieved without loss – nearly 450 RAF fighter pilots had been killed. Both air forces had been badly mauled and considerable damage done to various targets in England; but no decision had been reached, although that summer England had been at her lowest ebb. From now on, her power relative to Germany would increase and Germany's relative power decline.

But the attack on England was continued, in the most economical manner possible, in order to mask Hitler's proposed decision to find a theatre of war in which he could decisively employ his armies instead of having them play the part of passive spectators on the Channel coast. Invasion, a properly prepared landing, was threatened for 1941; meanwhile the Luftwaffe was to be rested and reinforced, ready for a major campaign in the spring, openly aimed at Britain, but actually at Russia.

By day, mostly in cloudy weather, small groups of bombers kept up the attack; but the main effort was made by the fighter-bombers. Some 250 Messerschmitt Bf. 109s and Bf. 110s – a third of the fighter force – were rapidly converted to carry bombs. Each jagdgeschwader converted three staffeln to the fighter-bomber rôle, the remainder supplied the escort. There was no time to train the pilots in bomb aiming and the total load was in any case only some fifty tons; although the attacks could be delivered very fast and so presented maximum difficulties to the defences, they had negligible effect. This was perfectly well understood by the pilots whose resentment was further fanned by the boastful, optimistic tones in which the battle continued to be reported at home and by criticisms, from Göring and from others, which implied that the German fighter force had failed to pull its weight during the summer and that resort to these measures was entirely their fault. This was hardly tactful, and it was also unfair; for the first time, there was a sharp criticism of those in authority.

The main targets were London and the south coast ports, but the population was hardly conscious of being bombed; very often, too, if intercepted, the fighter-bombers jettisoned at once. On the other hand, the Hurricane Wings were very often bounced by the escort. As a result of such an affair over London on 15 October, Satchell had to make a forced landing in a small field covered with anti-invasion obstacles. No sooner had he braked furiously to a stop than 'a fairly elderly VAD nurse leapt through the hedge, complete with toy pistol (belonging to her small son), which she pointed in a most terrifying manner'. She was followed within a moment by a horde of small boys, who surrounded the aircraft, calling out to each other, 'Coo! It's a Nurricane!'

In the same month, by a combination of bad weather and bad controlling on a day when Satchell was not flying, only four of his squadron came back. Satchell visited three of the four fatal crashes. The first two, an Englishman and a Pole, had gone in near Hampton Court, the former having jumped and parted company with his parachute. 'I went into the mortuary,' he wrote, 'and could not help feeling that he must feel cold lying there on the marble slab; he looked awfully peaceful and quite unruffled. I was then asked if I wanted to see the other pilot. The man lifted up a sack out of the corner of the room which was about half full of bits of flesh and bones, all a bit bloodied and charred, and smelling dreadfully.' Of the third pilot, half a headless torso remained.

On 6 November the last dog-fight took place over Portsmouth, the rival formations drawing great circles of white vapour across the blue sky; it was a clear case of the bounce, the attacked formation breaking violently, some upwards like coins spun casually from a finger. Then, in sixty seconds, four planes came down. Two Hurricanes and a 109 fell at a flat angle inland and one Hurricane dived straight in under full throttle, the rising, metallic whine seeming to tear the sky apart. The noise stopped abruptly. At the scene of the crash there was just a white gash in the soil, from which smoke drifted faintly away; a gang of small boys were busy filling their pockets with the tiny scraps of silver and green metal.

On 11 November the Italian Air Force, which had been training under Kesselring, attempted a daylight raid on a convoy off Harwich in which Donald Connacher was sailing as second mate of the *Charles Parsons*, his third ship of the Battle of Britain. 'Hurricanes met them and the Italians tumbled out of the sky like falling leaves,' he said. 'They didn't get close and they didn't hit a ship.'

The last notable dog-fight took place south of the Isle of Wight on 28 November, and Major Helmut Wick, leader of the *Richthofen Jagdgeschwader*, was shot down and killed; his death was always something of a mystery. The Spitfires of 609 Squadron, led by Michael Robinson, climbed to 30,000 feet before engaging. During the fight, Flight Lieutenant J. C. Dundas called over the R/T that he had got a 109; that was the last ever heard of him. When the Germans returned, Wick's number two claimed a Spitfire. The assumption is that Dundas shot down Wick and was in turn killed by the German leader's number two.

On this note, of honours even, the daylight Battle of Britain ended. According to British official reckoning, it was over at the end of October, after starting on 10 July, but both dates are optional. For the Germans, it had begun on 13 August and did not end until 22 June, 1941, when the Russian campaign began. On 25 November,

Dowding was replaced by Air Marshal Douglas, and within three weeks Park had been replaced by Air Vice-Marshal Leigh-Mallory, the manner of their replacement being hardly in keeping with the importance of the victory they had won, and a source of irritation to the pilots who had served under them.

The Battle of Britain has been frequently and loosely compared to Trafalgar. It was nothing of the sort. Nelson's fleet was enormously more formidable than the Combined Fleet of France and Spain, and the British annihilated their enemy without loss to themselves. Dowding had no such superiority and achieved no such result, although it seems that he was expected to do so. What Dowding and Park's battle more nearly paralleled was the victory of Howard and Drake in the Channel, when they engaged the Armada in a series of running fights, drove it off, badly damaged, and foiled for ever what slight chance of invasion there might have been. Even the ending is paralleled for, when it was still uncertain what had happened to the Spaniards, there were grumblings about 'our half-doing do breed dishonour', coupled with ill-informed technical criticism. There was even a sharp personal clash between rival Admirals – Drake and Frobisher. On the other hand, it was true that the fighter pilots who fought in the Battle of Britain had obtained a niche in history equal to that occupied by Nelson's seamen, as the first of the country's defenders against invasion, and in consequence that the Royal Air Force as a whole had come of age.

While the fighter-bomber attacks were going on, a proportion of the bomber force attacked London nightly; as the former began to die away, the night offensive took on a strategic character, ports and armament centres being the targets. The London 'Blitz', however, imposed a severe strain on the bomber crews because, no matter what the weather, at least a token force had to go to London. The strain of continual instrument flying told most heavily on the units equipped with Dorniers, as these were used in weather which was impossible for the Junkers and Heinkels, and the men became tired and resentful at having to carry the burden of the war virtually alone. A typical incident which occurred at the time was initiated by an oberleutnant of KG 3 who took his crew straight off an operation to a Brussels night club frequented by Party officials noted for Black Market dealings. He flung open the door and shouted: 'Officials – *Ortsgruppenleiter* – fur-dealers – OUT! Airmen may stay.' All the outraged Nazis could do was report him to his unit, which dealt leniently with the case.

During October the blockade aspect of the operations was given more priority, three geschwader being used for mine-laying. KG 30, based on Schipol and Eindhoven, was responsible for the Channel eastwards of the Isle of Wight and the east coast; KG 126, based on Nantes, operated west of the Isle of Wight and in the Irish Sea. The latter was led by Oberst Ernst August Roth, a torpedo bomber enthusiast who was later to command the forces which largely destroyed the Murmansk convoy PQ 17. He was given the entire torpedo bomber force of the Luftwaffe – four or five Heinkel 111s – and scored his first success against a tanker off the Isle of Wight in November. The most spectacular mine-laying operation carried out by all units was in December when they laid several hundred delayed-action mines of three different types – magnetic, acoustic and a combination of these two – in the Thames Estuary, sinking seven ships on the first day and causing considerable confusion.

London was bombed on every night except one between 7 September and 13 November, the average number of bombers being 160. On 14 November the first

provincial city was attacked – no fewer than 549 bombers
having Coventry as their target. This was a peak effort,
even the mine-layers being used. Otto Bechtle arrived
early, making his landfall at Ipswich and following the
River Orwell. It was a wonderful moonlight night, with
the towns and villages perfectly plain. Coventry was
blazing when he got there, but the scene was not yet
particularly impressive – from the height he was flying at,
it looked like a lot of scattered haystacks burning; each of
which was, of course, a building. He returned over
London, the city laid out below like a model and even the
smoke of the power stations clearly visible. Pathfinders
had led the attack and a beam had been laid across the
city: Paul Weitkus did not use it, the night being so clear
and there being the danger of night fighters hunting along
the beam. This was a particularly successful raid, causing
by direct and indirect means a twenty per cent drop in
aircraft production.

The mine-laying units used in the occasional peak
attacks often carried mines instead of bombs and as these
fell slowly by parachute the blast effect was very severe,
the explosion taking place above ground. But the main
weapon used in the night attacks was the incendiary
bomb, and during the winter most of the main cities had
about ten to twenty per cent of the built-up area burned
down. There were no epidemics, as prophesied, no abandonment of the cities by their population, as prophesied,
no panic of any kind. And no hope of the Germans
winning the war.

The last raid of 1940, on 29 December, provided a
dramatic climax to a memorable year. Both Bechtle and
White were over London that night, the former in a
bomber, the latter in a night fighter; for both of them, the
immense conflagration near St Paul's stamped the raid on
their memory. Instead of a black carpet of darkness

speckled with single, sparkling lights, there was an intense glow from a huge area, reflected red on the clouds, with searchlights weaving about, and bursting shells sending out drifting clouds of smoke. Several times, Bechtle's Dornier rocked violently, having either touched another aircraft or flown into its slipstream.

For White, conscious that the limitations of the night-fighting equipment made him more spectator than defender, the picture held an added poignancy from the fact that he knew the city and had affection for it. It seemed to him that the whole of London was on fire, an appalling and awe-inspiring sight, yellow and red flames swirling away over a vast area, St Paul's and the river lurid in their glare. He was honestly amazed, when driving through the city a few days later, to see how much of it was still standing.

Since England was alone and there seemed to be no reason why these attacks should not go on indefinitely until there was very little left, there might excusably have been some despondency; there was none. There was instead a stubborn refusal to admit even the possibility of defeat. It was this attitude which most surprised the Germans. In Bechtle's unit, for instance, there were three British prisoners of war employed in the mess. One of them, Bill, came from Tottenham, where his father owned a garage. Whenever the bombers returned from a raid, the three Englishmen were always waiting for them with the question, 'Where have you been tonight?' When the Germans tried to pull their legs with claims of 'London Kaput', Bill's invariable reply was, 'Tottenham is indestructible.' When an RAF night intruder found the German base and came roaring down on it, guns blazing, it had an appreciative audience – the three British prisoners, who stood at the door of the mess and cheered him on. 'They were quite certain that England would win,' said Bechtle.

Shortly before Christmas they had to be returned to their POW camp. The Germans bought them extra clothing and turned out to wave them goodbye. 'I'll never forget those three retreating figures, waving back at us,' said Bechtle, who also recalled that their football team never recovered from the loss.

There were many obvious factors which contributed to successful British resistance in 1940 – the decision, taken in 1935, to go ahead at high priority with radar research in face of opposition from Mr Churchill's nominee, Professor Lindemann, who favoured infra-red radiation; the work of Dowding in developing Fighter Command into a scientifically directed force; the all-important contributions of the Supermarine and Hawker companies, the latter going into production before an order had been received; the dynamic influence of Lord Beaverbrook, not only on actual production but on rapid repairs and modifications as well; the skill and valour of the fighter pilots; the matchless work of the groundcrews under pressure and under fire. But the basic reason was that the British people that summer were stirred by a unique and dramatic combination of events to fight and work as they had rarely done before. Under the often casual and superficially modest air which the British wear in public, they are an extremely proud and arrogant nation. They believed they were unbeatable, in any circumstances, by any force on earth. They had been seriously annoyed by suggestions that they were decadent, but were not prepared to resort to argument. They had been incensed by the assumption, among both friend and foe after the fall of France, that their end was near; they were not prepared to argue that, either. And fortunately – gloriously – even enjoyably – there was no need to do so. The situation provided them with the opportunity of proving everyone else resoundingly wrong by direct action. It was with almost savage pride that they set out to resist what seemed an overwhelmingly powerful and triumphant enemy. It was this feeling which gave that summer its epic quality, and it was this feeling which won the battle.

The atmosphere was totally devoid of that hysteria which sometimes accompanies a crisis, the streak of almost feminine cruelty which fear often tends to arouse. There was a certain amount of brutal 'hot air' spoken which was indicative only of a basic desire to fight; basically the struggle was waged in a decent and humane manner, and very few lost a sense of proportion. Mr Cooper, of Supermarine, witnessed a typical instance when a friend of his, a dominant and loud-mouthed personality fond of issuing lurid threats of what he would like to do to the Germans, actually had the opportunity of carrying them out. A wounded German airman landed by parachute in the street where they both lived, and Mr Cooper saw him free the man and then stand over him, protectingly, as a woman came out of a house, carrying a carving knife and screaming for vengeance. 'You touch him at your peril!' he roared. Then the incongruity of it struck everyone, and the scene dissolved in laughter.

Although the Battle of Britain did not win the war, but merely prevented the British from losing it, the effects were decisive in that they caused Hitler to abandon the assault entirely and march into Russia instead. After his early victories, when the Red Army was rapidly being destroyed, Hitler began to formulate plans for a second Battle of Britain, to take place when Russian resistance finally collapsed. Greatly expanded air and submarine forces were to carry out the attack, which was to culminate in invasion. It seems unlikely that it would have stood even as much chance of success as the first, as

Göring tacitly admitted in a talk with Sir Ivone Kirk-patrick just after the war.[1] Göring was contemptuous of the RAF's claims (which were not amended until much later), and regarded the air battle as a draw. The decisive aspect of it, he thought, lay in the fact that Germany's strength was relatively at its peak when war was declared and must thereafter relatively decline. The truth of this can be clearly seen in the production figures of operational aircraft for 1940 – in that year, Germany produced just over 8,000; the British, despite heavy damage to their industry, produced nearly 10,000, and their fighter production was nearly double that of the Germans. The Luftwaffe did not fade away as a result of the battle, it simply was surpassed by British production. 1940, there-fore, was Germany's only chance to win decisive victory, to use her temporary superiority to take advantage of the weakness in British defence caused by the pre-war political climate, bedevilled as it was on the one side by an incurably comfortable optimism, and on the other by an equally incurable naïve pacifism. The British normally do go to war in a partially unprepared state, but never had they been so ill-equipped as this. It was fortunate that the vital defensive component – Fighter Command – was not only up-to-date but able to achieve victory in circumstances so unbelievably alarming that they had never been considered when its pre-war strength had been planned.

Almost all the pre-war prophets had been decisively refuted by the first air campaign; there is no sign that they have learned their lesson. The same people continue to paint the same picture in the same phrases, with the nuclear rocket instead of the bomber carrying gas as their main weapon, and with a certainty unimpaired by the

[1] *The Inner Circle*, by Sir Ivone Kirkpatrick (Macmillan, 1959).

previous failure of their theories. These failed, basically, because they were not theories at all, and certainly not an appreciation of the situation; they were simply a romantic presentation of war. Gas was chosen, for instance, not on its merits, but for its emotional effect; fire did not seem so terrible (although it is), and therefore they did not bother to predict the incendiary bomb.

Only one man, to the author's knowledge, actually came near to predicting the Battle of Britain, and he was a tediously accurate German major who wrote of a hypothetical war between Britain and France in which a French *invasion*, with tanks and paratroops, was carried out, and beaten back into the sea by the overwhelming British air power; London and Paris were bombed, but the Londoners did not panic and that blow went for nothing. This was, of course, not admissible in pre-war London, where the authorities made every preparation for a panic evacuation. It was also distinctly unfashionable of him to talk about conventional military operations when everyone knew that these had been out-moded. 'When the next war starts,' proclaimed a writer in the *Contemporary Review*, 1938, 'and within a few hours of its starting, long before an Expeditionary Force could go into its first action, politicians, men, women and children, will be exterminated by the million. That fact is known.'

What had been conceived was an air war against main population centres, with terror as its object, the rival bomber fleets passing each other like express trains on parallel tracks, each intent on flattening its own target. What had been predicted was a bombing campaign; what had taken place had been a battle. The fight for air superiority had been the keynote; the fighter had been more important than the bomber, which had been directed at RAF targets, and because the German fighters had been unequal to their task, the German bombers had been beaten. Air war, it had been shown, was subject to exactly the same principles as any other type of war; the enemy forces could not be ignored, they had to be engaged and defeated. Only then could victory be exploited and the bomber play its full part.

In the night sky, initially, different conditions had obtained, for the defences had been so weak and ineffectual that the Germans did not need to fight for air superiority – they already had it. The targets here were mainly strategic – industrial centres and ports – and the general shape was much more like that of the Douhet concept. The Luftwaffe was unable to take full advantage of the situation, before the defences caught up, because it had not been designed for the task of 'total air war'. But Bomber Command, which was a strategic force, failed also in the strategic rôle; its achievements, where they were not merely wasteful, were mainly of tactical value only. When the wheel had turned full circle, the four-engined bombers pounded Germany, and much of Europe besides, into the dust, but there was no collapse and no surrender – the broken cities had to be captured by grimy infantrymen moving forward under cover of tanks and artillery. Then, and then only, did the white flag replace the swastika.

The Battle of Britain was unique in that it had set the precedent for civilian behaviour under air attack. Before it, the threat had been a nameless and shapeless horror grossly inflated by every available device of propaganda; when it was over, no one could ever look upon air attack in quite the same light again. The dragon was still there, still a dragon, still terrible – but no longer an argument for unconditional and abject surrender regardless of consequences. Triumphant defiance of the unknown was the real achievement of the British in their finest hour.

* * *

THE BOMBING CAMPAIGNS COMPARED

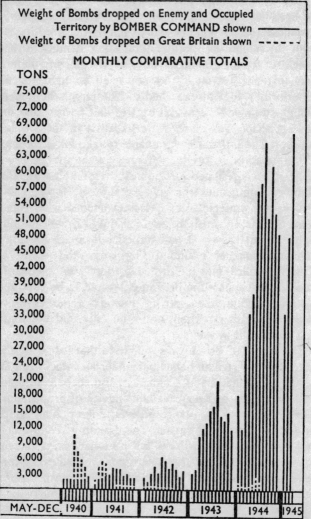

Weight of Bombs dropped on Enemy and Occupied Territory by BOMBER COMMAND shown ———
Weight of Bombs dropped on Great Britain shown ------

MONTHLY COMPARATIVE TOTALS

TONS
75,000
72,000
69,000
66,000
63,000
60,000
57,000
54,000
51,000
48,000
45,000
42,000
39,000
36,000
33,000
30,000
27,000
24,000
21,000
18,000
15,000
12,000
9,000
6,000
3,000

MAY-DEC. 1940 | 1941 | 1942 | 1943 | 1944 | 1945

Long after the war Barry Sutton returned to North Weald as Wing Commander Flying; they had Hunter jets and, to judge by the complaints, a fighter pilot was now no longer a hero but a noise. Still, not everyone had forgotten. In particular there was one old Cockney who used to clean out the offices; he was still there. 'I remember you,' he said to Sutton. 'Back in 1940. You took off and you never came back. 'Course you 'ad black 'air then.' He stroked his own head. 'Mind you, we're both getting on now. I'm 65 next month.'